HOW TO FIND A HOME
AND GET A MORTGAGE
ON THE INTERNET

Randy Johnson

HOW TO FIND A HOME AND GET A MORTGAGE ON THE INTERNET

Randy Johnson

John Wiley & Sons, Inc.

New York • Chichester • Weinheim • Brisbane • Singapore • Toronto

Copyright © 2001 by Randy Johnson. All rights reserved.

Published by John Wiley & Sons, Inc.
Published simultaneously in Canada.

This publication is designed to provide accurate and authoritative information in regard to the subject matter covered. It is sold with the understanding that the publisher is not engaged in rendering professional services. If professional advice or other expert assistance is required, the services of a competent professional person should be sought.

Library of Congress Cataloging-in-Publication Data:

Johnson, Randy, 1937–
    How to find a home and get a mortgage on the Internet / Randy Johnson.
      p.   cm.
    Includes index.
    ISBN 0-471-38072-5 (pbk. : alk. paper)
      1. House buying—Computer network resources.   2. House buying.   3. Mortgage loans.   4. Mortgage loans—Computer network resources.   5. Internet marketing.
    I. Title.

HD1380.6 .J64 2000
025.06'64312—dc21
                                                    00-038133

Printed in the United States of America.

10 9 8 7 6 5 4 3 2 1

*To my wife, Carole, for her support,
encouragement, and insight.*

CONTENTS

PREFACE

A man who had heard about my first book, *How to Save Thousands of Dollars on Your Home Mortgage,* called me and asked, "Is this a book for ordinary homeowners?" I replied, "No, because ordinary homeowners don't buy books. This book is for smart people."

Smart people buy books because they acknowledge that there is always something new to learn from experts. Indeed, I have talked with many of my tens of thousands of readers who have called, written, or e-mailed me with comments and feedback about the book. They seem to have one common characteristic: They are all smart people, many with advanced degrees. They praised the information and techniques in my book, and, based on their feedback, I think the title is accurate.

In this new book I have updated the mortgage information and have added lots of material about the homebuying process, including how to select and work with your real estate agent and how to ensure a trouble-free closing.

I have personally originated over one-half billion dollars in mortgage loans and have acted as a real estate agent on the sale of over $20 million in properties. I have gained my knowledge and developed these ideas in the trenches, so to speak. I believe that one of the strengths of this book is that my knowledge comes from being an expert myself, not from interviewing other people. I am pleased to share what I have learned with you.

Finally, the Internet has greatly expanded the capabilities of homebuyers and homeowners to get information never before available to them. I have had a mortgage Web site (www.loan-wolf.com) since July 1996, and have originated almost $20 million in Internet loans. I have been a keen student of how the Internet can be used to help buyers and owners cope with the problems that everyone faces in real estate transactions. My goal is to make two of life's most important financial decisions—buying a home and financing it—easier and more rewarding. To that end, I will show you (1) how to gather the information you need, and (2) how to use that information to make more intelligent decisions and ultimately to save yourself many thousands of dollars.

ACKNOWLEDGMENTS

I did not write this book by myself. The information and ideas I put forth here are the result of 20 years of dealing with thousands of clients, each of whom has added to my knowledge in one way or another. My clients have helped me think through the ideas and develop a methodology to help my next clients. For this, they have earned my enduring thanks.

I also want to thank the employees of the hundred-plus lenders I have dealt with over these same years. The good ones have become friends and are as frustrated as I am by the bureaucracies in which they operate. We have been united by a common bond of helping our clients.

I would also like to acknowledge those who made specific contributions to this book. First, Mike Hamilton, my friend and editor at John Wiley & Sons, was the inspiration for the book. He has provided encouragement throughout the process. I also want to thank Janice Borzendowski, who has a command of the language far better than mine and who made many corrections so as to make the manuscript more readable. Finally, I want to express my appreciation to Stephanie Landis of North Market Street Graphics, who edited the final manuscript for clarity and consistency.

If there are errors, they are mine alone.

INTRODUCTION

If knowledge can create problems, it is not through ignorance that we can solve them
—Isaac Asimov

What is wanted is not the will to believe but the wish to find out, which is exactly the opposite.
—Lord Bertrand Russell

CAN I REALLY DO THIS ONLINE?

Homebuying is a baffling, frustrating process not only for first-time homebuyers but for more experienced buyers as well. No doubt you've heard by now that people are buying and selling homes and getting financing on the Internet, and you are wondering whether using the Internet for these important activities is right for you. The good news is that the Internet can make these tasks easier and can simplify these processes and make them more efficient, economical, and rewarding. That said, using the Internet for real estate transactions is not something you can or should jump into without preparation.

In the first place, how best to use the Internet is not immediately obvious, and you can and will waste a lot of time before finding the sites and search methods that are most efficient and productive if you do not take time to prepare yourself.

Second, in addition to the uncertainty and doubt that surround the novelty of the Web for new users, you will probably confront legitimate concerns about e-commerce security, making you reluctant to proceed with commercial transactions in this unfamiliar environment.

Third, there is evidence that the anonymous nature of the Internet can work against the interaction between an individual and Internet companies, making it harder to develop relationships that promote effective communication—and, therefore, the results you achieve.

THE INTERNET AND THE CONSUMER

Internet consumers are frequently told that conducting business on the Internet empowers them. The trouble is, empowerment without education can be a dangerous thing indeed. The advent of online trading, for example, means anyone can buy stocks cheaply—but people often buy unwisely, hardly a productive demonstration of empowerment. To prevent this from happening to you in your real estate dealings, I want to educate you to use the empowerment wisely and well. This guide is written to familiarize you with Internet real estate resources, to reduce your anxiety about interacting with these resources, and to give you the confidence to work with these resources in a meaningful and profitable way.

This book is intended to be a valuable aid that enables you to enter the online real estate and mortgage sites well prepared to gather the information you need and to use rational processes leading to intelligent decisions so that you reap the fullest benefits from this new e-commerce channel.

The explosive growth of the Internet in the late 1990s has been nothing short of revolutionary, comparable in the minds of many to the invention of the printing press or the automobile. Initially a tool for the exchange of scientific information, then a curiosity—much like the home computer—the so-called Information Superhighway has fundamentally changed the way many people get the information necessary to their lives. Indeed, for many, the Internet is replacing newspapers, magazines, and even television as their preferred information channel. And the more the number of Internet resources increases, the more useful it becomes to users. The sheer amount of information now available has a downside as well, however. Thousands of new Web sites are being added every day, and the total number of pages has increased so rapidly that it boggles the mind. The figure is something like 500 million as I write this and will probably be over 1 billion when you read it.

THE GROWTH OF E-COMMERCE

More recently, another transformation of the Internet has occurred. It has gone from being a resource for the collection and dissemination of information to one for the conducting of business through Internet sites.

Indeed, the explosive growth of companies engaged in e-commerce has been the source of many news stories during recent years. Perhaps the most dramatic of these relate to the huge fortunes being amassed by the creators of e-commerce businesses. In many industries, investors in the stock market can value a one-store company higher than larger, well-known, established companies in the same industry. For example, unprofitable one-store barnesandnoble.com, with 701 employees, has a market capitalization of $2.89 billion, while its profitable parent, Barnes & Noble, Inc., with 29,200 employees, has a capitalization of only $1.73 billion. Whether investor enthusiasm for these e-stocks is warranted, only time will tell, but it is clear that e-commerce has captured the imagination of the American public and is here to stay. It will continue to shape the course of business in the foreseeable future.

In the last year or so, investors have begun buying stocks and bonds on the Internet. Online trading now accounts for about 15 percent of trading activity, and it has been reported that the online brokerage companies are spending $500 million in advertising per year to attract new customers. This is forcing fundamental changes in the stock brokerage business, as major players shift to accommodate the preferences of this new generation of traders and investors.

In more traditional fields of commerce, millions of consumers have become comfortable purchasing books and other relatively inexpensive items on the Net, probably as a direct correlation to their experience with catalog shopping and the promise of a money-back guarantee if they are dissatisfied. Likewise, people are favoring the use of the Internet to make airline reservations and to buy tickets; many are even selecting and purchasing cars on the Net. Most large and small retailers have established Internet presences. Today, in fact, if a public company does not have an Internet strategy, it will be discounted by Wall Street and the public alike. As consumer confidence in the security and reliability of the Internet grows, people will continue to expand their use of the Internet as their channel of choice for gathering data and making decisions on big-ticket items. Your choice to use the Internet in your search for a home or mortgage helps fuel that growth.

REAL ESTATE ON THE INTERNET

The biggest consumer markets of all—homebuying and residential mortgage lending—are shaping up as huge potential Internet markets. Consumers need information that is vital to their decision-making process about these life-changing choices, and much of it can be easily and quickly accessed from their computers at home or work, 24 hours a day, 7 days a week. At the Real Estate Connect 99 conference sponsored by Inman News features (www.inman.com), a premiere source of real estate news, evidence of the real estate industry's commitment to the Internet was abundant; both start-ups and established companies are investing hundreds of millions of dollars per year in technology and in organizations to capitalize on activity generated from the Internet. More than 1500 people attended this conference to share information that will shape the growth of this industry and to assure that they can stake out their companies' claims in this new e-commerce gold field.

SEARCHING FOR A HOME ONLINE

Historically, information on homes for sale was the tightly controlled, exclusive province of the real estate brokerage industry. If a prospective homeowner wanted to find out about homes that were available for sale, he or she was forced to call a real estate agent. Even in recent years, when control of the multiple listing service was loosened somewhat, it was done grudgingly by the real estate brokerage industry more as a result of court orders than from a desire to be helpful to homebuyers. Real estate professionals were afraid that they would be cut out of deals if buyers and sellers were able to meet and conduct business without the assistance of brokers—perhaps more significantly, without having to pay them. In fact, the opening of the marketplace and the facilitation of access to information holds the promise of improving communication between buyers and sellers and their agents, thus improving the market by making it more efficient for all parties.

The fears of the industry are now a moot point because, today, estimates are that virtually all homes listed for sale by the real estate industry are posted on the Internet. Those managing real estate Web sites not only report that millions of people access their sites every month, but that more of these people are actually doing business online, not just window-shopping. That said, there are still more shoppers than buyers today, because many shoppers are still reluctant to use this resource to its full potential, especially for such a big-ticket item as a home. That is why I have written this book: to give you the confidence to use this exciting new tool safely and successfully.

WHAT YOU SEE IS WHAT YOU GET

Thanks to recent technological developments, digital color images of properties for sale can be downloaded from a camera to a real estate Web site almost immediately. Sellers now have the ability to show online features of their property that, in the past, would have required printing expensive brochures. Buyers can get "live" previews of homes at their computers in their homes or offices. Buyers will seldom if ever make an offer to purchase without first inspecting the properties in person, but thanks to the Internet, homebuyers can start the process with far more information at their disposal, thus making them better prepared to make the right choice.

For example, a homebuyer can preview 25 or 30 properties online and narrow them down to 4 or 5 he or she wants to visit. In addition, other sites that facilitate the assembly of recent sales data in their neighborhoods will allow more homeowners to make independent decisions about the value of their own homes. Similarly, homebuyers who have access to the same comparable sales data and the ability to analyze the data properly will be better equipped to make offers and negotiate contracts on the homes they desire. This is a far better use of everyone's time than with the traditional homebuying process.

HOMESELLING

Most savvy sellers today want their homes listed on as many Internet Web sites as possible, where prospective buyers might see them. As a result, most real estate agents are listing their clients' homes on more than one listing service. In addition, there always have been and always will be for-sale-by-owner (FSBO) homes that are sold without the involvement of anyone in the real estate industry. Astute FSBO sellers will increasingly use the power of the Internet to assist with the marketing of their homes, and there are sites that give them access to home shoppers. Finally, a number of Web sites refer homesellers to competent real estate agents in their areas.

MORTGAGES ON THE INTERNET

Recent estimates suggest that as many as 10 percent of all mortgages may be originated on the Internet by 2003. That is a staggering $100 billion in mortgages annually. With the advent of automated underwriting, computerized valuation models, and the ability to send loan documents electronically to the closing agent, lenders have the capability to process and fund loans faster than ever conceived, and at lower cost than the more traditional lenders. The most advanced and forward-thinking lenders are already using many of these capabilities offline, so it is a relatively small step to using these techniques for customers who find them through the Internet.

Moreover, rate information is much easier to assemble and disseminate, with the added benefit that borrowers can shop anonymously, without having to make phone calls to lenders. Borrowers have never before had such easy and convenient access to rate information.

INDEX OF WEB SITES

One of the shortcomings of a book is that you can't put in working hyperlinks. Some of the URLs are long and complicated, and I know it will not be much fun to type them into your computer. Hence I have created an index of URLs at my Web site. When you want to go to a site—you'll be at your computer anyway—go to http://www.loan-wolf .com/urlindex.htm. (Be sure to bookmark the page for easy return to it in the future.) You will see every URL in the book with hyperlinks to the sites. No typing! I hope you like this feature.

SUMMARY

If there is a downside to this, it may be that the new mortgage processing systems promise to be more mechanical than user-friendly, and more clerical than personal. The Internet lenders are proceeding under the assumption that the Internet borrower is more interested in low cost than personal service, and the easiest way for lenders to reduce costs is to eliminate the most expensive person—usually also the best qualified one—from the transaction. The result? In this new world, borrowers will be dealing more with unlicensed, inexperienced "customer service representatives" than with licensed professional loan officers.

Unfortunately for the borrower, a number of mortgage decisions that every homebuyer must make—what type of loan to get, how many points to pay, when to lock in—are enhanced with professional guidance. Without this assistance, the borrower is faced with even more challenges. Thus, to the Internet borrower, the phrase, "You're on your own," will have more meaning than for those who seek the services of a hometown lender—which is another reason for this book. It will fill the gaps left by the new technology, allowing the solo borrower to be better prepared.

DECISION MAKING AND SALESMANSHIP

It reeks with the thick atmosphere of bargain and sale.
—HENRY ADAMS

The dominant influence that spawned the arts was the need to impose order on the confusion caused by intelligence.
—EDWARD O. WILSON,
CONSILIENCE: THE UNITY OF KNOWLEDGE

KEY POINTS

- Many subtle factors influence our decision-making processes.
- The desire for immediate gratification often overrides reason.
- Crafty advertisers can plant erroneous concepts that mislead.
- You will usually find a salesman at every decision point. Sometimes they help, sometimes not.
- Those who take time to educate themselves make better decisions.

Talking about decision making and the effects that marketing and salesmanship can have on the faculties of reason may seem unusual in a book about real estate and the Internet, but the purpose of this book is not just to help you gather real estate information. My objective is, first, to give you good ways to find real estate information, and second, to help you use that information to make better decisions. The majority of people make less than optimal decisions about their mortgages, and I want to ensure that you are not one of them by giving you a thorough grounding in the intricacies of that side of the business as well.

1

During the 20 years that I have been in the real estate–mortgage business, I have watched thousands of people make decisions. When it comes to choosing a home, most people know what they want. After all, we have lived in one home or another all of our lives, and we have a good idea about what we like and don't like. Conversely, I have watched people make monumental mistakes in strategizing how to buy or sell their homes, how to utilize the services of their agents, and how to negotiate the terms of sale, even basing their negotiating strategy on inaccurate assumptions about the other party's motivation. A typical example is the propensity of people to believe, in a tough market, that they can get "top dollar" for their home yet expect another seller to cave in and give them a "great deal." It doesn't work that way, folks. And when it comes to mortgages, people also have preconceived notions about what they want and how they can get it. These preconceptions are usually wrong.

IMMEDIATE GRATIFICATION

Most all of us suffer from a defect unique among American consumers: We prefer—often demand—the immediate gratification of saving money today versus the delayed gratification of getting a much larger benefit a few years down the road. Part of this is due to the fact that Americans love the idea of "sales" and "discounts." Another reason is that consumers are so used to seeing so many choices among products that are almost identical, they do not ask questions about quality and service. This carries over to the big-ticket items, including homes and mortgages. As to mortgages, people don't know how the mortgage industry is structured, they don't know all the choices the mortgage industry offers, and they don't know how to evaluate choices. Some homebuyers are so locked into a particular strategy that they do not listen to or use good information at their disposal. Let's face it: While it is important to make the best decisions you can in all areas of your life, it is especially important in selecting a home and financing it. The sheer size of the transaction means that it has the greatest impact on most families' financial affairs.

The bottom line is that whether you make a good decision or a bad decision can have awesome consequences. Though I talk here primarily about mortgages, this material can be applied to homebuying, as well as the purchase decisions you make in all areas of your economic life.

HOW PEOPLE MAKE DECISIONS

Cultural anthropologists and developmental psychologists have studied how early humans made decisions in the days when Lucy wandered out of Olduvai Gorge. Well, maybe not back that far, but, say, 5000 years ago. People make decisions based on their belief structures, an all-embracing view, or "how I think the world works." When you examine history, you can see that three main sets of belief structures have existed, leading to different methods of gathering and processing information that have evolved over the millennia.

The earliest humans had no concept as to how the world worked other than that times were good for a while and then times were bad for a while. Even worse, the normal life span was not long enough for people to pass on to future generations some of the important facts they had learned. In those perilous times there was no explanation of the changes from good times—adequate rain, abundant crops, plentiful game—to bad times—drought, absence of game, natural disasters, plague—so people created a world of myths, totems, taboos, and a host of gods that had to be propitiated regularly in the expectation that the gods would be pleased and either allow the good times to continue or bring them back. Some cultures even sacrificed virgins to assure good fortune during the coming seasons. As bizarre as this may seem to us today, it made perfectly good sense to cultures that did not have a good grip on the factors affecting their environments.

The Greeks and Romans, in their time, had sufficiently advanced to overcome some of the ill effects of the natural cycles. Aqueducts assured adequate water and a system of roads supported growing commerce as well as assuring the ability to move the army around to maintain order. Although the classical Greeks and Romans worshipped plural gods and hadn't totally abandoned the concept of sacrifices, they had moved on to goats and chickens, which must have permitted virgins to sleep more soundly. Even after the Renaissance, strange events showed that people's decision-making abilities still were rooted in some fairly bizarre beliefs. Galileo spent the last years of his life virtually under house arrest. He was saved from worse penalties only when he agreed not to promulgate his view that the Sun was the center of our solar system, a teaching that was contrary to the Pope's belief. We accept as common facts today things that were viewed with skepticism in earlier times. Those people weren't dumb! It's just that their belief structures, however flawed, profoundly influenced their decision-making processes.

In the modern era, reason and a reliance on scientific methods of analysis flourished contemporaneously with the Industrial Revolution and should have brought an end to the older belief structures. But science did not account for people's intransigence and resistance to change. When the Wright brothers flew at Kitty Hawk, some of the most highly regarded scientific minds of the day dismissed it as simply a fluke and stated that further advancement of this trickery had neither scientific interest nor the prospect of commercial success. That happened within the last 100 years.

Today, when millions of people invest billions of dollars in higher education, and half the homes in America have computers in them, you'd think that decision making would be highly evolved. When you ask people how they make decisions, most will give you answers that suggest that they carefully gather information and use shrewd decision-making processes based on reason. In practice, however, most people's decision-making processes are heavily influenced by emotion and factors that are buried deep within the limbic system of the brain. As often as not, the beliefs people hold about their economic decisions have been prompted by shrewd marketing types eager to induce consumers to make decisions favorable to a certain product or service. This applies to the mortgage industry, too.

The power of marketing influence is nothing short of phenomenal. Certain people, such as TV evangelists, politicians, and super-salespeople, seem to have an ability to mesmerize others—to get them to send in money, vote, or buy—that ordinary people cannot duplicate. You can call it charisma, if it has a positive purpose—or smooth-talking, blue-suede-shoe salesmanship if not—but you can recognize that it happens. Every week there's a story about some investment scam that bilks people out of their life savings. I'm sure you look at the victims and say, "How could those people have been so stupid?" The truth is that, given the right circumstances and the right idea, all of us can be victimized in similar fashion. We may not give away our life savings to some con artist, but both you and I have bought things we have never used and that have ended up at a garage sale the next summer. They may have been items of small economic consequence, but it happened, and we wasted our money.

The real estate sales and mortgage businesses are no different; they attract more than their fair share of salespeople who seem to have an inborn ability to find the weak spots in a consumer's mental defense network and prey on him or her. These people are an embarrassment to the honest professionals in the business, but they have been able to flourish because so many borrowers are willing to suspend their sense of disbelief long enough for the unethical real estate agent or loan rep to worm his or her way in.

No doubt one of the characteristics of the con has to be a cultivated sense of friendliness. "He was so nice, and he quoted us a great rate," people say, after they have been had. Of course! Do you expect the con to dress like a homeless person? Let me make the point another way. A sailor walks into a bar and a girl comes up and sits next to him and asks, "Hi, sailor. Would you buy me a drink?" Do you really think that she is only interested in being his friend? So it happens in the world of commerce too. That the worlds of friendship and commerce can be intertwined is not a bad thing, but you should not blithely assume that people who are friendly have your best interests at heart.

Psychologists have long known that the human brain can "create" images that it expects to see. For example, researchers put a subject in a dark room, display a paper with a bunch of dots on it, and tell the subject it is a picture of a bear. As the researchers increase the light, they instruct the subject, "Tell us when you see the bear," and sure enough, at some light level, the person says, "I see it!" Of course, when the lights are turned up all the way, everyone can see that it isn't a picture of a bear at all. What has happened is that the mind has filled in the spaces between the dots with its own expectations, creating for itself the picture of a bear.

This same phenomenon results in a characteristic shared by many American consumers, a quality that seems to make them particularly susceptible to what I call the "little con." As I mentioned earlier, Americans have a *need* to find a bargain; they *want* to find a bargain. Almost invariably, this desire expresses itself by their being overly price conscious, meaning they tend to be price shoppers as opposed to being value or quality shoppers. It seems easy for these consumers to come to the conclusion that there are no quality differences between consumer goods offered by different manufacturers, so they think that buying the one with the lowest price is smart buying. This is less a manifestation of greed than it is a reflection of Americans' innate willingness to believe that "if we shop hard enough, we'll find a bargain." Over 100 years ago, John Ruskin said, "There is no product that some man cannot make a little worse and sell a little cheaper, and the buyers who consider only price are this man's lawful prey."

It is this incessant need for a bargain that makes people jump for joy when they hear a "little con." They want to find a bargain, and when they hear something that sounds enticing, their mind "fills in the space between the dots" and they see the bear. Their minds become glazed over at their belief that they really have found a good deal. Their willingness to believe a little con means that there are always enough salesmen—those whose claims are not constrained by truth—to satisfy their needs.

This is particularly true in the mortgage industry. It is a somewhat unique business in that people shop on the basis of one price today, but the actual rate they are going to pay won't be set for 30 or 60 days. That means that the lender can quote a rate that is a total fabrication, and then blame the changes on variations in the market. As a consumer, your willingness to trust will make you not want to believe this, but some lenders—maybe even as many as half of them—routinely lie to customers about rates. If you call enough lenders, you're sure to find one of them. The most disturbing aspect of this is that a customer may have just talked with the most reliable, trustworthy lender in town, someone who knocks himself or herself out for his or her customers and really would get the consumer the best deal. But the rate shopper keeps calling until he or she finds the liar. From the earliest times in our history it has been so; hence the image of the frontier snake oil salesman is firmly and correctly a part of American folklore and history. Unfortunately, it is no different today.

BEHAVIOR CHANGES WITH KNOWLEDGE

The good news is that once consumers learn about a particular class of products, some of that need to find a bargain disappears. Every time you go to the store, you face an extraordinary number of choices. You have no doubt bought a cheap brand of a simple product—say, macaroni and cheese. It's so simple, you wonder how any manufacturer can screw it up. Unbelievably, they can, and so you go back to the higher-priced brand, the one you know is good. Maybe you've bought one of the $.79 screwdrivers you see near the checkout stand. They seem to last about six weeks, so if you keep replacing them every six weeks, you're spending over $6 per year on screwdrivers. Finally you "get it," and buy a $3 screwdriver with a lifetime guarantee, and the cost per month drops substantially. Simply put, once people get educated, they do a more sensible job of decision making. So how much should you be willing to pay for an education when you're about to pay $100,000 or $200,000 or $500,000 for a home and the mortgage to finance it?

The point is that this same gullibility goes on in the real estate business and the mortgage business, too. I have seen people get talked into buying a home that I didn't think was right for them and, sure enough, a year or two later, sell that home and buy the one they should have in the first place. Very expensive mistake! I've seen people mesmerized by all kinds of mortgage marketing hoopla, even by reputable companies. Let me give you some examples.

Millions of homeowners were talked into taking adjustable-rate mortgages (ARMs) tied to the 11th District Cost of Funds Index (COFI). The sales pitch was that this index was stable, whereas the other common index, the Treasury Bill index, was volatile. Believing that volatility was bad and that stability was good, millions chose the stable loan. The hitch? In a market environment where rates are falling, a volatile loan drops faster, which is exactly what you want. When people heard *stability,* though, they turned off the reasoning part of their brains before they could ask, "How much is this stability going to cost me?" The answer was that the 11th District Cost of Funds loans had a rate that was over 1 percent higher all during the 1980s than available but less well promoted alternatives. If you had a $200,000 loan, common in California, you paid over $2,000 every year for the privilege of having your stable loan. Obviously, the COFI loan, a great choice at other times, was not a bargain at that time. It was a rip-off.

Here's a more recent example. You probably heard about points, the up-front fee paid to a lender. One point is 1 percent of the loan amount—$2,000 on a $200,000 loan. This topic is covered in considerable detail in Chapter 14, "Understanding APR, Buy-Downs, and Discount Points." Because no one wants to spend $2000 if they don't have to, a loan with no points sounds like a bargain, doesn't it? Well, the full story is that the lenders raise the rate on these loans to above market levels. Why? For every $1000 the lender subsidizes your loan up front, you'll pay $3000 in extra interest over the next 10 years—a good deal for the lender, but bad for you. By the way, these days almost all lenders offer a zero-point option, but it's not a good one for most consumers, a point we'll also cover in Chapter 14.

Here's the latest gimmick. "Get your loan from us, and if the rate falls ½ percent, you can refinance at no cost." Sounds like another bargain, right? You bet it does, because a typical refinance transaction costs about $2000 plus points. You are being led—actually, misled—to believe that you are going to save over $2000 in the future, a compellingly attractive offer. I had a client who had heard about this loan and became fixated on it; it was all he talked about. At that time, a one-point loan would cost 7.375 percent, so the borrower was saying to himself, "If rates fall to 6.875 percent, I can refinance almost for free." When I investigated, I found it was very misleading, nothing more than a variation of the zero point–zero cost loan. The hitch was that the lender's posted "re-fi rate" was 7.875 percent, about ½ percent over the going rate. That means that rates would actually have to fall 1 percent from current levels—not ½ percent—to trigger the deal. If rates actually fell 1 percent, my client could get a "free" re-fi, but at a rate ½ percent higher than the market rate; and at that rate, there would be a $4,000 rebate to the originator on a $200,000 loan. Almost every lender in the western hemisphere would be willing to do the same deal any day of the week! So would I, so I told the client that I would refinance his home anytime he wanted, and we would use the posted rate at this lender's Web site.

This so-called bargain received tremendous press. A nationally syndicated columnist wrote an article about it that appeared in newspapers all across the country. A national magazine featured it in a box with the headline: "NEVER PAY TO REFINANCE AGAIN." Is that an attention-getter? How many people will be snookered by it? Lots, you can be sure, because the promise of anything free has a powerful appeal.

THE INFLUENCE OF ADVERTISING ON DECISION MAKING

Psychologists have long known that feelings of pleasure can be caused by the release of chemicals called endorphins. Spending money on things you want appears to cause the release of endorphins and thus is very pleasurable. Who would not attest to the enormous kick he or she gets from going on a shopping spree? How do you feel when you drive off of the dealer's lot with a new car? It smells good and feels better.

That fact is not lost on the marketers of consumer goods trying to get you to buy their products. If you are a first-time homebuyer, you're about to experience it again. When your transaction finally closes and you walk through the door of your new home, I guarantee that you'll feel the thrill as those endorphins charge around your brain!

A major influence on the decision-making process of many—perhaps most—Americans is the barrage of advertising to which we are all subjected. In most cases, at the heart of the typical advertising message is an appeal not to reason but to basic emotions of the consumer, perhaps trying to trigger those endorphins to flow. A primary target is self-image. Take ads for automobiles, which frequently tap into the subconscious belief that a man who drives a large, powerful car or a small, fast car will be more desirable to women. Let's face it; maintenance costs, mileage, and trade-in value, facts that should be important, are of minor importance for many consumers as they shop for a car.

You think it's different for mortgage advertising, right? Think again. Most of the beliefs people have about mortgages are nothing more than the flowering fruits of seeds that were planted by various mortgage industry forces via advertising and marketing. We'll explore a couple of them to illustrate.

First, when most people hear the word *mortgage,* they think, "30-year fixed-rate mortgage." If you think of a mortgage as a product, that particular one is the most expensive product of any offered by the mortgage industry. So why do most people, who want to save money, start their shopping process by asking about the loan with the highest rate?

In fact, the mortgage industry offers many loan programs—several hundred, at least—meaning that consumers, young or old, rich or poor, can choose the particular loan type that best fits their individual needs. But because so many people start out by shopping for the 30-year fixed-rate mortgage, they never ask about other types of loans. Their ignorance is exacerbated by the fact that many of the "loan officers" they talk with are so poorly trained that these supposed professionals do not understand the relative merits of the different programs themselves. Thus the loan officers are unable to counsel their customers wisely. Finally, as one lender told me, "If the customer says 'yes' to a loan quote, even if it's not quite right for them, what incentive is there for me to confuse him by bringing up more alternatives?"

THE POWER OF FNMA AND FHLMC

As to pricing, it is important to recognize that the Federal National Mortgage Association (FNMA or Fannie Mae) and the Federal Home Loan Mortgage Corporation (FHLMC or Freddie Mac) dominate the mortgage market for the most popular loans. These two companies are stockholder-owned companies that operate under special charters from the government. Because they buy a majority of the loans in the country, they are responsible for setting the rates on the types of loans that most homebuyers want—30-year and 15-year fixed rate mortgages. FNMA and FHLMC buy loans from banks, S&Ls, and mortgage bankers, then package them into "pools" of mortgages in a process known as *securitization.* They then sell interests in those pools to investors, such as pension plans, mortgage real estate investment trusts (REITs), and other purchasers of fixed-income securities. This is an oversimplification of a very complex topic, but essentially FNMA and FHLMC set the rates every day for the various loans they purchase. That establishes the market.

You will get your loan from one of the 25,000 "lenders" that originate loans, but a week later the lender will sell your loan to FNMA and FHLMC. If all lenders pay the same rate for their money, how much difference can there be in the rates they charge you? Very little. The base price is established, and the only thing your lender can control is how much it marks up the rate to cover its costs. The total amount is on the order of 2 percent, so even if a lender were to work for free, you wouldn't save very much. Specifically, there are never, ever any "sales" in the mortgage business as there are in the retail industry, where stores mark down prices 25 percent or 40 percent or 50 percent to move out the last of their inventory. As a result, there is far less difference in pricing between one large, ethical lender and another than most people think. The following is the result of a little survey I did. I called the top 30 lenders in my market to get their pricing. Figure 1.1 shows the results. Twenty-four of the 30 were at 1, 1.125, or 1.25 points.

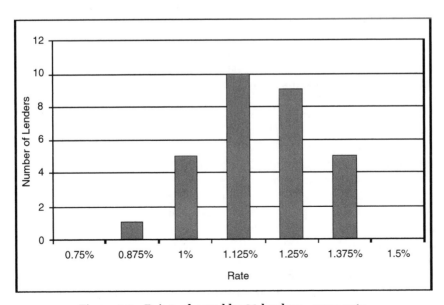

Figure 1.1   Points charged by 30 lenders—same rate.

You can see that the differences are almost infinitesimal. Remember, these are large, ethical lenders who just want to have your business. Sadly, there are other, mostly smaller lenders who have, shall we say, fewer ethical constraints on their approach to customers. If you end up doing business with them, they will try to get into your wallet and you will pay more. The good news is that many other smaller lenders operate more efficiently with lower overhead and can do business profitably with slightly better rates. (That's the lender that quoted 0.875 points.)

THE COMMODITY CONCEPT

A commodity is a product that has identical characteristics, regardless of its source. Wheat, oil, coffee, and pork bellies are commodities. Companies are limited in the way they market commodities because product characteristics and prices are equal. One bushel of wheat is the same as any other bushel of wheat. It is also true that one 30-year fixed-rate mortgage is identical to every other 30-year fixed-rate mortgage. This raises the question: If there are so many similarities in rates between lenders, why do people think that there are large differences? The answer is that the industry and most major lenders want to perpetuate the idea that there are significant differences so that consumers will spend time shopping for a loan, believing they can get a better deal. Why? Simply because lenders want their salespeople to have a shot at you.

Major lenders are not going to come out and say, "The loans we offer are identical to those offered by almost all of our competitors and, what's more, our rates and costs are the same as their rates and costs, too." Even though that is true, it would dramatically change the way they operate. Frankly, the industry likes it the way it is; lenders have learned to succeed in this environment, and no one wants to change it.

HOW LENDERS OPERATE

Because a company cannot say, "Our product is better," the correct, ethical way to compete in a commodity market is to establish a reputation of being trustworthy, or of being convenient, or of offering fast response, or some aspect of service that consumers find attractive. It applies to many industries where there are many, many producers of almost identical products. Unfortunately, though, it is far easier for a lender to promote itself by saying that its rates are better. On the Internet, for example, you'll find more than 20,000 mortgage Web sites, and, amazingly, *all of them* offer the lowest rates. How can they all be the lowest? They can't! In fact, by definition, half of them are worse than average. But lenders know that borrowers are looking for a bargain, so they promise one!

Perhaps you are wondering: What about the lenders that post their rates so you can comparison shop? Certainly some lenders are totally truthful in posting rates, but others almost never are. They just claim to have the lowest rates to entice the customer in the door. Then they do a bait and switch a week or a month later, when they are well into the process. For example, some companies with very high Internet visibility post very attractive rates to attract borrowers to apply. Everyone finds out later that only 2 percent of the applicants are "qualified" for loans at that rate. The other 98 percent are told they don't qualify and are offered higher rates. In fact, the lender never intended to fund more than that 2 percent, because the lender loses money on those deals and makes it up on the other 98 percent. This goes on all the time, offline and online. The point here—and it is an important point—is that you can't tell the difference between truth-tellers and liars, so don't rate shop!

THE BETTER SIDES OF SALESMANSHIP

The press regularly castigates any group of people who earn commission income. The way the media tell it, no one who earns a commission can be trusted. In contrast, the person who helps you at the bank is salaried. Can you trust him or her? Maybe, maybe not. The sign on the desk may say *Loan Consultant,* but this person is really a salesperson for that company's product. You'll never hear a bank employee say, "You know, I just don't think we offer a program that suits you." He or she will always tell you that the bank's program is perfect for you and urge you to buy. By comparison, the commission loan rep working for a mortgage broker doesn't care which lender or which program you choose; he or she gets a commission either way. That allows the ethical loan rep to stand back and give you impartial advice, to help you make intelligent decisions. Yet, because such a loan rep is paid a commission that is a percentage of the loan amount, the press has made it sound as if he or she can never put you ahead of the drive to earn a bigger commission. That's just not true. The best people in the business are happy that you came to them, and they won't steer you to programs just because they can earn more money. The reputable, competent professionals in the business make three or four times as much as their salaried counterparts, and they typically do three or four times the loan volume, too. In fact, the most successful reps, those who often make over $100,000 per year, would never, ever go to work for one of those large institutions that paid them a salary of probably less than half what they can make in commissions.

Salespeople make money by facilitating transactions. Most are honest and serve their customers faithfully. They also serve a variety of other, more useful purposes. First, they are the source of information about products and services you are interested in buying; they can fill in the gaps in your knowledge. Another often overlooked function is to get you off of dead center, to get you to *do* something. Often consumers need prodding, and, as I will discuss further in Chapter 7, "Finding and Working with a Real Estate Agent," salespeople can be of invaluable help in spurring both buyers and sellers into action, inspiring them with a sense of urgency when it is needed.

When you deal with successful professionals—as you should—you are going to be dealing with people who earn commissions, so get it out of your mind that there is something wrong with someone making money on your transaction. Concentrate on how much value you are receiving, how much these people's advice can save you. Usually that is many times what they are making.

SUMMARY

My purpose in exploring salesmanship and the decision-making process is to expose the subtle forces that have historically been very effective in planting ideas in the minds of so many people. By buying this book, you have taken the first step in expanding your knowledge and overriding some of those incorrect notions.

In my mortgage practice, I deal with many people who are in the top 5 percent of the populace in terms of income, assets, and education. Despite their advantages, they too have misconceptions when they arrive. And most of them end up with a different loan or select a different rate versus fee structure than what they had in mind when they walked into my office. The difference in what they were set to spend and what they end up spending after talking to me is many thousands of dollars per customer, which explains the title of my first book, *How to Save Thousands of Dollars on Your Home Mortgage.* I am equally sure that I can help many more people save money, too, via this new e-channel.

Before we get started saving you money, however, let me summarize what makes for a wise decision-making process:

- It is reasonable to get rid of your preconceived notions.
- It is reasonable to do research to determine which among the array of mortgages offered best fits the goals you have set.
- It is reasonable to carefully analyze the various rate versus fee alternatives your lender offers and select the one that makes the most sense for you.
- It is reasonable to work at finding the most opportune time to lock in your rate.

The way to save money is in the decisions you make about loan type, rate versus fee, and when to lock in, not in rate shopping. Yet a recent survey reported that 73 percent of Internet mortgage shoppers said that the reason they were searching for a loan on the Internet was to save money, as opposed to searching for better service, however that might be defined. Naturally, if lenders perceive that people are looking for a bargain, they will try to convince you that you can get a bargain from them. As a consequence, many lenders on the Internet are going to appeal to—even pander to—the consumer's expressed desire, a low rate. In my 20 years in the mortgage business, I have never seen such open and blatant appeals to the rate-conscious shopper. Be very cautious about this. Is it possible to get a good deal on the Internet? Absolutely—but educate yourself first! Recognize that the majority of the most easily identified Internet lenders are not going to be well equipped to give you much assistance. Remember, they perceive that they are in a price-driven market, not a service-driven market. In their drive to cut costs, they have eliminated most of the people who traditionally provided service. Being empowered means acknowledging up front that you're going to have to make these decisions yourself. Take good notes.

2

GUNFIGHT AT THE
INTERNET CORRAL

*In Italy for 30 years under the Borgias they had warfare,
terror, murder, bloodshed—but they produced Michelan-
gelo, da Vinci, and the Renaissance. In Switzerland, they
had brotherly love, 500 years of democracy and peace, and
what did that produce? The cuckoo clock.*
—ORSON WELLES AS HARRY LIME IN *THE THIRD MAN*

KEY POINTS

- The Internet is a new phenomenon, and both providers and users of information are still struggling to find the best ways of connecting with each other.
- The real estate and mortgage industries are among the largest, and the entrenched power structures are not always accommodating to change, especially if it is forced on them.
- Many of the real estate industry's most cherished assets are under attack.
- The tools are in place to forge more productive relationships between principals and their agents, and consumers need to be more proactive in these relationships.

At the Real Estate Connect 99 conference I mentioned in the introduction, everybody who is anybody in this field was there and made presentations at various events. At the time, the first Internet lender had just gone public with an immediate market capitalization of $1.5 billion. Everyone at the conference could smell the money and the excitement was palpable. Economics notwithstanding, there are still some important issues to be resolved before the real estate industry fully integrates the Internet into the way it interacts with its customers.

Over the past few years, Realtors, through their 800 local and state associations, and nationally through the National Association of Realtors (NAR), have resisted efforts to make public the information on properties that their member brokerages had listed for sale. "If you want to buy a home, you have to call one of our members," they seemed to be saying. Their efforts failed, of course, and the public has access to the information—which, in part, makes this book possible. However, this resolution of this battle between consumers and the real estate sales industry was not reached willingly, but in many cases as a result of court orders.

As this war to control information is waged across the country, it seems that the final battle is being fought on the Internet. The NAR and the large real estate brokerage companies still believe that the information on homes listed with member real estate companies is proprietary information that can be sold for a profit. The purpose of this chapter is to introduce you to some of the players and the way this dispute is playing out.

REALTOR.com is the official Web site of the NAR. The NAR has contracted with a company called RealSelect to manage its Web site. RealSelect's parent is a company called Homestore.com, which also manages similar Internet databases for homebuilders and apartment owners. Homestore.com entered into a number of agreements with various multiple listing services (MLSs) and various real estate brokerage companies that gave RealSelect exclusive rights to display on a nationwide basis the listings of these real estate companies on the REALTOR .com Web site. It further provided that the managements of its companies would discourage the listings from being displayed on other Internet Web sites.

As inducement to these entities to enter into these exclusive agreements, Homestore.com apparently offered them shares of Homestore.com stock at favorable prices that promised tremendous profits when the company finally went public. Then, according to at least one lawsuit that was filed, Homestore.com reneged on one of those promises. Ultimately this suit was settled, with Homestore.com reportedly giving the plaintiff company 250,000 shares of stock at a market value of $17.5 million. Why am I telling you this? Because you need to be aware of the implications about the control potentially being exercised over the information on the listing of your home.

You might think that information about your home is *your* information, but many industry forces take the position that, when they configure that information in a format compatible with the MLS computer or the Internet, it becomes their information, data they can sell to others. Selling your name to other companies may be legal, but I am bothered by privacy implications of it, especially if it is done without your permission or knowledge. And this isn't like the Department of Motor Vehicles selling lists of drivers to direct mail companies for 2 cents apiece. We're talking about substantial referral fees, the result of which, real estate executives hope, is to dramatically increase their companies' profits.

This state of mind concerning control over information and its manipulation continues to this day. At the Real Estate Connect 99 conference, I heard Alex Periello, president of Coldwell Banker, say:

> *"Brokers are realizing for the first time that the national vendors that we provide to them and the local ones they secure are willing to pay them a great deal of money to have access to their customer base. So they are taking advantage of that. Now a word of caution in all of this—that is the exciting part of the business—a word of caution is that any perceived threat to this now from anyone including online service providers, mortgage companies, anyone else that interacts with that customer, any threat to this by the real estate community would be viewed as a hostile action."*

This might prompt you to think one of the following: "Wait a minute! I chose them and contracted with them to sell my home or to represent me in buying it, not to have their hand in my wallet in all these other transactions"; or, "My agent's company is supposed to be getting my home as much exposure as it can, not restricting it. The Internet is supposed to be about free access to information"; or, "Information about *my home* is *my information,* and I resent someone else trying to make a million bucks off of my listing." If so, then I think you are on the right track. In our society, the consumer ought to have free choice about which companies to do business with, not be subjected to pressure by those who stand to earn kickbacks from referrals.

THE FUTURE

There are over 720,000 real estate agents who are members of the National Association of Realtors. They pay dues and fees to help run their local boards that administer the local MLS; and some of those dues go to the NAR. At a rough cost of $500 per realtor, we're talking about national revenue of $360 million, plus or minus a few million. Membership allows agents to enter their listings into the MLS through their computers and to search the MLS database for properties for their buyer clients.

What happens when every agent has his or her computer connected to the Internet and all of the listing data are on the Internet? Then imagine that each agent has software that facilitates posting listings directly to the Internet databases and to performing property searches on the Internet databases instead of the database at the agent's own local board or association.

How long will it be before agents to say to themselves, "Gee, doing this on the Internet is a lot easier and cheaper than the traditional way"? At that point, the local databases managed by the agents' MLS databases become of marginal value to them. Then, how eager do you think they'll be to shell out $500 or so every year for membership in their local association, their state association of realtors, and the NAR? Case in point: In my home state of California, out of 196,000 real estate licensees, only 92,000 are also members of the California Association of Realtors.

Does this mean the end of organized real estate? Hardly. But the Internet is about empowering individual homeowners and homebuyers, giving them access to more information and more control over their own destinies. Will they still need expert advice? You bet they will, and there will always be experts around to help them—for a fee. I think that real estate experts will begin to offer a selective array of services from which the consumer can choose those he or she wants and pay a fee for just those services. The fallout for the industry is that those agents who are experts, who provide value to their clients, will be worth every penny of the fees they earn and will prosper, whereas the marginal companies and marginal agents that continue in the traditional fashion will be history. What the exact outcome will be and which players will be standing when the smoke clears is not readily apparent. I do suspect that some of those entrenched in the current power structure do not like what they see.

Keep in mind, too, that the players who make the entire industry work are the real estate lenders. Simply put, no money, no real estate business. During the 1980s there was a real partnership between the real estate sales folks and those with the money. The real estate pros knew the buyers and they called on the mortgage pros to finance their deals. That all changed during the 1990s, however, when the real estate forces began exerting more control over the lending process. The lenders were relegated to more of a background role. I heard Sharon Millet, then president of the NAR, say recently that lenders' income from loan origination was too high, that they were making too much money. I'm not exactly sure what she meant, but I think she was implying that the real estate brokerage industry could run the lending function more efficiently than the lenders.

Did the lenders take this power grab lying down? Hardly. They responded to this pressure by marketing directly to the consumer, a trend that is likely to continue. In fact, the mortgage lending community is better organized to control business in this arena than the more highly fragmented real estate sales industry, so it will be interesting to see how this all plays out. And the stakes are very high. Consider all of the real estate data in the country and the value of these data to so many businesses and government entities. Appraisers and taxing authorities want to know the value of a property when it is transferred. City and county governments want to track all the parcels within their jurisdictions. Title companies that insure properties want to track their potential liabilities. The federal government wants to track which properties are in flood zones and which are in areas of toxic contamination. School districts want to track homes in each district. The list goes on and on, and the value of maintaining highly accurate information is important to these entities. Currently, control of this information is highly fragmented, as are the lists of homes for sales spread across hundreds of local MLS databases. Probably in the next five to 10 years some force or forces—perhaps not just those companies who are current players—will bring some cohesiveness to this arena. The results will be both interesting and important to the entire industry and to consumers.

SUMMARY

When you consider that Homestore.com was willing to give stock worth $17.5 million to a real estate company for exclusive access to its agents' listing information, you don't have to be a rocket scientist to see that the use of the Internet for real estate transactions is shaping up to be a battleground with a lot at stake.

Your task, as a consumer, is to be critical about what you see and read on the real estate Web sites. The adage still applies: Don't believe everything you read. You need to be proactive in managing the marketing and sale of your home in order to assure that your agent and his or her company use the Internet fully to your advantage. Buyers will have to learn new ways of finding homes and utilizing the services of their agents. As on the Serengeti Plain, e-commerce is a broad and somewhat unexplored world in which different animals are on the move. Some are predators, so others need to be wary to avoid becoming prey. Both danger and opportunity are lurking in the tall grass.

GETTING INFORMATION ABOUT COMMUNITIES

It is the mark of an educated mind to be able to entertain a thought without accepting it.

—ARISTOTLE

KEY POINTS

- Every community is a collection of neighborhoods with numerous and sometimes widely varying characteristics. It is important to find one that fits your needs.

- Look at all the factors relevant to each community, as the choice you must make will almost invariably involve prioritizing those factors, then compromising on the less important. Rarely, if ever, will all your criteria be met. The vast quantities of data available on the Internet do not translate to all data being valuable, and much of the information may be difficult to interpret.

- Don't rely solely on statistics to make your decision; it is important that you judge the characteristics of a community by "feel" as well. Trust your instincts.

Every sizable metropolitan area is a collection of subcommunities, varying from inner city neighborhoods to nearby suburbs to outlying areas. Even smaller towns may have significant delineations. The first step someone moving to a new area must take is to learn about the differences between a given community and other nearby communities. It is vitally important for homebuyers to understand these differences if they are to make intelligent decisions when making the major investment in a home.

Those moving within the same community or to a nearby area already have a head start in this process, but for newcomers, community characteristics can be a mystery. And let's face it, the costs of making a mistake are huge; a family making a 10 percent down payment on a home and then finding out that they made a serious mistake will face costs of 6 percent to 7 percent of the home's value, effectively wiping out their equity. That precludes a further move for most people, regardless of the seriousness of the error. For that reason, it is important—make that essential—for those moving to a new area to do enough research to assure that when they finally select a new neighborhood, all involved will be happy with the choice.

CHOOSING A COMMUNITY

Perhaps you think the choice of a community is based on obvious criteria: "We want to live in an area that's close to work, where home values are increasing, where the schools are good, where shopping is convenient, where the crime rate is low, where property taxes are low," and so forth. Do I really need to tell you that it is never that easy?

Affordability is almost always a factor, because those who got there before you have already determined the values in that neighborhood. The most affluent can afford to move to the most prestigious areas, but for the rest of us, how much we can afford will force us to make trade-offs. For example, families with children in high school might stress the quality of the high schools and might want to focus on finding an area where their children will be in a school system that will afford them the greatest opportunities for advancement into the college of their choice. Older couples would probably want to find areas where they can have easy access to health care, shopping, and the opportunity for socializing with people in their own age group.

The point is, you must prioritize your needs. Start by making a list of those criteria that are most important to you and your family. The following comprise a list of the most commonly considered. Write these down and add any that are particular to your situation, then begin setting your family's priorities.

- Housing value appreciation potential
- Resale value and other economic factors
- School system
- Crime rate
- Commuting time
- Median income
- Other demographic factors
- Shopping
- Legal issues
- Environmental issues

We'll look at each of these in more detail, and then I'll point you to Web sites where you can find helpful information on each of these criteria.

Housing Value Appreciation Potential

Across the country, housing values have increased so much in the last 20 years that it has become abundantly clear that a home is not just a place to live; it is also an investment. Assuming that you will want to sell sometime in the future, your down payment on your next home will be your equity in the current one, so you need to be concerned about resale value when you buy. You want the value of your home, and thus your equity, to appreciate faster than average, or at least as fast as the average of other neighborhoods. Some areas in any community are past their prime, while others are just entering theirs. Don't misunderstand: I don't mean that older communities are necessarily bad. In fact, such areas have an appealing charm due to, among other factors, diverse architecture, larger lots, and mature trees, which newer tracts do not have. What I am saying is that some communities have excellent qualities that are apparent to larger numbers of homebuyers than others, and, because the demand is higher, the prices are going to be under more upward pressure. If you are lucky enough to buy in one of these communities early, you can look forward to higher appreciation than those who buy in less desirable areas.

Condominiums and Townhomes.   Studies show that most people prefer to live in single-family homes—the typical detached homes on their own lots. The problem is that in most desirable urban and suburban areas, land values have risen so high that developers must build homes in higher density just to make them affordable. So, though most people might prefer single-family homes, when they find out about prices, they realize they may only be able to afford a condominium or a townhome. The problem with the value and appreciation of these units is that most owners are not able to differentiate their units from all the others in the complex. In brief, it is safe to assume that one unit will appreciate just about as quickly or as slowly as every other in the complex. This is not necessarily bad, just a factor to take into consideration.

Another factor in condominium projects is the percentage of units occupied by renters, as opposed to owner-occupied units. When you get a higher percentage of renters—over 30 percent—you should be concerned about a problem. Owners of those rental units may not be as committed to the appearance, maintenance, and upkeep of the complex as you and the others who live there. Second, from a more pragmatic standpoint, most lenders are quite cautious about lending in projects where the percentage of renters is high, and others won't lend at all.

They fear that a severe bump in the economy might compel those absentee landlords to default not only on their mortgages but on their association dues as well, thereby putting the economic viability of the complex in jeopardy. If you are interested in any condominium or townhome, find out this information right at the beginning. You'll have to do some digging, as it is doubtful you will ever find this statistic on the Internet, particularly if it's bad. Even your agent may not know this information, but you can have him or her research this important topic before showing you property. The complex's association management office or off-site management company may be able to determine the number of renters by counting the number of units where the monthly dues statement is sent to an address other than the unit itself.

Planned Communities.   In many areas, even neighborhoods composed of single-family homes can still be considered to be planned communities. Like condominiums, they have a community association and covenants, conditions, and restrictions (CC&Rs) that govern many facets of what a homeowner can and can't do with his or her home. For example, a common restriction is that an architectural review committee has to approve any additions or changes to a home, and sometimes even a new paint color. The upside of such strict governance is that the general appearance and pride of ownership may be more evident in such communities, translating into higher values. Statistics demonstrate that housing values in such communities appreciate faster than in nonplanned neighboring areas. Of course, these communities may not be the best choice for someone who feels that such rules, restrictions, and bureaucracy are an infringement on personal freedom.

High-Cost Communities.   For people moving to or being transferred to highly desirable areas—the San Francisco Bay area, currently—home values can be two or three times those for comparable housing in other sections of the country. The good news is that these areas frequently are also areas of future appreciation. Thus, if you can afford to live in such an area, your home will probably be a good investment. My point is to think long term when scouting communities. Obviously you do not want to jeopardize your family's financial future by living beyond your means, but sometimes "buying up" can also mean increasing your return on investment (ROI).

__TIP__ Refer to Chapter 6, "Estimating What It's Worth," to learn about Web sites where you can access information on housing values for your area. Are they increasing, declining, or static? Also, ask your real estate agent to show you statistics on how long properties in the area stay on the market. The first sign of a slowdown is when homes don't sell as quickly as they used to, as indicated by the number of days on the market before a property sells.

Resale Value and Other Economic Factors

If you have ever had the misfortune of being forced to sell a property at a disadvantageous time, you know how upsetting it can be. I've had to do it, and I wouldn't want to do it again. Neither should you. My point here is that if, for example, you are being transferred somewhere for a short period of time—say two to four years—and your employer does not have a relocation policy that includes buying your home if it doesn't sell quickly, be very careful when assessing the prospects for resale. If they don't look good, I recommend that you rent for a couple of years; this can be done without much risk.

Consider, for example, the early 1990s in the Greater Los Angeles area, when residents experienced the loss of over 350,000 jobs in the aerospace industry after the relaxation of Cold War tensions resulted in tremendous cutbacks in defense spending. This occurred at a time when real estate values were already declining, thus exacerbating the situation. Ten years earlier, when oil prices dropped, we saw a similar situation in "Oil Patch" states such as Texas and Colorado.

Economic downturns can affect small towns even more dramatically. I was on a fishing trip in Dillon, Montana, when the local sawmill announced that it was shutting down, eliminating 80 jobs. That doesn't sound like a lot of jobs if you are a big-city resident, but it was devastating news to this small community. Though some chose to tough it out, others had to move to find work. Even if your job is not one of the 350,000 or 80, do you want to try to sell your home when everyone else is trying to sell theirs? I didn't think so.

To find out about such factors in a community, you can access the economic statistics at the Department of Commerce at www .commerce.gov and two of its bureaus, the Bureau of the Census (www .census.gov) and the Bureau of Economic Analysis (www.bea.doc.gov). Don't feel intimidated by the avalanche of data. A short study of personal income, housing starts, and the like can give you an indication if your area, or the area you're considering moving to, is growing or static. No, you can't predict the future, but you certainly can qualitatively assess the community's long-term prospects. In addition to these sources, newspapers report these kinds of statistics, and most newspapers these days have Web sites.

School System

I recall reading that when the 50 states made their annual reports to the U.S. Department of Education, every single state reported that its schools were above average. Who are they kidding? Do the math: 25 were above average and the other 25 were below average. Understandably, school administrators don't want to admit that any schools under their supervision are below average, so be aware that as a prospective homeowner, you will be deluged by information, all of which says,

"The schools in this area are excellent." It's up to you to confirm that this is true; do research to determine the facts.

For starters, be sure to look beyond school district data, because there may be some variation in schools at different grade levels within the same district; grade schools might be good but the intermediate or high schools might not be as good, or vice versa. There may be important differences between, say, two high schools in the same district.

In addition, be sure to check the school district boundaries and the boundaries within the district. I can remember a big brouhaha when a builder assured its homebuyers that their children would be attending the particularly desirable nearby high school. That was important to a number of the buyers who knew that school was one of the very best in the state. What the builder didn't know was that the school district was redrawing its boundaries and that the new tract was being assigned to another high school! Homebuyers who take the time to do the research can be spared similar disappointments.

Finally, and perhaps most important, when you get close to a decision, visit the schools your children will be attending. The principal or other administrator will be glad to spend a few minutes with you and give you a tour. Take with you information you have gathered and check it against what you see and feel.

Crime Rate

One of the bright statistics of the 1990s is the drop in the national crime rate. Nonetheless, it is still a factor. No one wants to live in an area frequented by drug dealers, gang-bangers, and worse. Later in this chapter, I'll give you some Web sites to go to for information on crime rates in this category, but there is nothing like talking to friends, neighbors, and coworkers.

NOTE   There is a difference between violent crime and other types that may not have much impact on you. For example, my hometown has the reputation for being the national center for telemarketing scams and investment fraud. That shouldn't deter you from buying a home there, just from talking to the wrong people.

Commuting Time

Unless you are a glutton for punishment, determine precisely what the commute time will be from your new community to your job, whether by public transportation or by car. Make sure to do this during rush hours. Once you arrive to begin house hunting and when you zero in on an area, try the commute. If necessary, switch to a motel near your proposed home. Several days of this will tell you if the commute will be tolerable. Be sure to talk with neighbors who take a similar route to work. Don't invest in a new home only to spend all your free time on the road.

More recently, condominium projects are being built that are practically within walking distance of a number of businesses. In my area, there are four or five very attractive, successful projects that are nominally within an office/industrial area. Certainly, they offer benefits, but the lifestyle is different from that of purely residential areas, so again, you have to weigh your priorities.

| TIP | Regardless of the length of your commute, why not pass the time more profitably by listening to audio books during your drive? They are a lot more interesting than talk radio and other commute-time diversions. Check your local library or the various audio book companies such as Books on Tape and Recorded Books, both of which have huge catalogs of rental tapes that will keep you occupied, better informed, and calmer behind the wheel.

Median Income

So many aspects of our lives are determined by economics and our views about money that it is important to many homebuyers to find a neighborhood of their financial peers. I'm not promoting a "keep up with the Joneses" philosophy, but, realistically, it is a factor to many in America today. If your income is significantly higher or lower than that of your neighbors, you may find that you don't have much in common with them and end up unhappy and forced to face an expensive move. You need to be cognizant of the psychological factors that shape your family's behavior and find a neighborhood that matches your beliefs.

Other Demographic Factors

I used to live in a neighborhood where every family except one had a couple of school-age children. This couple was a generation older than the rest of us and, friendly as we all were, at that stage in life, most of our social life revolved around our children. The result was that our interactions with this older couple were infrequent and relatively superficial. Looking back, I suspect sometimes they wished they lived among neighbors their own age.

Today, conversely, I live in a community where most people are senior citizens, not because it is a retirement community but because the development is 30 years old. Many residents are original homeowners, so of course they are all 30 years older than they were when they first bought their homes. Though there are a handful of families with school-age children, they have very little to do with their neighbors, not because they aren't lovely people, but because they have so little in common, so little to talk about. I think that you see my point: You will increase your family's happiness by buying a home in a neighborhood where most of the people have a lot in common with your family.

Shopping

As much time as Americans spend shopping, you may be surprised to learn that, when people are house hunting, convenience to shopping is an often overlooked consideration. If you choose to live 10 miles out of town, implicit in that decision is the assumption that you won't be running to town every time you forget something on your shopping list. Though it's common practice now in the newer suburbs for master developers to build shopping centers as they build new residential tracts, making shopping convenient in most cases, nonetheless, you ought to check on their progress. In a relatively newly developed community near us, about 5,000 people live in an area where a shopping center was indicated on the community's master plan. Five years later, the promised site is still an empty lot and the residents have to drive an inconvenient distance to shop.

If you're thinking of buying in an older community, you may have to recognize that you may be limited to the offerings in smaller stores because developers just don't put large chain outlets in these neighborhoods.

Legal Issues

If you are considering moving to an area that is fully developed, you probably won't have to deal with zoning issues; but if you are interested in an area where there is a lot of vacant land, you'd be well advised to familiarize yourself with the city's or county's plans for this land. You do not want to find your new home backing up to a mall or to a street that is about to become wider, busier, and noisier. You can find out this type of information at your city hall or at the county planning office.

Of course, some development will be more readily apparent. In my area, a major debate is raging over a potential new airport. Regardless of the merits of the arguments, the emotions of the participants are running high over the impact of such a development. As an outsider, you don't want to be the person buying the home of the first resident jumping ship in advance of a mass exodus and the resulting crash in values. Be informed and you won't be devastated to find yourself in the eye of a land use storm.

Environmental Issues

Sometimes it seems as if the federal government keeps statistics of every square inch of our land, to keep it safe from environmental polluters. Then, just when you become complacent, you hear on the six o'clock news about some strange new contamination problem in a town near you. There are Web sites you can access to determine whether there are any such problems in your area. The first is the Environmental Protection Agency (EPA). Go to their site at www.epa.gov, plug in the zip code of the area you want to check to learn whether it has any Superfund cleanup sites or other such sites, selecting the Enviromapper function. A map quickly appears that shows the location of potential problem sites and hazardous waste sites. I was alarmed that there are 58 in my zip code alone, and there will be some in your area too. Luckily, when you investigate further, chances are that most of these sites will turn out to be local gas stations, dry cleaning establishments, photo finishers, and car dealerships. In my area, even one of the schools and the offices of several doctors are considered hazardous under the EPA definition! More helpful is the environmental profile function, which has charts and statistics for such items as air quality, drinking water, surface water, hazardous waste, and toxic chemical releases.

Another site you should check out is the Environmental Defense Fund at www.scorecard.org. Type in a zip code and find out about various risks caused by environmental hazards in that area. Again, however, use common sense when evaluating information, as a little investigation will show you that the risks are highest where the most people are, which is where the jobs are, which is why you are thinking of moving there.

A third site worth a look is www.nearmyhome.com, which has reports that assess the risk of such natural threats as earthquakes, fires, and floods as well as threats posed by environmental pollution. The cost to consumers is $4.95 for each report. Engineering and insurance companies as well as commercial real estate lenders use these data, and they are certainly worthwhile to you as a consumer. Before you spring for them, however, ask your real estate agent if his or her company already has a contract with the provider so that these reports will be provided to you for free. And be aware that in some states, such as California, sellers are legally required to disclose certain hazards, so you may get a report like this anyway. The point is, you want to know about an environmental problem before making an offer on a home, not after it is in escrow.

An environmental problem that is not likely to be fully disclosed is that relating to water—not its quality, but where it goes. Water might drain from a nearby property onto yours, or water might not drain from your property, or subsurface water might come to the surface on your property. During the dry season—nine months long in my area—how would a homebuyer know what happens during the wet season? A client of mine was doing a final walk-through one day before closing on a home when he noticed water seeping from under the front walkway. He hoped it was water from a sprinkler that had been left on too long, but it wasn't. The home's concrete pad was sitting on a natural spring that came to the surface during the wet season. My client was lucky to see this, and naturally, he didn't buy the property. You might not be so lucky, so be sure to ask about all the possible risks.

THE PERSONAL TOUCH

After you have zeroed in on a neighborhood, go there one Saturday, park your car, walk around, and meet some of your potential new neighbors. You'll be surprised what you can find out. I know someone—not a client—who bought a home without doing this kind of personal review. Worse, she bought through an out-of-area real estate agent who knew nothing about the area, much less the home. She called me to cry on my shoulder because the house she had bought was next to that of a family whose teenage son practiced on his drums four or five hours a day. If the seller had personally reported this to the police, the seller would have been obligated to disclose this nuisance to potential buyers, but, as it was, drumming is not against the law so the buyer had no recourse. It was the seller's reason for moving; all the neighbors knew about it, and all she had to do was ask.

In contrast, a client of mine who wanted to make an offer on a property in a particular area did take the time to walk the area. One resident he talked to told him about the Neighborhood Watch program in the area, which he took as a good sign. He didn't stop there, he kept asking, and among the things he found out was that the sellers of the house he was considering had had their car stolen twice from in front of their house. Next!

MAKING A CHOICE

Choosing a community, then, like choosing a home, is an exclusionary process. You begin by assuming that any community would be satisfactory, then start excluding those that do not meet your most important criteria. What you will be left with are several that would meet your needs. The first step is to collect general information.

Collecting General Information

A quick and slick way of accessing general community information is by going to www.realtor.com. Click on Find a Neighborhood and you'll get to the page shown in Figure 3.1, where you can search from a map, by city and state, or by zip code. I typed in Huntsville, Alabama. Figure 3.2a shows the result. Note that you can zoom in or out of whatever area is shown on the map to include a larger or smaller area.

TIP   If you are seeking school data, some real estate sites will only work with a county, not a city or a zip code.

Note that in Figure 3.2a is the slick "criteria match" section. In the Neighborhood Qualities section, you can type in a specific zip code to

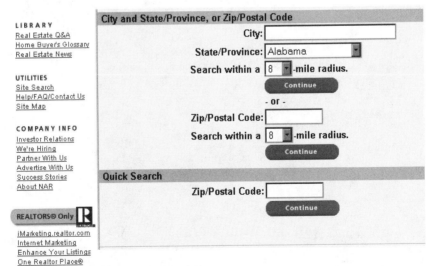

Figure 3.1   REALTOR.com Find a Neighborhood page.
(Courtesy of Homestore.com.)

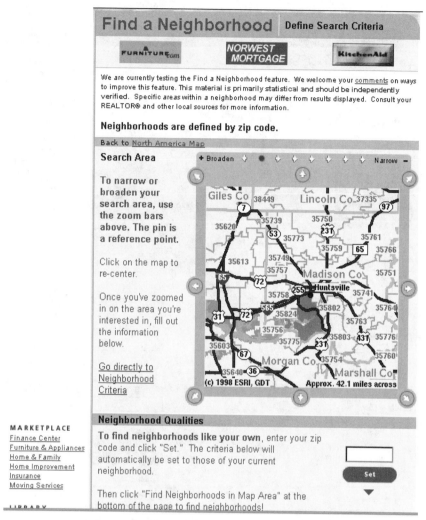

Figure 3.2 (*a*) **Area map of Huntsville, Alabama.**
(Courtesy of Homestore.com.)

locate areas near Huntsville that most closely match your current residence. Alternatively, you can enter data in the bottom half of the page (as shown in Figure 3.2*b*) that allow you to define neighborhood characteristics you want and to rank their importance to you. For this example I chose best schools and high income.

When you have finished, go to the bottom of the page and click on Find Neighborhoods in Map Area. This prompts the computer program to compare the characteristics of your hometown neighborhood or the

MOVING SERVICES

LIBRARY
Real Estate Q&A
Home Buyer's Glossary
Real Estate News

UTILITIES
Site Search
Help/FAQ/Contact Us
Site Map

COMPANY INFO
Investor Relations
We're Hiring
Partner With Us
Advertise With Us
Success Stories
About NAR

REALTORS® Only ℝ

iMarketing.realtor.com
Internet Marketing
Enhance Your Listings
One Realtor Place®

Then click "Find Neighborhoods in Map Area" at the bottom of the page to find neighborhoods!

──────────────── OR ────────────────

Define the qualities you want in a neighborhood and rate how important each quality is to you. **For qualities with a 1-5 rating, consider 1 to be the best.**

Click to Select

School Performance	Unspecified ▾
Crime Risk	Unspecified ▾
Rural/Urban Profile	Unspecified ▾
Cultural Amenities	Unspecified ▾
Households with Children	Unspecified ▾
Age of Population	Unspecified ▾

Home Features

Now define the kind of homes you're looking for. **This is a general, overall picture of homes in the neighborhood and may not reflect features of specific homes.**

Click to Select

Home Cost	min	Unspecified ▾
	max	Unspecified ▾
Age of Homes		Unspecified ▾
Square Footage		Unspecified ▾
Minimum Bedrooms		Unspecified ▾

Type of House	☐ Single Family
	☐ Condo
	☐ Townhouse

When you've made your selections, click "Find Neighborhoods in Map Area."

To start over, click "Reset Form."

[Find Neighborhoods in Map Area]   [Reset Form]

School data provided by The School Report. All other data supplied by MonsterDaata.com, Inc. It is not guaranteed and should be independently

Figure 3.2 *(Continued)* (*b*) Neighborhood criteria page.

criteria you entered with those of areas near Huntsville. It ranks the areas and displays a map where all the zip codes are displayed. Those with the highest correlations will be shown color-coded on the map. In this case, zip code 35816, which has a 74 percent correlation with the criteria I established, showed up shaded on my computer screen, as shown in Figure 3.3.

If you click on the Quick Summary button, you'll get a statistical summary of characteristics of that neighborhood as shown in Figure 3.4.

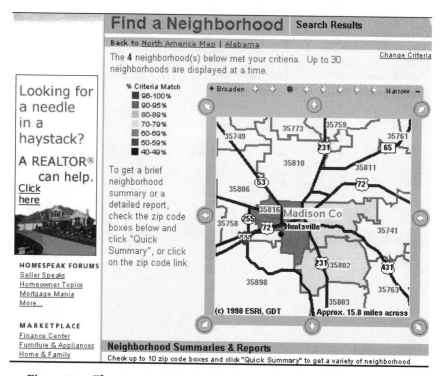

Figure 3.3   The area near Huntsville that matched my search criteria.
(Courtesy of Homestore.com.)

Finding Out about Housing Values

When you have reduced your search to specific properties, you will want
to read Chapter 6. At this stage, however, you want to make sure that you
are looking in the right section of town. Every community has a range of
values, so if you can afford a home in the $150,000 range, excluding areas
where the average values are significantly higher or lower than your target range can save a lot of grief and time wasted looking in the wrong part
of town. To find areas in the community where the housing is in your
price range, you can enter in your price range—say, $150,000 to $175,000.
The search results will show you the zip codes that have homes in your
price range. If you haven't been prequalified by a lender, you should also
do an affordabilty check. Refer to Chapter 12, "Qualifying."

As I said earlier, these sites show summary characteristics, which
may be enough data to narrow down your search. If not, you might benefit from more detailed information. You can go to the sources for the
REALTOR.com Web site, at www.2001beyond.com for school data, and
www.monsterdaata.com for the rest.

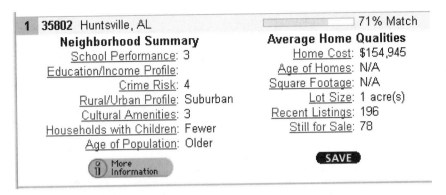

Figure 3.4   Quick summary of characteristics for this zip code.
(Courtesy of Homestore.com.)

If this process appeals to you, start by practicing with the area you now live, comparing your hometown with other nearby areas and zip codes to get a feel for how the process works. Then you'll be better able to use the site to interpret and analyze the data on your new hometown. Again, the purpose of this exercise is to get a rough idea of the characteristics of potential communities. As in the home search, your goal here is to exclude areas that do not meet your criteria as well as include areas that do.

Other Neighborhood Information Sites

HomeAdvisor, at www.homeadvisor.com, has an excellent neighborhood search feature that portrays the data in a slightly different manner. This part of the Web site is not available directly from the home page, so you have to go on a short journey. Click on Homes for Sale—Find and compare homes and neighborhoods in the upper left portion of the home page. On the next page, under House Hunting Tools on the left side, click on Look up a neighborhood. You will then reach the page shown in Figure 3.5 to initiate a three-step search process.

Enter a state and region, and in the criteria section, enter crime rate, school test rating, and neighborhood type in the appropriate drop boxes and radio buttons. Then click the See Results button to access the page with the search results, shown in Figure 3.6. Note that HomeAdvisor defines neighborhoods by zip code. You have three choices here, noting the radio buttons denoted Demographics, Crime, and Schools. In this case, we'll follow the Demographics button to find communities most closely matching the search criteria. If you click on the Crime or Schools buttons, you'll get a similar layout of results in those categories.

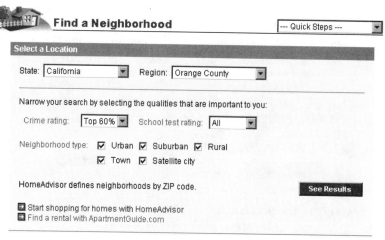

Figure 3.5   HomeAdvisor's Neighborhood Finder page. (Courtesy of HomeAdvisor.)

In the demographic layout, you can click on a community that interests you for more information. I clicked on Aliso Viejo, and went to the Neighborhood Details page shown in Figure 3.7. Note that some of the same statistics are shown along with a map that details the precise location of the community in the region. By clicking on See surrounding neighborhood, you can go to a more detailed map that shows school locations. You can also click on these links:

- Find homes in and around this neighborhood
- Find rentals in and around this neighborhood
- Find real estate services in this neighborhood

to see about the availability of further services. The topic of finding a home will be covered in detail in the next chapter.

At the bottom of the page are listed more particular neighborhood types. In this case, you can see that 25.54 percent of the residents of this area are listed as Upward Bound. When you click on that, you can see that Upward Bound is defined this way:

Young, college-educated, computer-literate, dual-income, frequent-flying executives and professionals describe those in "Upward Bound." Most of this group is married, with pre- and school-age children, and live in new, owner-occupied single-family homes.

Demographics for Neighborhoods 1 to 10 (52 total)									
Neighborhood	On Map	Listings	Type	Population	Primary Employment	Median Income	Households	People per Household (Avg.)	Median Age
Aliso Viejo - Laguna Beach, etc. (92656)	❶	160	Suburban/Satellite City	30026	Professional	$53,735.00	13189	2.27	37.3
Anaheim (92899)	❷	0	Suburban	37872	Professional	$79,758.00	12458	3.03	38.2
Anaheim - Anaheim Hills (92807)	❸	129	Suburban	37872	Professional	$79,758.00	12458	3.03	38.2
Anaheim - Anaheim Hills (92808)	❹	101	Suburban	18223	Professional	$81,123.00	5904	3.07	36.5
Anaheim - Sunkist (92806)	❺	30	Urban/Suburban	31960	Professional White Collar	$50,290.00	11291	2.81	34.6
Brea (92821)	❻	50	Suburban	34705	Professional	$62,689.00	12826	2.7	36.9
Brea (92823)	❼	8	Suburban	1343	Professional	$66,429.00	528	2.54	46.7
Capistrano Beach - Dana Point (92624)	❽	62	Suburban/Satellite City	9678	Professional	$66,774.00	3582	2.61	40.8
Corona Del Mar (92625)	❾	144	Suburban	14682	Professional	$95,172.00	6685	2.19	46.2

Figure 3.6   HomeAdvisor's Neighborhood Demographics page.
(Courtesy of HomeAdvisor.)

After the description are listed more particulars about people in this category. Among the characteristics, you'll find that they own BMWs, have beepers, watch Murphy Brown, and 17 other facts. You can mine these data for fun, and it's an interesting way to find out if the people in a neighborhood are like you.

If you're through examining the demographics of this area, remember that you can go back to the Neighborhood Results page to check out crime and school statistics. If you are not finding quite what you like, you can also go back to the first screen and change the input variables so as to change the results. These are potentially very useful tools, particularly for those who are less familiar with an area and are trying to narrow down their search.

HomeSeekers.com, at www.homeseekers.com, does not have a general neighborhood information search model, but it does have a school search feature that links directly to The School Report (www .schoolreport.com), discussed later. CyberHomes, at www.cyberhomes .com, has a direct link to SchoolMatch (www.schoolmatch.com) but does not have more general neighborhood information.

The Census Bureau

You want facts? The Census Bureau has facts, tons of them. Raw data from the most recent census may be found at www.census.gov/.

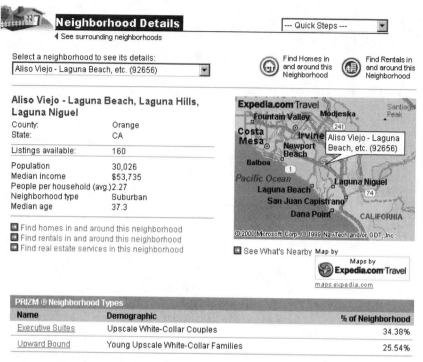

**Figure 3.7   HomeAdvisor's Neighborhood Details page.
(Courtesy of HomeAdvisor.)**

Current readers will find data from the 2000 census as they are made available. Once at the U.S. Census Bureau home page, find the American FactFinder section, click on the state you wish to see, and you will be presented with a map. Zero in on the county you are interested in and you will get to a page containing an index to demographic factors such as population and income for the county. To get more detailed information, go to www.venus.census.gov/cdrom/lookup/, where you will have the ability to look up more data than you thought possible, such as:

Median household income

School enrollment, educational attainment, and employment status

Period of military service

All in all, the Census Bureau will show you over 200 ways to slice and dice the data. Arguably, the data may be a little obtuse for some, but there is probably no other way of finding that 584 people in my hometown spent between 15 and 19 minutes commuting to work. You can see how your proposed commute compares with that of your neighbors.

A Better Way to Get Census Data

As interesting as these data are, it's a pretty grueling task to study them. Luckily for you, private enterprise strikes again. Not only do the folks at EPIC Relocation Services LLC update the data on a regular basis as new data become available, the format is far more user-friendly. This excellent service is at www2.amshomefinder.com/. Type in the town you are interested in, and two types of reports will be provided. The first is an abbreviated report. You get a map and a data summary like the one shown for my hometown in Figure 3.8. You can also get a colossal report, page one of which is shown in Figure 3.9. This particular portion shows the statistics for Households & Income. The data are largely from the U.S. Bureau of Census and other sources, although it is far easier to read and comprehend. I found the material here fascinating, and I think you will too.

MORE DETAILED DATA

School Information Web Sites

As school quality is of interest to everyone with children and those who want to sell their homes to others who have children, let's examine in more detail the various school sites discussed earlier. The following sites have information on schools nationwide. These sites are supported by revenue from real estate agents and other providers of services to homebuyers so that the information can be free to homebuyers looking for school information. The sites want to attract more real estate agents who will pay an annual fee to be associated with the sites. The bottom line is that, in accordance with the economic model for this type of Web site, information you provide about yourself will be sent to these service providers, who have paid the site to be in business to distribute information they want. When you order a report on a school in a particular town or zip code, you can expect a call from a friendly agent saying, "I understand you are looking for a home here." Personally, I find nothing wrong with this as you are notified up front that this is the case.

2001Beyond at www.2001beyond.com/bin/home.idc/ is better at comparing school districts than individual schools within a district. If you haven't yet decided which of several districts to move to, this service may be helpful. In smaller areas where there aren't many choices, this type of report may suffice. In the upper right corner of the home

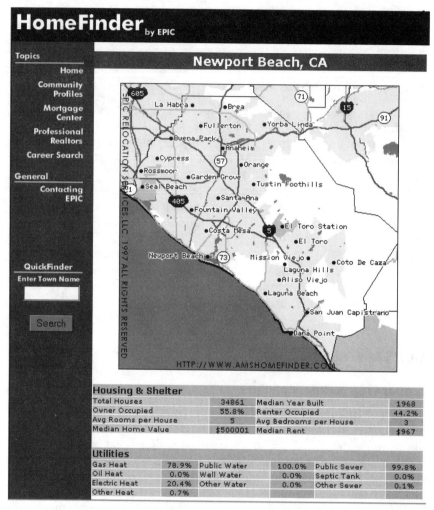

Figure 3.8   AMS HomeFinder report page.
(Courtesy of EPIC Relocation Services LLC.)

page, you'll find a box where you can scroll down to a state and hit GO. At the next screen, you'll need to know the county in which you are interested, not the city, so choose a county. Then you can compare up to four different schools within that county. Figure 3.10 shows what the Public School Snapshot page looks like.

The site goes on to list the elementary and middle schools associated with each high school. Additionally, you may get information on various aspects of the districts, such as at which grade various educational features become available in the curriculum. If you want more in-depth studies, you must pay $4.50 for each report or $6.50 for

HomeFinder by EPIC

Topics

- Home

Community Profiles

Mortgage Center

Professional Realtors

Career Search

General

Contacting EPIC

Demographics

Total Population	66643	0 - 18 yrs	14.2%	19 - 64 yrs	70.4%	65 & Over	15.5%
Born Instate		46.4%	Born out of state		53.6%
Per Capita Income	$45434	Median Household Income	$60374	Median Family Income	$81929

Industry

Retail Trade	15.3%	Finance, Insurance, Real Estate	18.3%
Construction	5.3%	Communications, Public Utilities	0.9%
Transportation	2.8%	Agriculture, Forestry, Fisheries	0.9%
Wholesale Trade	5.3%	Public Administration	1.2%
Manufacturing	13.4%	Business & Repair	6.6%
Personal Services	3.6%	Entertainment	2.0%
Health Services	7.1%	Education	6.7%
Mining	0.2%	Other	10.7%

Education

Public Elementary School	34.4%	Public Secondary School	80.1%	Public University	84.6%
Private Elementary School	65.6%	Private Secondary School	19.9%	Private University	15.4%

School District Information

NEWPORT-MESA UNIFIED	Lowest Grade: KG	Core Expenditure per pupil: $3303
P.O. BOX 1368	Highest Grade: 12	Current Expenditure per pupil: $4806
NEWPORT BEACH,CA 92663	# of Schools: 26	
714-000-3450	# of Teachers: 664.40	Total Expenditure per pupil: $5145
	# of Students: 17447	Instruction Spending: 59.00%
	Stud/Teach Ratio: 26.30	Support Services Spending: 37.90%
		Non-Instruction Spending: 3.10%

QuickFinder

Enter Town Name

Search

Transportation & Commuting

Car or Carpool	90.0%	Bus	0.7%
Rail	0.1%	Walked	2.2%
Streetcar / Subway	0.0%	Other	6.5%
Rush Hour	7:30am to 7:59am	Avg time to work (min.)	22

Airports

NEWPORT BEACH POLICE	Private Heliport	1 mi. from downtown
HOAG MEMORIAL HOSPITAL	Private Heliport	

New Community Profile Search | Get A Colossal Report

Figure 3.8 *(Continued)*

up to four reports. You have a choice of a number of separate reports. Figure 3.11 shows what a sample page of the School Overview looks like.

The School Report is at www.theschoolreport.com. On the home page, again you to click on the state you want and then hit Go. At the next screen you may click on either a city or county to get statistics about the high schools in that county. Figure 3.12 shows the summary for the various school districts in my county.

By clicking on a school district, you can get more specific information about various schools. There is a hitch here, because to get this information, you need to fill out a questionnaire with your name, address,

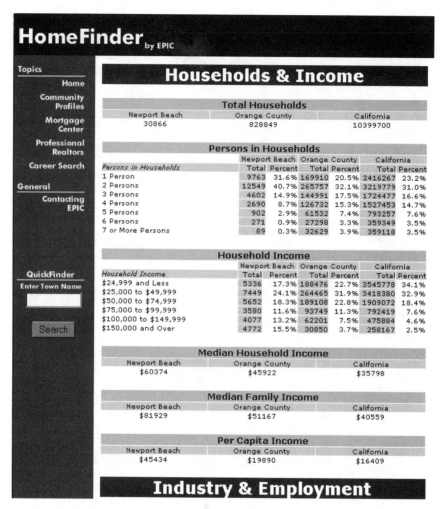

Figure 3.9   Part of AMS HomeFinder's colossal report. (Courtesy of EPIC Relocation Services LLC.)

phone numbers, and so on. When you submit this information, you may think that you are going to get a report immediately, but that is not the case. A real estate agent or other service provider who has signed up for your area will mail it to you and follow up with you. Another good feature is the ability to get a map of the high school area showing the locations of the elementary and middle schools that are associated with that high school.

SchoolMatch is at www.schoolmatch.com. To get to a district, you have to go through a relatively exhausting search by state, then by school system, as all school districts are listed alphabetically within the

Public School Snapshot

Compliment's of 2001BEYOND and **2001BEYOND HOME SITE**

Click here for the 12 page report that covers over 200 facts

Public School Snapshot
Highlights

School Year 1999-2000 District	University Irvine	Laguna Bch	NewportHbr	Cor.delMar
Lowest Grade Level	K	K	K	K
Highest Grade Level(a)	12	12	12	12
District Statistics				
Student Population	7367	2528	6919	3388
Student/Teacher Ratio	26	24	29	28
Average Class Size				
Grade 1	20	20	20	20
Grade 8	31	25	29	29
School Awards				
National Merit Finalists	26	2	2	2
Seniors with SAT Scores	74	58	51	74
(% prior year)				
Math	634	541	553	569
Verbal	574	551	537	540

School Directory

**Figure 3.10   2001Beyond Public School Snapshot page.
(Courtesy of 2001Beyond.com.)**

state. Then you get only bare details and have to pay $34 for a complete report.

My feeling is that these sites are less useful than one would hope for. In contrast, the best school site I found on the Internet is that offered by School Wise Press at www.schoolwisepress.com. At this point, the service offers information only about California schools, but perhaps coverage will be expanded. If not, my readers who live in or are moving to California will find this of real help, and others can see what a good site can offer. Not only can you find out information about each school, you can compare all the schools in a district, examining

The School Profile
School Overview

School Year 1998-1999 District	Mt. Carmel Poway	Poway HS Poway	R.Bernardo Poway	Ramona Ramona
Information updated as of	FEB 1998	FEB 1998	FEB 1998	FEB 1998
Lowest Grade Level	K	K	K	PS
Highest Grade Level*	12	12	12	12
District Statistics				
Dollars Per Student	3955	3955	3955	4175
Student Population	20903	19144	14536	6570
Teacher/Professional Staff	1336	1173	899	571
Student/Teacher Ratio	27	30	29	27
Median Years of Teaching Experience	12	12	12	10
School Statistics				
Elementary Schools	16	14	11	6
Average Population	746	792	793	629
Mid/Jr. High Schools	4	3	2	1
Average Population	1442	1604	1505	1010
High Schools	1	1	1	1
Average Population	3200	3250	2800	1788
Average Class Size				
Grade 1	20	20	20	20
Grade 8	33	33	33	30
High School English	29	32	32	28
High School Math	29	32	32	28
High School Science	29	31	32	28

Figure 3.11   2001Beyond School Overview page.
(Courtesy of 2001Beyond.com.)

the test score ranking, percentage of students less proficient in English, and so forth. Figure 3.13 shows the report for the elementary school my children attended. Note that it shows school test scores and lots of other data, not just the school address and phone number.

Figure 3.14 shows a ranking of high schools in the county displaying reading proficiency—how students in each school scored on the California state reading tests. Reports like this can really help parents zero in on a school that can fit their children. Much more information is available at this site, and I hope that other companies will use this as a model for developing similar services for other states.

Another choice for those outside of California would be to go to the State Department of Education in your state. The nomenclature varies from state to state, so the best way to find the site is to go to one of the directories such as dir.yahoo.com/government/u_s_government/ state_government/ or www.go.com/webdir/u_s_state_governments?lk= noframes&svx=related. Then go to the state and from there to the De-

Orange County, CA School Districts

After viewing this information, click here to get a FREE in-depth School Report for any school districts you select.

The Real School Report

SATs

Orange County, CA Districts	Total Student Population	Average Elementary School Population	Student Teacher Ratio	Average Class Size - Grade 1	Average Class Size - H.S. Math	Computers in Elem. Classroom
Anaheim ESD-Anaheim	8506	945	22	28	33	-
Anaheim ESD-Katella	4965	827	22	28	32	-
Anaheim ESD-Loara	5872	838	22	28	36	-
Anaheim ESD-Magnolia	781	781	22	28	34	-
Anaheim ESD-Savanna	2996	998	22	28	36	-
Brea-Olinda	5921	508	23	28	30	K
Buena Park	5343	738	23	31	32	4
Capistrano-Aliso Niguel	12292	776	22	29	30	K
Capistrano-Capistrano Vlly	15657	755	22	28	28	K
Capistrano-Dana Hills	11094	789	22	28	36	K
Capistrano-San Clemente	11951	810	22	29	29	K
Centralia-J.F. Kennedy	3149	524	22	30	33	K
Centralia-Savanna	589	589	22	30	36	K
Centralia-Western	3016	603	22	20	35	K

Figure 3.12 The School Report county report page. (Courtesy of Homestore.com.)

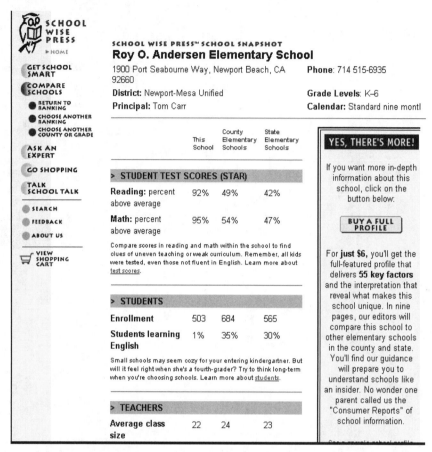

Figure 3.13   School Wise Press school snapshot. (©2000 Publishing 20/20. Source: School Wise Press, http://www.schoolwisepress.com.)

partment of Education. The information varies greatly from state to state, but most people will find the information quite useful.

IMPORTANT I'm going to repeat the suggestion I made earlier in this chapter. Regardless of how much research you do, regardless of how many facts you collect, there is simply no substitute for visiting the school that your children are going to attend. Seeing the classrooms and meeting a teacher or two can be illuminating. Also, if you have children in elementary school, go to the school when school lets out and talk to the mothers who are waiting to pick up their kids. If they are like most parents, they will tell you exactly how they feel. You might also get the name of the president of the PTA and get more insider information that way.

Top 75 Schools in Reading: High Scoring Students

Percent of students scoring, on the 1998–99 STAR test (also known as the SAT-9), in the highest group nationally (with scores higher than the 75th percentile), showing percent of low-scoring students in comparison. Students still learning English (designated as LEP in the column farthest to the right) students are shown for reference. For a fuller explanation and search tips, please see the footnote.

CLICK ON A SCHOOL NAME TO LEARN MORE.

RANK	SCHOOL	DISTRICT	% STUDENTS SCORING	% HIGH	% LEP
1	Andersen	Newport-Mesa		69%	1%
2	Bonita Canyon	Irvine		67%	4%
3	Alderwood	Irvine		65%	5%
4	Turtle Rock	Irvine		64%	6%
5	Harbor View	Newport-Mesa		63%	1%
6	Vista Verde	Irvine		62%	3%
7	Santiago Hills	Irvine		60%	4%
8	Canyon View	Irvine		59%	12%
8	Eastshore	Irvine		59%	7%
8	Nohl Canyon	Orange		59%	4%
11	Valencia	Saddleback Valley		58%	1%
11	Laguna Road	Fullerton		58%	15%
11	Deerfield	Irvine		58%	7%
14	Lincoln	Newport-Mesa		57%	2%
14	Arroyo	Tustin		57%	0%

Figure 3.14   School Wise Press high school reading statistical report. (©2000 Publishing 20/20. Source: School Wise Press, http://www.schoolwisepress.com.)

City Guides

Another way to check out cities is to go to cityguide.lycos.com/. You can navigate from a world map down to state and finally to town in that state. From there you can get to a general community page. If the city has its own Web page, you can generally find a link to it. Figure 3.15 shows the home page for Colorado Springs, Colorado, at www.colorado-springs .com/. Note the large number of hyperlinks to other pages.

Yahoo! has its city information at dir.yahoo.com/Regional/U_S_ States/. When you navigate to get to the city, or, failing that, the county you're interested in, you will see a number of different categories. Remember that Yahoo! is a directory of Web sites, like a phone book but with lots of subcategories. Navigating the site may be a little tedious, but there is a lot of information there and it may well be the best way to find information of a more business nature.

Finally, you can go to any of the many search engines such as AltaVista (www.altavista.com) and type in the city and state you are interested in, and you will probably be rewarded with a few hundred Web pages, many of which may have relevant information.

Crime Statistics

The best way to find crime data is to go to www.crime.org. Go to State Links and check to see whether your state is listed. You can also go to the home page of the Department of Justice's Bureau of Justice Statistics at www.ojp.usdoj.gov/bjs. Additionally, as you did with the education search, you can go to your state's Web site and continue your search for crime statistics. Finally, go to your county's or city's Web page. Sometimes the police department will post local crime statistics, the information that is most important to you.

WELCOME TO THE CITY OF COLORADO SPRINGS' ELECTRONIC COMMUNITY ACCESS PROJECT... a system that provides all citizens greater access to municipal government and public services and information. The system is easy to use; just click on the buttons to the sides of the mural to enter the desired areas. Enjoy this new way to receive information and services, and let us hear about your ideas and comments for improving the system.

Figure 3.15   Colorado Springs home page.
(Courtesy of the City of Colorado Springs.)

SUMMARY

The characteristics of a community will have an important effect on your family's well-being. The sites mentioned in this chapter will give you a leg up on your search for the ideal community that matches your family's needs. Having said that, quality of life is an intangible concept that transcends statistics. While these data can help you, have your antennae up when you visit each neighborhood and you'll make a better choice.

4

FINDING AND BUYING A HOME

I do not feel obliged to believe that the same God who has endowed us with sense, reason, and intellect has intended us to forgo their use.

— GALILEO GALILEI

KEY POINTS

- Buying a home is an exclusionary process. You have to eliminate most properties you're offered because they do not meet your criteria.

- Your objective is to use the information available on the Internet to make the homebuying process easier. You want to spend less time traipsing around and more time concentrating on those properties that interest you and that have the greatest potential of being right for you.

- Most homebuilders now post the details of their construction projects on the Internet. You can see floor plans, photos, conceptual drawings of the elevations, and pricing. Preliminary shopping no longer entails visiting dozens of model home complexes.

- In addition to traditional listings, thanks to the capabilities of the Web, you can also find out about for-sale-by-owner (FSBO) properties, as well as those available as a result of foreclosure at banks and government agencies.

Before we begin discussing how to find and buy a home, let's establish our objectives. I'm going to open the discussion with two assumptions: First, I assume that you agree that of the homes listed for sale at a given point in time, most will not meet your needs. Thus, the homebuying process consists of eliminating most of the data you accumulate, because only a very small percentage of homes will interest you enough for you to consider looking at them, much less buying them. I'm also going to make a second assumption: Even though you know you will discard most of the data about current listings, you still want to be sure that you get a look at 100 percent of the properties that are on the market in your price range. Human nature is such that if you know you are seeing only 90 percent of the properties, you will be positive the perfect property is in that other 10 percent. Thus you want to be assured that the methods of *e-homelooking* (my term for this process) I introduce here will give you the greatest chance of seeing all of the available properties on the market in your area that meet your most important criteria, as discussed in Chapter 1, "Decision Making and Salesmanship." Let's get started.

TIME IS OF THE ESSENCE

In my career, I've noticed that a number of home-hunters are fairly casual about the process. They don't seem to have a sense of urgency or to realize the importance of timeliness in this process. In fact, you are embarking on a competitive endeavor; you have competitors out there, other families whose needs are very similar to yours. Therefore, to be successful, you must be willing to move swiftly when you need to, when your search finally holds the promise of success. Every real estate agent you meet can tell you stories about clients who let the right property slip away because of inaction and had to watch it being sold to another buyer who had a better understanding of the importance of urgency in a homebuying transaction. Keep in mind: *The objective is to buy the property!*

With that in mind, the first lesson I have to teach here is not about how to use the Internet to help you find a home, but how to develop a plan that has an end—a goal—in sight: to visit properties and make an offer as soon as you find one that is right for you and/or your family. To that end, with the exception of FSBOs (homes listed for sale by owner)—and sometimes even in those cases—recognize that you are going to need the services of a real estate agent.

Right about now I'm sure some of you are thinking: "But the reason I'm reading this book is to learn to use the Internet so I *don't* have to work with an agent, someone who will pressure me." Let's talk about this. I'll use the analogy of buying a car to make my point. When we go to a car dealership, most of us hate it when a salesperson comes up to us as soon as we walk through the door. We just want 30 minutes or so to look. Eventually, we want to talk with the salesperson, just not yet. It's the same with buying a home. And learning about e-homelooking will enable you to do that—to conduct your search in a comfortable environment where you are in control. You can do some research for yourself and begin to formulate some ideas about what you want. Then, at some future date—next week or next month—it will be time to call an agent. After all, most of the homes you will be looking at will be listed with an agent. The seller, in effect, will be paying for your agent, so you might as well get a good one to represent you. This brings me to my next point: As you look at properties, you should also be engaging in a search for an agent to represent you so that when you narrow your search, your agent can arrange for you to see the property, give you advice about the property and the neighborhood, develop a negotiating strategy, present the offer, negotiate the deal, and, upon acceptance, make sure that you are protected and that the transaction closes smoothly. The issue of agent selection is so important that I have devoted an entire chapter to it. Refer to Chapter 7, "Finding and Working with a Real Estate Agent," for more insight and suggestions on this topic.

SEARCH PROCESSES

A lot of the information in this section will seem obvious to those who have bought homes in the past, but I'm stating the obvious to ensure that those less familiar with the homebuying process are up to speed. At any given point in time, there are more than 1 million homes listed for sale in America with real estate professionals, and perhaps another 100,000 offered for sale by owner. Of course, only a small percentage will be in your search area, but we're still talking about a lot of homes available for consideration and purchase. With that in mind, I repeat my admonition from the beginning of this chapter: The search process is an exclusionary one. Your job is to eliminate those homes that don't meet your criteria. What you have left are the ones you want to investigate further.

This is a good news–bad news situation. The good news is that the process of preliminary searching is a piece of cake thanks to computers. Each property's characteristics are entered into a very large database, which is organized around those characteristics. This means you can say, for example, "Let me see all of the three-bedroom, two-bath homes with a double garage priced between $175,000 and $200,000 in Huntsville, Alabama, and rank them by price." Almost instantly, you will get a list of all the properties that meet those criteria. Is this easy or what?! You then examine particular details of each home listed, often displayed with the home's location on a map and usually in color right in front of your eyes on the computer screen. Without stepping outside your door, you can determine, "This one is ugly!" "That one has a terrible kitchen that will cost money to remodel." "This one is located too far from work." "This one is on a busy street." "This one looks nice but appears to be way overpriced, and it has a pool and we don't want a pool." Finally, you'll hear yourself say, "Aha! Look at this one! Let's go see this one." What could be simpler?

But don't forget, I said there was bad news. Here it is: You will not find all these properties listed in one convenient database. For reasons too complicated to go into here, this is just not the case. (This may change in the near future, but at the time of this writing, there is no one-stop shopping database for real estate properties.) The other problem is that the data usually originate in one of the 800 multiple listing services (MLSs) in the country. Because there are different database systems at these services, these differences will also be reflected in the way data are displayed and organized when they get uploaded to the Internet. Fortunately, however, though there are differences in how the search parameters are organized on the various Internet Web sites, once you learn how to query one site, it's not too difficult to figure out the others; they're all similar.

A second element of bad news involves the vagaries of e-commerce. In the first place, as you can imagine, managing a million or so listings is quite an undertaking, not to mention expensive. In spite of the fact that the real estate brokers are going to make a large commission on any homes they sell, many do not want to cough up the cash to put their listings on the Internet—not if they don't have to, and they don't. These services are free to the seller and his or her agent. This raises the question: If it's free to the seller, and if the buyer doesn't have to pay for access either, how do these sites make any money? The answer is that, in most cases, they hope to earn money either by selling you something else you are interested in or by selling advertising to another company that hopes that you will see its ad and buy whatever it is selling. The result? When you visit these sites, you may feel like a salmon swimming upstream, with a lot of bright, shiny lures dangled in front of you. Welcome to the world of e-commerce.

Know What You're Looking For

So now you know what's good and what's bad about going online for real estate information. To maximize the good and minimize the bad, the next point I want to stress is this: Before you begin cruising specific sites, and before you look at any properties, set some objectives. Keep in mind that you are going to get much more information than you can use or remember. I recommend you break these objectives into three categories:

- Must have
- Would really like
- Would be nice, but could do without

An excellent sample wish list can be found at www.realtor.com/aspcontent/wishlist.asp. Print out this list, work on it with your family, and then use it to evaluate every property you visit. And be sure to share the list with the real estate agent you select.

Next you'll need a method of collecting information, and, when you get to the point of comparing homes, a list of questions to ask about each home. A very good checklist is available at homeadvisor.msn .com/ie/homes/seehome.aspww.home. (This site is also accessible via the House Hunting Process section at HomeAdvisor; go to Compare and Contrast, item 4, Listing Notes.) Write down the answers to these questions for each and every property you visit, because as sure as the Sun rises in the east, your memory will begin to fail after you've seen a few homes. Therefore, I suggest you make a number of copies of this list and fill out one for every property you visit. In addition to helping your memory, this will also enable you to check the features of each home against the criteria you established in your objectives.

NOTE   At this point, you should have already examined your credit report. If not, skip over to Chapter 13, "Checking Credit," and start working on it. You should also have calculated how much down payment you can afford, including what you might be able to get from the Bank of Mom and Dad. You should also check out qualifying in Chapter 12, "Qualifying," so you know what you can afford and what the mortgage industry will let you borrow. And, if it's time to select a lender to work with and to get preapproved, read the information on mortgages in Chapters 9 and 10, "Getting a Mortgage on the Internet: Parts One and Two."

Locating a Property

Having an address is one thing; knowing where a property is, is another. As you begin your search, let's say you like the home at 456 Maple Street. But where the heck is Maple Street? How far is it from work? Even when you have a detailed map of the area you are searching, finding a property on a street may not be that easy, particularly if you do not know the numbering system. For example, is 456 at the north end of town or the south end? Though many of the homebuyer sites we will examine have mapping functions, these can leave a lot to be desired.

One possibility is to invest in a CD-ROM map program such as Rand McNally's Streetfinder, which makes it easy to find properties and to determine whether they really are in your search area—or, if not, how far away they are. You can also find similar mapping services on the Web. I especially like www.mapquest.com, which enables you to locate nearby features including automatic teller machines (ATMs), restaurants, veterinarians, or the closest Blockbuster outlet, to name just a few. Another good service is Vicinity.com's Mapblast service, at www.mapblast.com/mblast/index.m. You type in an address and it displays a map of the area. At both sites, you can zoom in and out or move the map around to see what you want about the location of the property in question. You can also print out a map to take with you if you are searching from afar and haven't visited the area yet.

HOMEBUYER WEB SITES

Real estate listings are available at only a modest number of sites on the Web. My intent has been to include and cover all of the most comprehensive sites, the ones that have the most listings. There may be more in the future, though it is going to take a considerable investment to overcome the advantage currently enjoyed by the early entrants who have staked out a position in the field.

NOTE I'm sure you have done enough Web surfing or have read enough books about the World Wide Web to understand the necessity for the following caveat: My goal is to include the most accurate, up-to-date information here, but the Web is always changing, so some of the sites may have changed by the time you read this.

Before we begin to explore these sites, a few comments are in order to help you get the most from your online real estate house hunting:

- In my discussion of these sites in this chapter, I concentrate principally on the property search engines. Additional features offered by these sites, such as community data, mortgage information, and so forth, are addressed in the chapters devoted to those subjects.

- These services naturally boast about the number of listings they contain, but whether the number is 1.3 million, or 1 million, or 750,000, what's important to you is how they cover your specific area of interest. If you are looking for a home in Minneapolis, you want to learn about houses that a service has listed there, not the million-plus that are listed in other areas.

- Each of these sites has unique qualities, and you will probably find something of value in all of them, so leave no site unseen.

REALTOR.com

REALTOR.com, at www.realtor.com, is the official Internet Web site of the National Association of Realtors (NAR), meaning the association's 720,000-plus members—or Realtors, as members may call themselves—can post their listings here. The properties are uploaded to the Internet from each multiple listing service, where individual agents enter their property for sale. I'm told that properties contained in over 650 out of a total of 800 MLSs are shown here. Some of those MLSs have exclusive relationships with REALTOR.com, meaning that those listings are likely to be displayed only at this Web site. REALTOR.com is managed by Homestore.com, which also manages other affiliated real estate sites.

NOTE As the main Web site for the NAR, REALTOR.com has been designed to satisfy and meet the needs first of brokers and salespeople who are members of the NAR, and second of the clients whose properties they list. Currently in third place is the homebuying customer. This may be a subtle difference, but I think it is one to keep in mind.

REALTOR.com offers a full range of services, as you can see by looking at its home page, shown in Figure 4.1.

To find the area of the country you want to search for a property, click on the FIND A HOME button and go to a map of the United States, where you can select a location; alternatively, pick a location from the drop box. At the next screen, you can either click on a subarea of the state you want or enter the city and state, the search radius, or just the zip code. (Note that the MLS search function there is useful only to Realtors or others who already know the MLS listing number of a property from a previous search, perhaps at another site, and want to see if more information is available here.) A word of warning: Querying these databases can sometimes be disconcerting. For example, when I entered my town's main zip code, I got a "no listings" message; then, when I put in the city name and state, I got 24 listings. My point is, use as many search alternatives as you can to ensure that you get all the information that is available.

The number of responses you get will depend upon the search radius. When the radius was 4 miles, I got over 500 properties. When I narrowed it down to 1 mile, I got 85 properties, a little more manageable (see Figure 4.2). Once you refine the properties in your narrowed-down search, you'll probably want to go back and widen the search.

Next, and still without narrowing the search criteria, I plugged in Huntsville, Alabama, our example city from Chapter 3, "Getting Information about Communities." As you can see in Figure 4.3a, I got 523 listings. Be sure to note that the Other Preferences search criteria choices changed significantly, as shown in Figure 4.3b. This reflects the distinctiveness of properties in the different areas. Gone, for example, is Ocean View, clearly not a Huntsville characteristic. But now options include lot sizes from ½ acre to 20 acres or more, not property features you'll find in my densely populated hometown.

You can then refine your search to a property type, price range, number of bedrooms, and so forth. You don't want to plow through 500 properties, so you can now use these other criteria to narrow the search and eliminate those properties that don't meet your needs. The downside to this is that, just because of semantics, you may pass up something that might work. Maybe the four-bedroom home you want is listed as three bedrooms and a den. So be careful not to narrow your search too tightly. You also have to be realistic about the size of the sam-

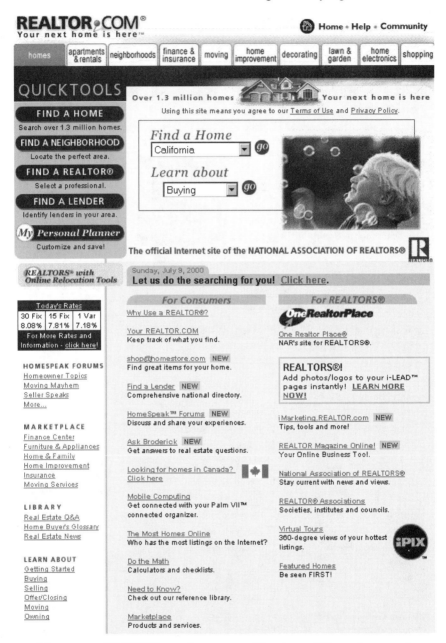

Figure 4.1   REALTOR.com homepage. (Courtesy of Homestore.com.)

ple you want. I typed in a price range and bedroom count to whittle down the 500 listings to just 11—maybe too narrow. The first listing of the 11 is shown in Figure 4.4.

Here are shown a summary of information about the home and the agent contact information. Usually you will have to click on the More

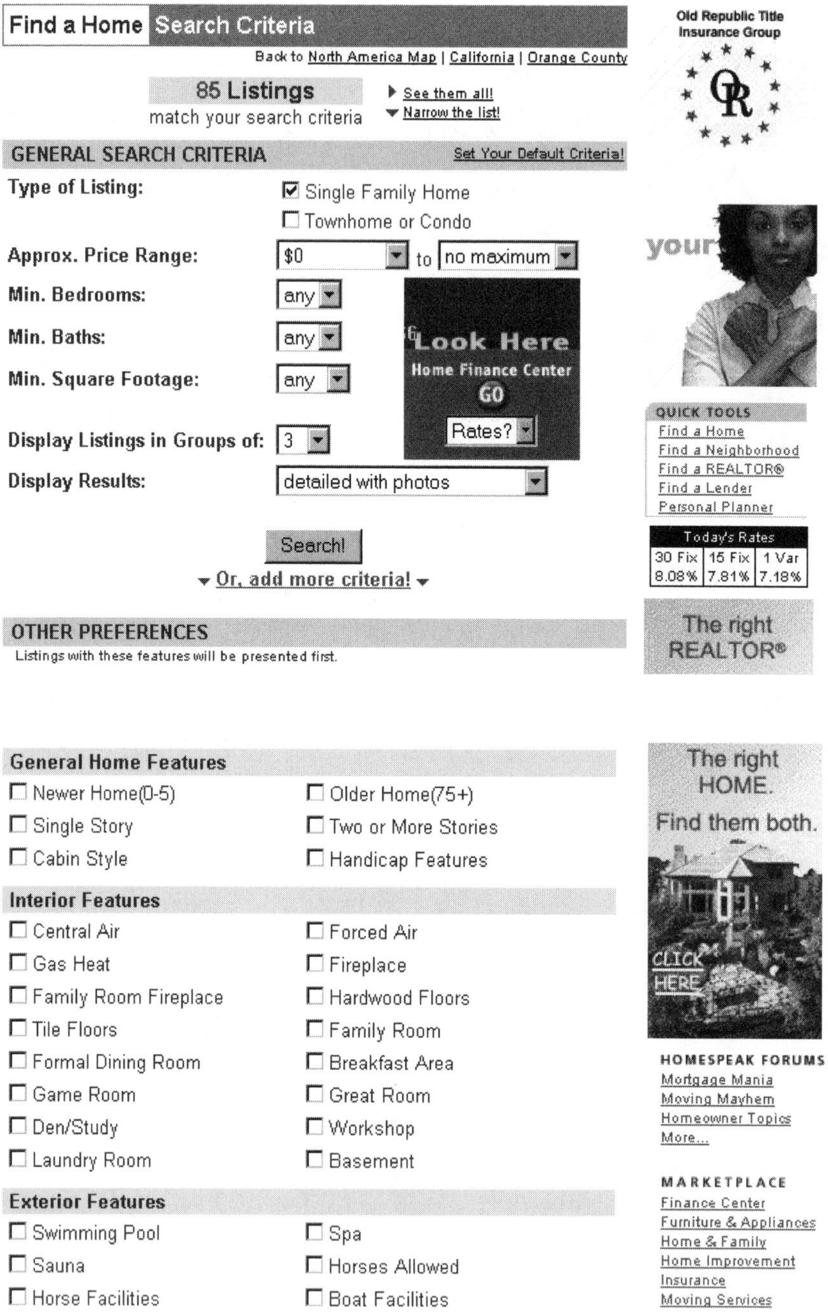
Find a Home Search Criteria
Back to North America Map | California | Orange County
85 Listings
match your search criteria
See them all!
Narrow the list!
GENERAL SEARCH CRITERIA
Set Your Default Criteria!
Type of Listing:
Single Family Home
Townhome or Condo
Approx. Price Range:
$0
to
no maximum
Min. Bedrooms:
any
Min. Baths:
any
Min. Square Footage:
any
Look Here
Home Finance Center
GO
Rates?
Display Listings in Groups of:
3
Display Results:
detailed with photos
Search!
Or, add more criteria!
OTHER PREFERENCES
Listings with these features will be presented first.
General Home Features
Newer Home(0-5)
Older Home(75+)
Single Story
Two or More Stories
Cabin Style
Handicap Features
Interior Features
Central Air
Forced Air
Gas Heat
Fireplace
Family Room Fireplace
Hardwood Floors
Tile Floors
Family Room
Formal Dining Room
Breakfast Area
Game Room
Great Room
Den/Study
Workshop
Laundry Room
Basement
Exterior Features
Swimming Pool
Spa
Sauna
Horses Allowed
Horse Facilities
Boat Facilities
Old Republic Title Insurance Group
your
QUICK TOOLS
Find a Home
Find a Neighborhood
Find a REALTOR®
Find a Lender
Personal Planner
Today's Rates
30 Fix 15 Fix 1 Var
8.08% 7.81% 7.18%
The right REALTOR®
The right HOME.
Find them both.
CLICK HERE
HOMESPEAK FORUMS
Mortgage Mania
Moving Mayhem
Homeowner Topics
More...
MARKETPLACE
Finance Center
Furniture & Appliances
Home & Family
Home Improvement
Insurance
Moving Services

Figure 4.2 REALTOR.com turned up 85 listings for my area in California, based on general search criteria only. (Courtesy of Homestore.com; © SoCal MLS.)

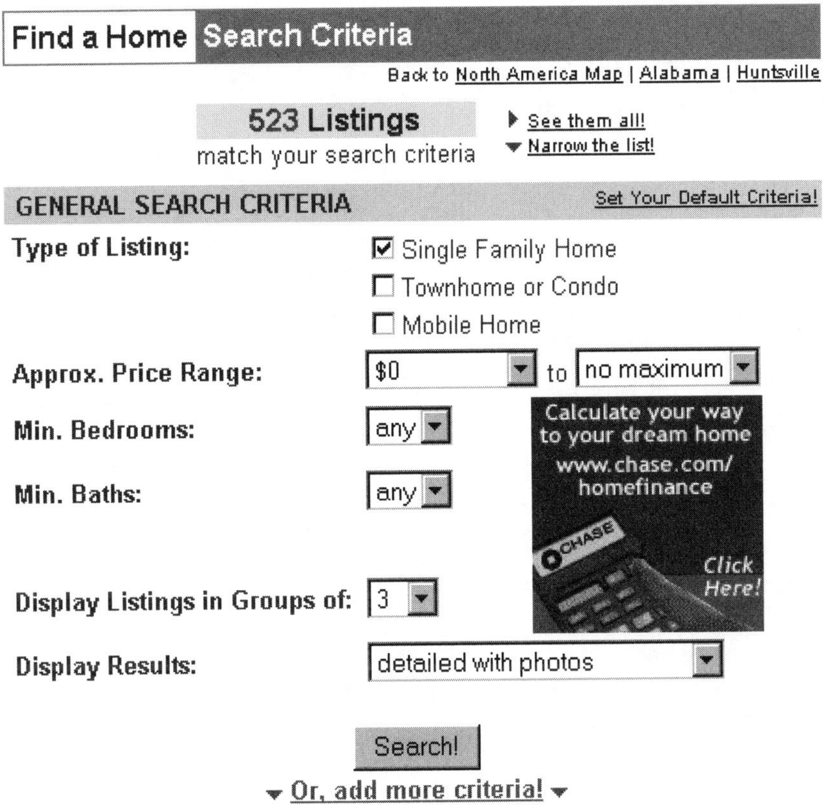

Figure 4.3   (a) A general criteria search gave me 523 listings for Huntsville, Alabama. (Courtesy of Homestore.com; © SoCal MLS.)

Info button for details on bedroom size and many other features of a home. I did that and went to the supplementary page, which shows a better picture of the home instead of the thumbnail. Additional details of this home are shown in Figure 4.5.

There is also the option of pinpointing this home's location on an area map by clicking on Map. You can also get a thumbnail sketch of information about the specific area and schools by clicking on the appropriate hyperlinks. (Note, however, that to get more information about the city and schools, I recommend you use the tools described in Chapter 3 rather than those offered here.) Finally, you can e-mail this listing to your spouse or real estate agent.

A great feature here is the Personal Planner, accessible from the Quick Tools box in the upper left of the page, which enables you to choose SAVE THIS LISTING, SAVE THIS REALTOR, or SAVE THIS OFFICE by clicking on the link. This adds the information to your planner. You can also enter two addresses into your personal planner—say

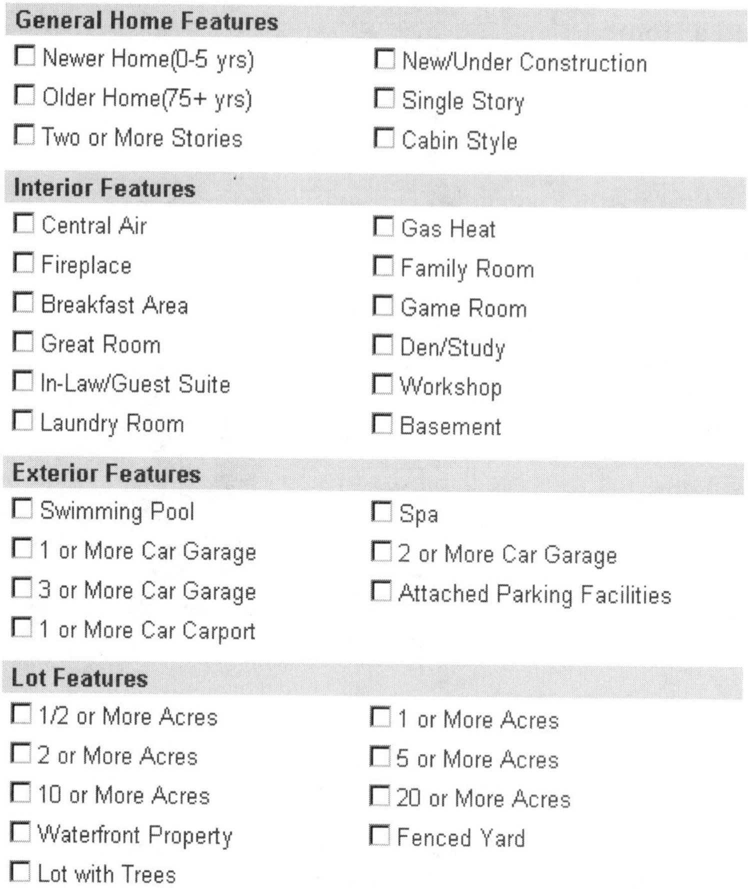

General Home Features

- ☐ Newer Home(0-5 yrs)
- ☐ Older Home(75+ yrs)
- ☐ Two or More Stories
- ☐ New/Under Construction
- ☐ Single Story
- ☐ Cabin Style

Interior Features

- ☐ Central Air
- ☐ Fireplace
- ☐ Breakfast Area
- ☐ Great Room
- ☐ In-Law/Guest Suite
- ☐ Laundry Room
- ☐ Gas Heat
- ☐ Family Room
- ☐ Game Room
- ☐ Den/Study
- ☐ Workshop
- ☐ Basement

Exterior Features

- ☐ Swimming Pool
- ☐ 1 or More Car Garage
- ☐ 3 or More Car Garage
- ☐ 1 or More Car Carport
- ☐ Spa
- ☐ 2 or More Car Garage
- ☐ Attached Parking Facilities

Lot Features

- ☐ 1/2 or More Acres
- ☐ 2 or More Acres
- ☐ 10 or More Acres
- ☐ Waterfront Property
- ☐ Lot with Trees
- ☐ 1 or More Acres
- ☐ 5 or More Acres
- ☐ 20 or More Acres
- ☐ Fenced Yard

Figure 4.3 *(Continued)* *(b)* **As the area of your search changes, so too do the Other Preferences options.**

the husband's work address and the wife's work address. Then, every time you pull up a property, the distance between that property and the two addresses you entered will be listed—a slick feature for those who want to minimize commute time.

I highly recommend you make use of this feature, because if you start printing out information on every listing that you like, before you know it you'll have papers strewn all over the table and floor and you won't be able to make heads or tails out of them. Once you have looked at, say, 40 homes and saved 8 of them, you can go back to review them, starting the elimination process. For example, property 8 may be a clear-cut winner over 2 and 3, but you can't know that until you see 8. You can discard 2 and 3. Finally, the personal planner will

7    $369,900   Irvine, CA 92614   **More Info**

Beds: 3 Baths: 2.5 Sq. Ft.: 1762   MLS No.: S215329   **100% match**

Show me more!

This two story detached home built in 1987 has 3 bedroom(s), 2.50 bath(s) and is approximately 1762 sq. ft. Rooms include a family room, formal dining room, breakfast nook, master bedroom suite, laundry room, foyer. Other features include fireplace(s), breakfast bar, cathedral/vaulted ceilings, window treatments. This home has a 2 car garage. Recreation amenities include community swimming pool(s), community spa(s), community tennis court(s). The lot is fenced.

For more information, contact...

REMAX PREMIER REALTY
Office: 949-451-1200
Fax: 949-857-2847
Email us.

Figure 4.4   The first of 11 homes in Irvine that matched my price range and required number of bedrooms. (Courtesy of Homestore.com; © SoCal MLS.)

advise you of any new listings that meet the criteria you established—but you'll have to return to the site; it will not send you an e-mail.

Another attractive feature at REALTOR.com lets you can save the information you have just gleaned from the site. Note the sections My Searches, My Realtors, My Neighborhood, My Articles, and My Contacts. Of course, saving the information pretty well ties you to the site, which is one reason why the feature is there. Nonetheless, it still is a very useful feature.

Some of the other materials at the site were not so obvious to locate. At the top of the pages you will see the following links: GETTING STARTED, BUYING, SELLING, OFFER/CLOSING, MOVING, and OWNING. These are the doors to further educational and informational pages. When you click to enter any of these areas, you will get a list of about a half-dozen subcategories. For example, under OFFER/CLOSING there were some excellent suggestions in these subcategories: Making an Offer, What the Offer Contains, and so forth. I found them to be well written and helpful. There's also a Real Estate Q&A where more than 100 commonly asked questions are listed alphabetically and answered succinctly.

In summary, REALTOR.com's fully functioned features for finding properties are excellent, and navigation difficulties in earlier permutations of the site have been remedied.

Property Description

$369,900 Located in BORGATTA, Irvine, Zip Code: 92614. ITALIA.

This two story detached home built in 1987 has 3 bedroom(s), 2.50 bath(s) and is approximately 1762 sq. ft. Rooms include a family room, formal dining room, breakfast nook, master bedroom suite, laundry room, foyer. Other features include fireplace(s), breakfast bar, cathedral/vaulted ceilings, window treatments. This home has a 2 car garage. Recreation amenities include community swimming pool(s), community spa(s), community tennis court(s). The lot is fenced.

Additional Information

Living room fireplace	Curbs & gutters
Gas range and oven	Attached parking
Built-in oven	Automatic garage door
Dishwasher	Model: PLAN 3
Central air conditioning	See agent for details on association fees
Forced air heat	School District: IUSD
Wall to wall carpeting	Elementary School: IUSD
Ceramic tile flooring	Jr. High School: IUSD
Block fencing	High School: IUSD
Tile roof	

**Figure 4.5   Clicking down to greater levels of detail.
(Courtesy of Homestore.com; © SoCal MLS.)**

HomeAdvisor

Microsoft's entry in the world of e-real estate is HomeAdvisor, found at www.homeadvisor.com. This site is operated by HomeAdvisor Technologies, Inc, which is owned by Microsoft and four of the country's largest lenders. You might ask, "What is a software company doing in the real estate information business?" Well, it might be there to sell software. Just think of those 720,000 Realtors and other agents who aren't NAR members, each of whom is running his or her own small business. What do they all need? Computers, and the software programs that turn those computers into valuable business tools. Then consider the market for a software program that would enable all those agents to upload listings to the Internet, to receive inquiries about those listings from interested buyers and their agents, to communicate with customers, to manage the closing process, to create a "paperless" process, and who knows what else. Now you can understand Microsoft's interest in the online real estate marketplace. Furthermore, realize that real estate and mortgages account for something like 10 percent of the gross domestic product, involving over 10 million transactions annually. Even if Microsoft captures only a tiny sliver of that large number of high-dollar-volume transactions, it can be a potential profitable business. Thus it makes sense for the software giant to enter the online real estate competition.

To that end, HomeAdvisor is intended to be a universal Web site; that is, valuable to anyone interested in buying and selling properties and getting mortgages. Take a look at the HomeAdvisor homepage, shown in Figure 4.6. Click on the Homes for Sale area (top left of the graphic) and you will be taken to the Find and Compare Homes page as shown in Figure 4.7. Enter state and city names, hit Go, and you will get a list of communities within that region. You can then click on the ones that interest you. A nice feature of HomeAdvisor is that it alerts you with a symbol next to a particular neighborhood or town when there are no properties in its database. This can be a real time saver.

You can skip a few of the intermediate steps if you already know the zip code of the area you're interested in searching. You can enter it and a price range, as I did here, and go immediately to the summary page of the listings that meet your criteria. The first 6 of 13 listings are shown in Figure 4.8.

Note that the listings locations are shown on the map, a helpful feature. Addresses will be listed for some properties as well, also help-

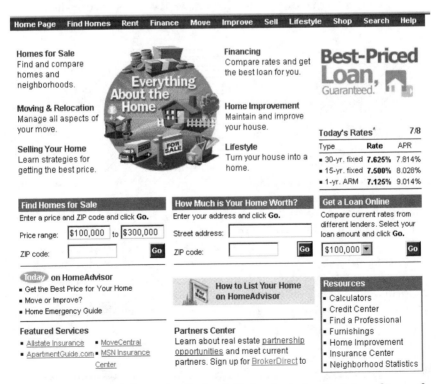

Figure 4.6   HomeAdvisor is Microsoft Technologies' entry into online real estate. (Courtesy of HomeAdvisor; © SoCal MLS.)

Homes for Sale

Decide to Buy
- Get Pre-Approved
- Rent Or Buy?
- Budgeting to Buy
- Find an Agent

House Hunting Tools
- Get the estimated value of any home
- Look up a neighborhood
- Review My Homes List
- Get new listings in e-mail
- Take a Virtual Tour
- Work With an Agent
- Know What You Want

Roadmap
A step-by-step guide to finding and buying a home.

Find and Compare Homes

Search for homes in: ⦿ United States ○ Canada

State: California

Region: Orange County

Price range: $300,000   to: $375,000   Go

Search by MLS number: **Find a specific home by address:**
        Go   Street:

Search by ZIP code: City:

92614   Go   State: California   Go

Apartments and Rentals
Find an apartment or rental in your area.

Home Buying Advisor
Checklists, tips, guides, and Q&As to help you through the home buying process.

**Figure 4.7   The Homes for Sale page on the HomeAdvisor site.
(Courtesy of HomeAdvisor; © SoCal MLS.)**

ful in case you want to drive by them. (I have blanked out the addresses for reasons of confidentiality of their owners.) Note also that homes that have a picture in the detail will have an icon of a little camera, as in property #3.

At the upper left, you can click on Location to modify the search area. Even more helpful is the ability to refine your search by defining other characteristics. For example, you might only be interested in a home of over 2000 square feet, or with a certain number of bedrooms or bathrooms. Finally, in the lower part of that screen, you can specify other features you want in your home—say a fireplace, garage, or central air conditioning. When you have done this, properties meeting your new criteria will display a red star (★). The Web page notes: "Because listing providers may not provide all of the details about each home, homes with no stars may have some or all of the features you are interested in." You can broaden your search again by increasing the price range or the search area, as you will remember that this search is of properties only in one zip code.

At this point, you can click on a property to get more details about the listing. Figure 4.9 shows one of the homes turned up in this search. You can see enough detail on this property to know if it interests you. If the street address of the property is given, the map will show the location of the property; if not, the map will be centered on the zip

Fireplace features:	Living Room	Estimated lot size:	3024 (approx), 3024sf
Bedroom 2:	Main Floor Bedroom	Stories:	Association Spa
Parking:	Direct Garage Access	Parking spaces:	2
Features:	Cathedral/Vaulted Ceilings, Home Warranty, No Common Walls, Planned Development	Roof:	Composite
		View:	Park/Greenbelt View
		Community:	Community Tennis
Heating:	Forced Air		
Pool/spa/sauna:	Community Pool		

Neighborhood Information

Zoom into: Street ▼

Microsoft **Expedia** Maps

Maps by maps.expedia.com

Distances
HomeAdvisor calculates the distance between this home and the addresses (map points) you enter.

➡ Add your own Map Points to customize this section

theatre   1,797.0 miles

Demographics
Population: 23,073
Neighborhood type: Suburban
Home Listings: 66

➡ Research neighborhood school and crime statistics

Find Local Shops and Services
Select a category and click **Go** to find a business near this home.

Parks & recreation ▼   **Go**

 Home Search Results | --- Quick Steps --- ▼ |

Modify Your Search

Price range:	Location:
$300,000	Change the location of your search.
$375,000	

Bedrooms:	Other criteria:
Any number ▼	Age, size, type, preferences...
Bathrooms:	
Any number ▼	

Go

Homes 1 to 10 (10 mapped)
Expedia.com Travel

13 homes found. Here are homes 1 to 13:

$302,000 Irvine, 92614 **❶**
Single-family, 3 bedrooms, 2 baths, ~1300 sqft, built 1988.
Single Story Model, 3RD Bedroom Currently A Den, Corner Loca...

$310,000 Irvine, 92614 **❷**
Single-family, 3 bedrooms, 2 baths, ~1344 sqft, built 1971.
Wood Flooring Throughout. Completely Remodeled Kitchen W/ C...

$312,000 ▆▆▆▆▆▆▆ Irvine, 92614 **❸** 🏠
Single-family, 3 bedrooms, 2.5 baths, ~1571 sqft, built 1980.
Freshly Painted Interior, Formal Dining Room Has Been Conver...

$330,000 ▆▆▆▆▆ Irvine, 92614 **❹**
Single-family, 3 bedrooms, 3 baths, ~1428 sqft, built 1987.
This Floorplan Won An Architectural Design Award. Shows Gre...

$337,500 ▆▆▆▆▆▆▆▆▆ Irvine, 92614 **❺**
Single-family, 4 bedrooms, 2.5 baths, ~1428 sqft, built 1969.
Office Could Be 4TH Bedroom. Master Bedroom W/Plantation Sh...

$345,000 ▆▆▆▆▆ Irvine, 92614 **❻**
Single-family, 3 bedrooms, 3 baths, ~1500 sqft, built 1991.
Wonderful Single Family Home In A Great West-Park Area. Thi...

Figure 4.8   The results of the search.
(Courtesy of HomeAdvisor; © SoCal MLS.)

code. You can also add your own Map Points—for example, your work address—to customize this section, although this is of less value if you do not know the street address of the property in question (as is the case in many instances). Many homeowners and agents do not want to put their addresses on the Internet because they do not want people knocking on their doors unannounced wanting to see the property (nor do they want to advertise to thieves). At the bottom of the screen is a drop box that you can use to find local shops, parks, and other amenities close to the home. Unfortunately, the site's feature that allowed you to add properties to your personal list of favorites has been eliminated.

HomeAdvisor also offers the Home Tracker, accessible by clicking on the option below the real estate agent's information. The value of this option is that you can enter the characteristics of the house of your dreams, and when a home that meets those criteria comes on the market, you will be notified automatically by e-mail.

| *TIP* | When you select an agent to work with, ask him or her to sign up for Home Tracker too, to ensure that your agent will be notified of this information when you are and will know what you know!

Not surprisingly, I found the agent contact information to be less comprehensive at HomeAdvisor than at the NAR's own Web site, REALTOR.com. Still, agents can sign up for the Broker Direct program, which allows them to post listings on the HomeAdvisor Web site in case their MLS has an exclusive arrangement with REALTOR.com. Probably because of those exclusive arrangements, HomeAdvisor does not have as many listings as REALTOR.com. (Later I'll explain why you will find that you have to look at all of the real estate Web sites; no single site has all the properties listed.)

Overall, the quality and scope of the homebuying information available at HomeAdvisor is impressive, if hard to find. On the home page, there is a Resources box toward the lower right. Click on Calculators or Credit Center and a drop box that says Quick Steps will appear in the upper right. Click on Advisor to view an outline of topics. When you click on a topic, a number of relevant questions (75 in one case and over 100 in another when I checked) will be answered. You can check the ones that interest you. True, the answers tend to be quick, one-sentence responses, but they can give you a jump start on your investigations.

In summary, with HomeAdvisor Microsoft has made a bold statement to the real estate industry that it intends to be a major player in this arena. Its site is particularly consumer friendly, and Microsoft surely has the money and expertise to maintain HomeAdvisor as a first-rate site that you will want to use.

HomeSeekers.com

HomeSeekers.com was an early entrant into this business, and, to date, its only independent service. It suffers somewhat because its competitors

**Figure 4.9   An online view of a potential property.
(Courtesy of HomeAdvisor; © SoCal MLS.)**

are better known. But being less well known does not mean that Home-Seekers is less valuable to you, the home-hunter. HomeSeekers.com has formed relationships with a number of MLSs (not all, because of exclusivity arrangements with other services). So, although the site might list few homes in one area of the country, it might list 100 percent of the available homes in another—perhaps the one you are interested in. For example, it had only three listings in Huntsville, but more than 500 in my home market in California. My point: Include HomeSeekers.com in your online search.

In the not-too-distant future, probably all the same data—albeit in different formats—will be available at all sites. Until that day, agents may have to circumvent their brokers and their exclusive MLS contracts to give their clients better exposure. HomeSeekers.com has made it easier through its proprietary software package, which, among a host of other functions, allows real estate agents to upload listings to the Home-Seekers.com site. It has also recently partnered with HomeAdvisor, so you may find the same listings at both sites depending on the contractual relationships with the various MLSs. The HomeSeekers.com home page is shown in Figure 4.10.

Note that you can either type in the name of a town or click on a state to get to a particular area. Once at the appropriate screen, you can enter in price and other criteria to meet your needs (see Figure 4.11).

Perhaps you'll want to start out by selecting only those listings that you can visit via a virtual tour (described fully in the next chapter), available under Your Options. When you hit Search Now, you will see a summary of the first listings in that category, as shown in Figure 4.12. By clicking on the price at a listing, you go to a page dedicated to that property. I picked the one priced at $319,900 to display in Figure 4.13.

If you click on Location, you will get a map showing where the property is situated, even if the exact address of the listing has not been disclosed. You may find that the data on each house are a little less comprehensive at HomeSeekers.com than at other sites, but if you find a home you like, copy down the MLS number. You can then go to other sites, enter that number, and get more information about the home by going directly to that listing, bypassing the search function.

You'll also find there is a little less agent hoopla at this site, but HomeSeekers.com has partnered with a company that provides instant contact with agents who have signed up for the service. Call or e-mail, and an agent is paged and can call you back instantly. Or, if you prefer, you can have HomeSeekers.com e-mail you when new homes meeting your criteria are listed.

Other notes about this site: Listings are updated daily, definitely a plus; another plus is that this site is somewhat easier to navigate than the others described; it is less complicated and less cluttered, an advan-

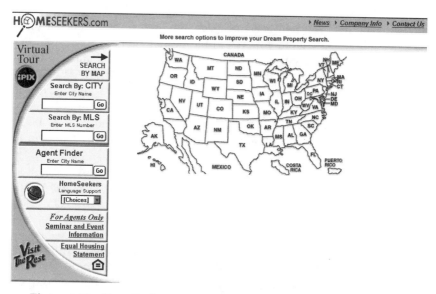

Figure 4.10 HomeSeekers.com is an independent service well worth checking out. (Courtesy of HomeSeekers.com, Inc.)

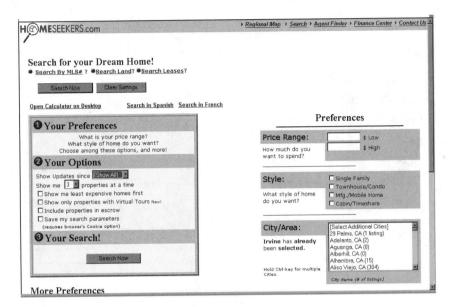

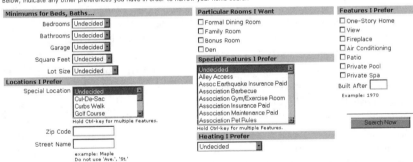

Figure 4.11   At HomeSeekers.com, you can specify all your preferences.
(Courtesy of HomeSeekers.com, Inc.)

tage at times. On the negative side, there are virtually no educational materials, and the finance area consists of a link to its lender "partner." Finally, HomeSeekers.com is to be applauded for being the first site to have a mirror site in Spanish, making the power of this process available to those who are not proficient enough in English to navigate the other sites.

CyberHomes

CyberHomes, at www.cyberhomes.com, was created by Moore Data Management Services, recently acquired by VISTAinfo, an environmental database service. Moore runs the computers that store the list-

Homes which met your search!

Previewing 1 thru 3 of a total 3 homes found

Click on the image to view detailed information

	$319,000
	Irvine 92620
	3 BR / 2 Ba
	1531 SF (approx)
	Single Family
Southern California MLS	**$319,900**
	Irvine 92612
	3 BR / 2 Ba
	1665 SF (approx)
	Single Family
	$319,990
	Irvine 92612
	3 BR / 2.50 Ba
	1800 SF (approx)
	Condominium

Previous	**New Search**	Next

Figure 4.12   Summary data for homes.
(Courtesy of HomeSeekers.com, Inc.)

ing databases for more MLSs around the country than any other provider. Perhaps as a result of this association, CyberHomes can state that its listings are updated every day, an important factor in a hot market. Take a look at the CyberHomes home page in Figure 4.14. Click on a state to go to the search page, shown in Figure 4.15.

In addition to the standard search criteria—price range, number of bedrooms, area—you can also search by radius or address. The radius search solves one major problem of database searches: how the criteria are defined within the database. If a database is organized around zip codes, for example, you might miss a good listing if the location you are in is near the boundary of two zip code areas, or if it is located in a larger city where there may be post office designations that exist within political boundaries. The radius search lets you either enter an address as a starting point or pick a point on a map and define the radius of your search. This will be very helpful when you have pinpointed an area and want to see all the nearby properties. Similarly, the address search function allows you to enter a street and find out the listings on that street. This is a lot easier than navigating through a search process that is defined by town or zip code.

To demonstrate how this works, first, I clicked on California, then on Orange County, then on Radius Search to get to the page shown in Figure 4.16. Rather than put in an address, I went to the map. Note that it is centered in the middle of the county. I chose to go to Irvine, which is south and east of this portion of the map, so I clicked on Center Map on the left, then moved my mouse to the lower right corner of the map

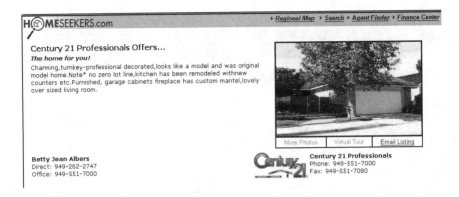

**Figure 4.13   Home details displayed in clear, easy-to-read format.
(Courtesy of HomeSeekers.com, Inc.)**

and clicked. I had to do this several more times until I got to the area I wanted. I then clicked on Set Origin Center on the left to determine the center of my search radius. This is a densely populated area, so I set the search radius at 5 miles, then set the price range and other criteria, as you can see in Figure 4.18.

NOTE One feature at CyberHomes is particularly intriguing. Note the category Listed since: in the upper right corner of the center section. This feature allows you to check new listings—say those listed in the last 7 days—without having to plow through all of the other homes you have previously rejected. Note that this useful feature is not apparent until you get to this page. If your search takes longer, this can be a real timesaver. Be sure to look for it.

Because I had narrowed down the search area, I left the other

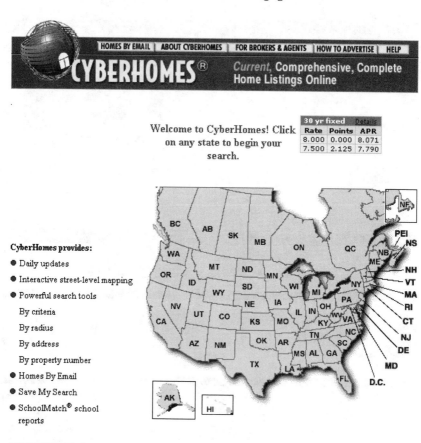

Figure 4.14 The CyberHomes home page.

search criteria open so as not to be too restrictive. The search produced one property, which is displayed in Figure 4.19.

I clicked on the property number for the one that interested me—P159702—and got lots more information on the property, as you can see in Figure 4.20.

In summary, the search features at CyberHomes are excellent, offering choices not available elsewhere, and the timeliness of the data is unsurpassed. Importantly, thanks to CyberHomes' relationships with a large number of MLSs, more information will probably be made available in the future. My criticisms are that the photos of properties are small, there is zero educational information, and the financial toolkit consisted of links to the Web sites of "strategic partnership" mortgage companies. But you, dear reader, have other ways of getting that information.

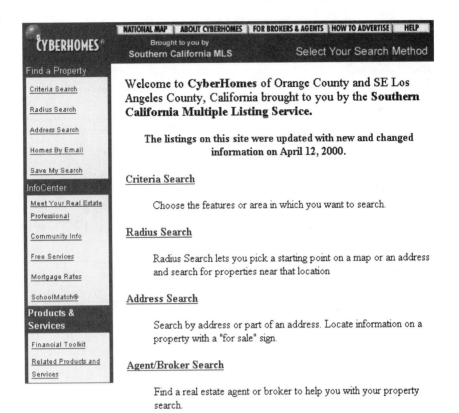

Figure 4.15   Search CyberHomes by three methods.

HomeScout

HomeScout, at www.iown.com, is the home search tool of iOwn. Though principally a mortgage site, the goal of HomeScout is to concentrate on home ownership, as the name iOwn implies. To that end, in addition to iOwn's Realtors Center, where agents can post their own listings, HomeScout is also linked to HomeSeekers.com, and to the following less well known sites: The Real Estate Book (www.realestatebook.com/), RealEstateVillage.com (www.revillage.com), Who's Who in Luxury Real Estate (www.luxury-realestate.com), New Homes Direct (www.newhomesdirect.com), and the FSBO site, Owners.com. In effect, via this site, you can search several databases at once, which is an advantage.

When you type in your search criteria, the results are returned as shown in Figure 4.21. For the first cut at looking at properties, I find this very pleasing tabular format quite useful, particularly if the search criteria end up producing 150 homes. Be aware that the listing information itself may be on another computer, so when you click View listing

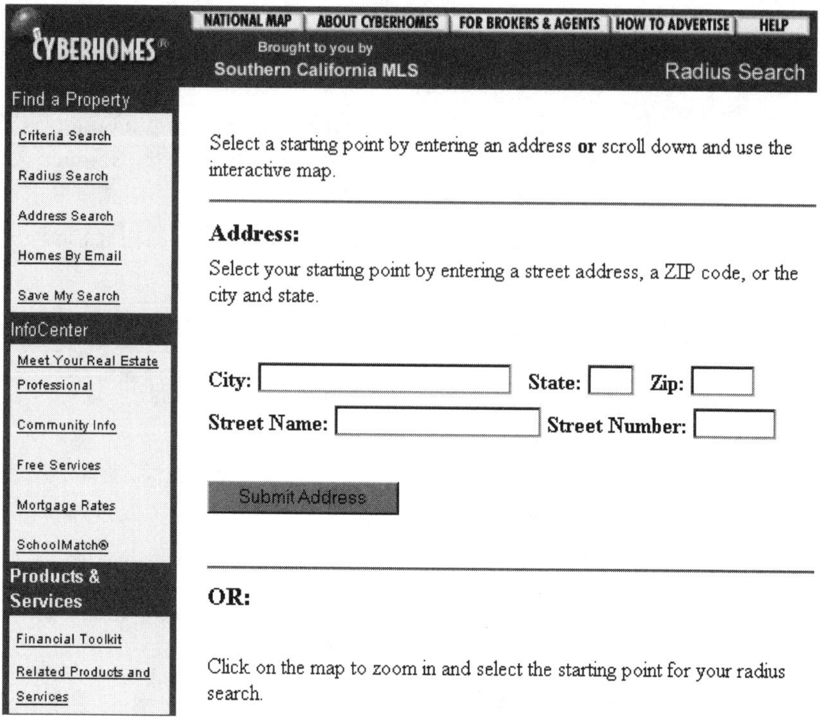

Figure 4.16   Navigating the CyberHomes map.

for any of the properties, you will follow a hyperlink to the Web site that actually hosts the listing information, say, HomeSeekers.com.

The site also has a good array of educational tools, and has recently established links to providers of related services such as insurance, home inspection, and moving.

Other Sites

There are several other sites I want to mention in this section. They do not have as many properties listed as the ones already covered, but you should check them out nonetheless.

HomeHunter is a little unusual in that it is offered only through the Web sites of local newspapers. Because the layout of the search results is easier to analyze than at some of the other sites (see Figure 4.17), it's worth checking out. To see whether HomeHunter is under contract with a newspaper in your area, visit the site at www.homehunter.com.

HomesDatabase.com is the site for Metropolitan Regional Information Systems, Inc., at www.homesdatabase.com. This is the MLS service in the Mid-Atlantic states, Maryland, and parts of Pennsylvania, Virginia, West Virginia, and the District of Columbia. The site is well

OR:

Click on the map to zoom in and select the starting point for your radius search.

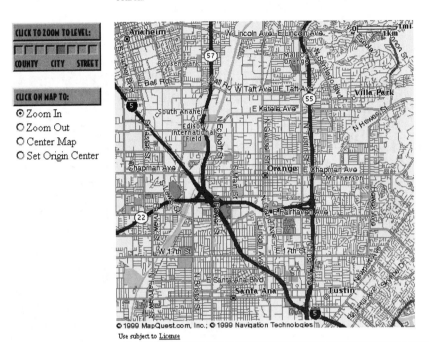

Figure 4.16   *(Continued)*

organized, so you can cut to the chase and find properties easily. Currently, it has 65,000 listings in these areas, so, if applicable, add this Web site to your resource arsenal.

The Real Estate Book at www.realestatebook.com, RealEstateVillage .com at www.revillage.com, and Who's Who in Luxury Real Estate at www.luxury-realestate.com, are, as previously mentioned, the databases of home listings that can also be accessed through HomeScout at iOwn.com. However, you may want to visit these sites individually for educational and other material.

REAL ESTATE COMPANY WEB SITES

Any real estate company that intends to stay in business in the twenty-first century will have a Web site. It's that simple. Therefore, assume that any company worth dealing with will have some kind of Web presence. Theoretically, the larger the company, the more resources it will have to

Figure 4.17   HomeHunter information is less comprehensive.

devote to developing a well-organized online offering. Of course, you'll find wide variation in quantity and quality. To be perfectly honest, I'm not sure why any buyer would use any of these Web sites for a property search. Each company-owned site shows only its own listings, which is good for them, but probably doesn't do much for you other than subject you to more sales pitches. Here's a sampling:

Cendant is the world's largest franchiser of residential real estate brokerage offices in the country. Each of its operations has its own Web site: Century 21 at www.century21.com, Coldwell Banker at www.coldwellbanker.com, and ERA Real Estate at www.era.com. Given their

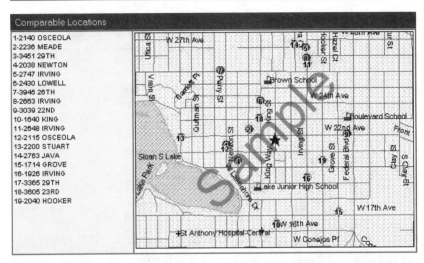

Figure 4.17 *(Continued)*

common ownership, you'd think that these sites would be similar, but, as of this writing, they are different. Of the three, I found that the ERA site was the most friendly and displayed the properties in the most effective manner.

Prudential's real estate operation is at www.prudential.com/ realestate. Perhaps because it is part of a large financial services company, the main site offers slightly different options from some others, including excellent tips for moving and a section devoted to retirement living. Unfortunately, when it comes to finding a home, you're shunted right back to REALTOR.com.

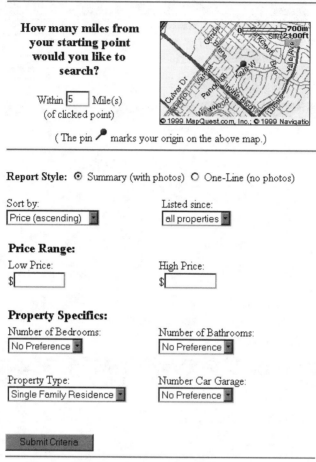

How many miles from your starting point would you like to search?

Within 5 Mile(s)
(of clicked point)

(The pin ✎ marks your origin on the above map.)

Report Style: ⦿ Summary (with photos) ○ One-Line (no photos)

Sort by: Listed since:
[Price (ascending) ▾]   [all properties ▾]

Price Range:
Low Price: High Price:
$[   ] $[   ]

Property Specifics:
Number of Bedrooms: Number of Bathrooms:
[No Preference ▾]   [No Preference ▾]

Property Type: Number Car Garage:
[Single Family Residence ▾]   [No Preference ▾]

[Submit Criteria]

Figure 4.18   Homing in on an area to search and picking search criteria.

RE/MAX, at www.remax.com, seems to be more directed toward its agents than the public; as at the Prudential site, you'll be sent back to REALTOR.com when you go house hunting.

Better Homes & Garden Real Estate was acquired by GMAC and is now a part of the GMAC Real Estate network. The home page is at www.gmacrealestate.com. As at Prudential and RE/MAX, a property search request does nothing more than divert you to the REALTOR.com Web site.

A New Alternative

Homeroute offers a novel approach at www.homeroute.com. At this site you can go to the Dream Track section and hire an agent who, for a reduced commission, will help you make an offer on a home *not* on the

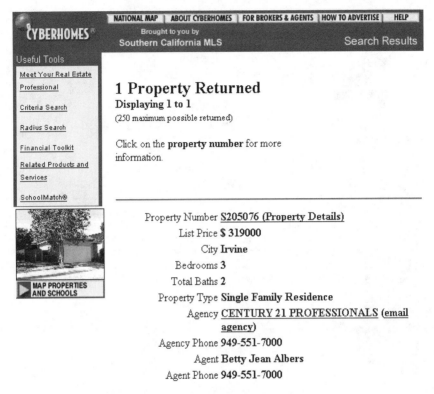

Figure 4.19   Results of search.

market you would like to buy. Of course, the seller of your dream home may not even be considering selling and moving, but you never know what might happen. You may get lucky and buy your dream house because you were willing to be a little more creative in your search labors.

EVALUATING THE SITES

Each of the sites discussed in this chapter would have you believe that you need only go to that site to find the home you want. Don't you believe it! REALTOR.com certainly has the most listings, but HomeAdvisor, HomeSeekers.com, and CyberHomes each has a sufficient number to merit your attention in the search process. In addition, the search processes vary and you might find one appeals to you more than the others. As noted earlier, there are other sites to consider as well. To evaluate the efficiency and coverage of these Web sites, I developed a test. I went to my local MLS and got a list of properties on the market in my area. I then went to each of these Web sites and

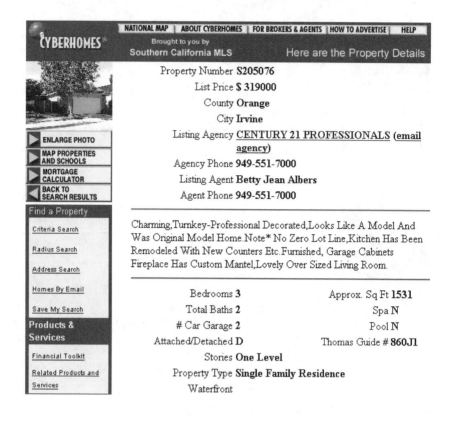

Figure 4.20   Getting down to details for a single property.

entered the search criteria I felt would most closely resemble the list of properties I had chosen. (This was not meant to be an exhaustive test, and I'm sure the results will be different for various areas of the country.) The results are shown in Table 4.1.

As you can see, no single site listed all the properties I chose. Though most of the properties showed up somewhere, I do not know why more of them didn't show up in more places. One probable reason is that the local MLS is organized around districts, while search engines may be organized around cities or zip codes. I repeated this kind of search in other areas as I was doing research for this book, and, though the results varied somewhat, the bottom line is: Use all of the search engines to find all the properties in your target area.

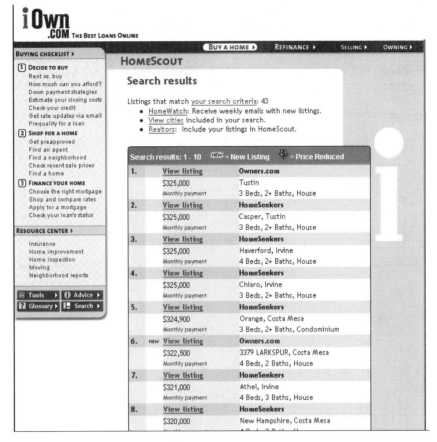

Figure 4.21   HomeScout properties are linked to other real estate sites.
(© iOwn Holdings, Inc. 2000.)

HOMEBUILDER SITES

One advantage homebuilders have over local real estate agents is that they know exactly what they are building, where, and how much it will cost—at least for today. In addition, there are fewer builders than real estate companies, and, collectively, they construct fewer homes every year than are sold in the resale home market. Consequently, it is easier to assemble and manage data on new homes than on resale homes.

The Web site of the National Association of Homebuilders, the industry's largest trade association, is at www.homebuilder.com. When you visit the site, you will note that, except for color, this site's graphics are almost identical to those at the REALTOR.com Web site. Why? Because they are both managed by Homestore.com.

Table 4.1   Ranking the Real Estate Web Sites

		MLS		
Property	REALTOR.com	HomeAdvisor	HomeSeekers.com	CyberHomes
1	x	x		
2	x			
3	x		x	x
4	x	x		x
5	x	x		x
6	x	x	x	
7	x		x	x
8				x
9		x	x	
10				
11	x		x	x
12	x	x	x	
13	x	x		
14	x	x		
15	x		x	x
16	x	x	x	x
17			x	x
18			x	x
19	x	x		
20	x			
21			x	x
22	x	x		
23	x			
24				x
25	x		x	

The site claims to have 136,000 listings, and the search process starts out the same as on the homebuyer sites. Though the front page gives you a choice of finding properties under the categories of New Homes, Builders, Custom Builders, or Planned Communities, regardless of which you select, you will go to a map to select a state and then to a map of that state with the market areas listed. The resulting Market Area map is the same, regardless of the route. You can then search by featured builder or by establishing a geographic search area such as a city or county and then itemizing other variables such as bedroom count in your search criteria. A word of caution: I found it easy to miss homes because I didn't know exactly how to ask the questions. You could too and end up with a smaller list than you might like. You might be interested in homes in the $200,000 price range, but if a builder has a model at $199,990, it may not show up in the search. Remember, this is an exclusionary search process, so you should do a broader search first, then narrow it down after you're sure you've included all the possible homes. Keep track of the names of builders who have projects in your area.

Unlike REALTOR.com, which has a fairly universal format for all listings, homebuilder.com merely has summary data about builders, projects, and homes. Any in-depth search will take you via hyperlink to the builder's own Web site, for example www.fieldstone-homes.com. These sites are usually very well organized, so it would be pointless for www.homebuilder.com to replicate them. If, as I recommended, you've kept a list of companies that are building homes in your preferred area, you can go to the Preferred Builders page where you can link directly to those Web sites. You might find doing your house search at each builder's site more useful, too.

Builders' Web sites vary significantly in their sophistication. Some are quite simple, containing just a list of projects and locations, and directions to the sales office. Others have incorporated the snazziest capabilities of the Web. For example, at www.riversgate.com/models/model10_frame.html, you'll see that this builder not only includes a picture of each model but a floor plan and a virtual tour of the home, utilizing the 360° digital camera view of the home's exterior and interior. No doubt as more builders learn what consumers are looking for on the Web, they too will refine their site offerings. If you end up finding a home this way, be sure to pass on to the builder an evaluation of the Web site so the builder can improve it.

Two other homebuilder sites to check out are NewHomesDirect, at www.newhomesdirect.com, and NewHomeSale, at www.newhomesale.com. Both have contracted with a smaller number of builders than homebuilder.com, but that doesn't mean that these sites are less useful.

FSBO WEB SITES

The Internet is going to be important not just to real estate professionals, but to people who want to sell their homes themselves—the for sale by owner (FSBO, pronounced *FIZZ-bo*) sellers. In the past, the seller had limited—and decidedly unsophisticated—marketing tools available: a sign in the front yard, an ad the Saturday paper, and perhaps flyers distributed throughout the neighborhood. Obviously, such methods reach only a very local market. The Web, however, has global reach, and FSBOs too can take advantage of that scope. Now buyers contemplating a move anywhere in the country—or the world—can look at FSBO properties. For that reason, it is conceivable that FSBO sellers will find that the Internet benefits them more than any other class of seller.

The best-known FSBO site is at www.owners.com. This is a very well-organized site that offers a great deal of help both to the buyer and to the seller. By definition, you are going to find properties here that you find at no other site—a good reason for going here. There are numerous listings, and, more important, they do not appear to be distress properties. If anything, they are quality properties; and if such a property is priced right, it will sell more quickly because of this additional exposure.

As a buyer, you search properties first by state, then by county or market area. My search of Orange County turned up 229 listings—not bad. You can have the list sorted by price, city, county, bedrooms, or square footage. Unfortunately, you can't discard cities you don't want; you can only go through the pages alphabetically until you reach the city you want. This isn't a problem, however, in less densely populated areas, where only a handful of properties might be listed. A listing typically carries a notice if the seller will entertain offers from buyers who are represented by an agent, also noting whether buyers without agents can receive preferential pricing.

Even though the services of owners.com include the ability to post up to five pictures, I found a surprising number of listings that did not include a picture of the property. I don't understand this, because it makes your job as a buyer more difficult, which is exactly the opposite of what a seller wants. All in all, though, I found the site to be an excellent resource.

Three other FSBO sites are FSBO.net at www.fsbo.net; www.fsbo-homes.com; and www.fsbonetwork.com. The last one is a network of FSBO magazines.

While the number of listings at FSBO sites will never come close to the volume at the Web sites managed by and for real estate professionals, any serious homebuyer should check out the listings at these online offerings. To repeat, you'll find properties at these sites that are found nowhere else on the Internet. My only injunction is that the FSBO seller may have decided to do it him- or herself because he or she believes "none of the real estate brokers realizes how much my house is worth." In those cases, the chances are the agents *do* know what the house is worth, it just doesn't conform to the seller's opinion. You don't want to be the dodo that pays 5 percent under the asking price when the house was 15 percent overpriced to begin with. Again, do your research about values, using the tools discussed in Chapter 6, "Estimating What It's Worth."

AUCTION SITES, REOS, AND OTHERS

Given the phenomenal success of the auction sites eBay and price-line.com, there may be a real future for online real estate auctions too, but not yet. The most significant home auction site attained notoriety when it conducted the first online auction of over 100 properties being sold by a government agency, but it is changing direction. Properties sold via online auctions in the future are likely to be those with a large number of units to sell quickly—banks selling their real estate owned properties (REOs) acquired through foreclosure, developers trying to clear out the last units of a project, and so forth. The nature of the auction process hinges upon two variables. The first is that potential bidders know what they are bidding on, such as an 1889 Gold $5 coin in a particular condition or a certain collectible doll. Real estate is different; every property has a unique location and unique characteristics, which means that a buyer has to do considerable research. Second, there must be enough bidders. One bid per property is not going to make a market attractive to sellers. To be successful, an auction Web site must collect enough listings to create critical mass—to attract enough buyers to make the process work. If you are auctioning 20 condos in the same project, there is a greater likelihood of attracting a larger number of buyers. One company whose site does offer this service is the Real Estate Disposition Corporation. You can see whether there are any upcoming auctions in your area at the site at www.r1redc.com. A site that offers access to REOs is www.foreclosureseekers.com, managed by HomeSeekers.com.

The potential for a buyer is that he or she can assume that a seller has already tried traditional selling methods and failed. The seller is thus trying at auction to liquidate the property at distress prices. You have to ask yourself if you want to buy a distress property on an as is basis with little or no warranty, in the case of REOs, and potentially with little recourse to the seller. The benefit is that these may be the best places to find a home at a bargain price, especially if you are a fixer-upper type of person.

HomeAuction.com at www.homeauction.com is currently available only in the state of Washington. Sellers are charged a 3 percent commission if the home sells. This is no different from a typical broker; however, if HomeAuction.com is successful in creating a high-traffic auction site, it will be providing many more buyers than a local broker. Stay tuned.

Finally, government agencies that wish to sell surplus properties or ones they have acquired through foreclosure routinely post on them on the Internet. In some cases the homes are listed with local real estate companies and thus can be accessed using the normal methods already discussed. In the cases involving the Department of Housing and Urban Development (HUD) and the Department of Veterans Affairs (VA), bids must be made through a broker.

Housing and Urban Development	www.hud.gov/local/sams/ ctznhome.html
Department of Veterans Affairs	www.vba.va.gov/bln/loan/ homes.htm
Federal Deposit Insurance Corporation	www2.fdic.gov/drrore/
General Services Administration	propertydisposal.gsa.gov/Property/ about/welcome.html
Internal Revenue Service	www.treas.gov/auctions/irs/real1 .html
Small Business Administration	www.sba.gov/prop
U.S. Army Corps of Engineers	www.sas.usace.army.mil/hapinv/ index.html
Fannie Mae	www.fanniemae.com/homes/ index.html
Freddie Mac	www.homesteps.com

SUMMARY

Most people search for homes by having a real estate agent screen them first, or by taking the home listings section of the Sunday paper and traipsing around looking at model homes and open houses. Most of these homes will not meet your needs, but you don't know that until you see them. This is an inefficient and frustrating method. Searching for homes on the Web is a far easier and more effective and efficient process. That is why I'm writing this book—to motivate homebuyers to begin to participate in the exciting world of e-homelooking and to assist them in making the wisest use of this resource. As more homebuyers recognize the power of the Internet, its use in the researching and marketing of homes will explode. In future editions of this book, I would like to incorporate the experiences of homebuyers, both their successes and frustrations. Please let me know about your Web real estate travels by e-mailing me at feedback@loan-wolf.com.

In the next chapter, I will explain the value of the online real estate marketplace to sellers.

SELLING A HOME ONLINE

Man's capacity for knowledge is finite, but the amount of ignorance is infinite.

—RANDY JOHNSON

Education is the progressive discovery of our own ignorance.

—WILL DURANT

KEY POINTS

- Most of the publicity about real estate and the Internet has focused on what the Internet can do for buyers, not for sellers.
- If they take the proper steps, sellers can ensure that their properties are exposed to the greatest number of potential buyers.
- Advances in digital photography allow buyers to view property details interactively.
- The Internet offers terrific help for for sale by owners (FSBOs), the homeowners who wish to sell their homes themselves.

Why do people list their homes with real estate agents, and why are they prepared to fork over a 6 percent commission for the service? For one simple reason: Real estate agents know who the buyers are. Furthermore, because most buyers do contact an agent to help them, if your home is not listed with a real estate agent, he or she obviously won't show your home to potential buyers.

Let me say at the outset that the best agents work hard and do a terrific job of maximizing value for their sellers; in short, they are well worth their commission. That said, however, by definition, half the real estate agents are below average, and of course it's those who give even the best ones a bad name. It's the "one bad apple spoils the whole bunch" syndrome. That is why selecting the right agent is important, and why I devote Chapter 7, "Finding and Working with a Real Estate Agent," to the topic. Internet or no, a highly qualified real estate agent can and will make your real estate transactions go more smoothly and successfully. That's not to say, however, that some sellers, in some markets, can't benefit from marketing their homes themselves. So in this chapter I also describe online help for the FSBOs, as well as auction sites.

COVERING THE WEB

When you list your home with a real estate company, you want to make sure that your agent includes your home on as many Web sites as possible in his or her overall marketing plan. As I stated in the introduction, as consumer confidence in the security and reliability of the Internet grows, people will increasingly make it their channel of choice for gathering the data they need to make real estate–related decisions. That means that increasing numbers of homebuyers will turn first to the Internet to seek information about properties in areas that interest them, which of course means sellers have to be there.

As a seller, to reach the large numbers of online shoppers, you want to assure that your home is posted on all real estate sites. Why? Because most homebuyers do not visit all the sites where homes are listed. In the first place, no seller should assume that any buyer knows about all the relevant Web sites. Buyers are not in the business; they're consumers, so they rarely are aware of all that's available to them. The fact is, many buyers may visit only one Web site, and if your home is not on that one Web site, your property will miss out on exposure to a lot of buyers—perhaps one who would be interested in your home. To repeat: If you want all buyers to see your home, you must list it on all the real estate Web sites.

As I mentioned, most real estate companies now have their own Web sites to promote their listings; many real estate salespeople have Web sites, too. You want to be listed on these as well.

Whose House Is It Anyway?

Now you know you need to list your home on all relevant Web sites. That seems easy enough, given the computer capabilities that enable you to submit and copy Web content quickly and easily. But there's a catch (isn't there always?). Recall what I discussed in Chapter 2, "Gunfight at the Internet Corral." At the time of this writing, the real estate brokerage industry is engaged in an idiotic attempt to monopolize information, as it did when it resisted allowing multiple listing service (MLS) data to be made public. In this case, the MLS in your area and your brokerage firm may list their properties only on the REALTOR .com Web site, not all of the national Web sites.

Does this enrage you? It should. The information about your home for sale is *your* information, not the salesperson's, not the broker's, and surely not the company's, whose headquarters may be thousands of miles away. The company may only be the franchiser of your local company. But the powers that be in the real estate industry are taking the position that when they put the information into the MLS or Internet format, it becomes their information, not yours. This begs the question about the proper role for an agent—to give the property maximum exposure. It is not in your best interest for your agent's company or anyone else to restrict access to this information, whatever the rationale. I hope that by the time you read these words, the courts or the U.S. Department of Justice will have redrawn the lines and this will be a nonissue.

In the meantime, ask prospective agents about their company policy regarding on which Web sites they post their listings. If they say that their policy is to post your listing on all pertinent Web sites, request that this be put in writing as part of your listing agreement; specifically, request the agent to list the sites on which your property will be posted by name or by Web address. The following is some simple language you might use in such an agreement with your agent.

In connection with the listing of the property at (*home address*), (*name of broker*) agrees to provide listing information to the following Web sites:

- REALTOR.com
- HomeSeekers.com
- HomeAdvisor
- CyberHomes
- HomeScout
- (*Name of regional database*), at (*Web address*)
- (*Name of broker*), at (*Web address*)
- (*Name of agent*), at (*Web address*)

This can simply be a little letter of understanding between you and your agent, to clarify his or her responsibilities. If you want it to be a legal part of your listing agreement, show it to your attorney and ask him or her to incorporate this language in an addendum to the listing contract to make it legally binding under the laws of your state.

But you're not through yet. After you come to this agreement with your agent, get on the Internet and confirm that you can find your listing at each Web site you have agreed on. If you can't, chances are that buyers won't be able to find it either.

Next, discuss with your agent how he or she intends to respond to inquiries from online buyers. For example, research has shown that, for whatever reason, prospective buyers seem reluctant to use the "respond by e-mail" options at property listings. Some agents list just their name and a phone number, whereas others provide more contact options. Figures 5.1 and 5.2 show examples of the latter, on the REALTOR.com and HomeAdvisor sites, respectively.

Note that each agent has made it easy to get more information about the property. In addition to the agent's e-mail address (sometimes more than one), the office phone and fax numbers are listed.

That may not be enough, so don't be afraid to suggest that the agent's home phone number, pager number, and/or cellular phone number appear there also. Having a number of contact methods is important. Most people are hesitant about contacting real estate agents in the first place, and those who are doing so via the Internet are perhaps even more so. Therefore, you want to make it as easy as possible for buyers to contact your agent once they decide they want more information about your property.

How important is response time? I recently saw a program demonstration during which a prospect filled out a short form at a listing page; immediately thereafter, a voice message was sent to the listing agent's cell phone. The tinny, computerized voice said, "John Jones is interested in listing 14050. His phone number is 415-555-1234 and his e-mail address is johnj@xyz.com." Is instantaneous response essential? Human nature being what it is, probably yes. A study of car sales on the Internet demonstrated that if a salesperson called back within 8 hours of an inquiry, he or she had a 37 percent success rate in closing; if the salesperson waited 24 hours to respond, the success rate dropped to 17 percent; at 48 hours, the success rate fell to 8 percent—or, put more powerfully, the failure rate climbed to 92 percent. I think that the importance of response time in selling homes isn't much different. In summary, as a seller, you want an agent

Figure 5.1   REALTOR.com agents offer several ways to contact them.
(Courtesy of Homestore.com.)

Corona Del Mar $799,000
CORONA DEL MAR CA 92625

Bedrooms:	4
Bathrooms:	4
Listing number:	639446
Property type:	Single-family
Stories:	1
Parking:	3 Car Garage, Attached, Garage Door Opener
View:	Ocean, Bay
Pool/spa/sauna:	Private Pool, Private Spa
Elementary school:	LINCOLN
Junior high school:	CDM
High school:	CDM
Copyright:	Copyright(C) 1999 Orange Coast Association of REALTORS(R), Inc. Information herein deemed reliable but not guaranteed.

Listed by: ROBIN TENCH
REMAX REAL ESTATE SERVICES
rtench@homesoc.com
(949) 720-7339 phone
(949) 720-3821 fax
E-mail the listing agent about this home

⊟ Get listings by e-mail with Home Tracker.
⊞ Add this home to Your Favorite Homes.
⊞ E-mail your agent about this home
⊞ E-mail your co-buyer about this home

Figure 5.2   HomeAdvisor makes it easy to get in touch with its listing agents. (Courtesy of HomeAdvisor.)

who will respond to you in a timely fashion; more important, you want the agent to respond to buyers as quickly as possible.

LISTING IN LIVING COLOR

Real estate marketing has come a long way since the "3 BR-2 BA home on quiet street" two-inch by half-inch ads in the Sunday newspaper. The graphics power of the Internet means that you can place an in-depth ad with color photos online 24 hours a day, 7 days a week. And, with the advent of digital cameras, you can take a picture of a property and upload it almost immediately to all the Web sites showing the home.

In addition, broader bandwidths and faster download speeds enable virtual tours and 360° views of the exterior and interior of online properties, giving homebuyers today an unprecedented ability to check out the features of properties without leaving their current home. For a view of the very latest in this technology, I recommend that you check out Interactive Pictures Corporation at www.ipix.com and VRViews at www.vrviews.com. I think you will be blown away at what you see.

How do you get pictures like this of your home on the Internet? From a technological standpoint, here's how it works. A photographer takes a picture using a digital camera with a "fisheye" lens that captures everything from floor to ceiling and side to side, so-called 360 × 360 views.

Then the camera is turned exactly 180° and another picture is taken. When the two images are combined, you get the 360° view you can see at the Web site. The process is repeated for each view—perhaps the front and rear of the property, the living room, the kitchen, and the master bedroom. As to taking the pictures, there are two methods. Camera equipment worth several thousand dollars is required—too much of an investment for an individual agent, perhaps, but not for the whole office. The alternative is that a professional will come to the property and take the pictures. This may be a better move until everyone learns how to do it.

Virtual tours offer an important benefit to sellers: When a listing offers a virtual tour, buyers stay at the listing longer, intrigued by what they see. This is a tremendous positive for you as a seller, because it makes you stand out from your competition and I believe it will translate into faster sales. Adding a virtual tour to your listing will cost in the neighborhood of $100, but it is customary for the listing agent to pay for this. So definitely discuss—perhaps insist on—this capability when you interview agents. Any competitive real estate company will be offering this option to its clients who ask for it.

HOMESELLER SITES

Because of the organization and concentration of power in the real estate community, it is arguably easier to assemble information for the benefit of potential homebuyers than it is for the disparate and unorganized body of homesellers. Consequently, until recently there were few sites dedicated to the homeseller. Following is a sampling of homeseller sites.

HomeGain

HomeGain, at www.homegain.com, uses a simple methodology. Sellers want to find agents who are experienced in their area, and agents want to find people in their marketing area who are interested in selling. That's what makes a market, and in the case of HomeGain, that's what makes a Web site. Figure 5.3 shows HomeGain's home page.

If you are interested in selling your home, go to HomeGain and enter a property profile, including all the pertinent details of your property. HomeGain will send your information to registered agents in your area, who in turn will submit proposals to you back through the Home-Gain Web site. You can review and evaluate the proposals, then contact those agents whose proposals seem reasonable. The profile you submit is treated as confidential material; your name and phone number will not be given to agents, so they cannot call you unsolicited. You control the contact with the agents, an advantage for many people.

HomeGain is still in its early stages of development; nevertheless, it looks like it will be a valuable tool for sellers, and I recommend you give it a try.

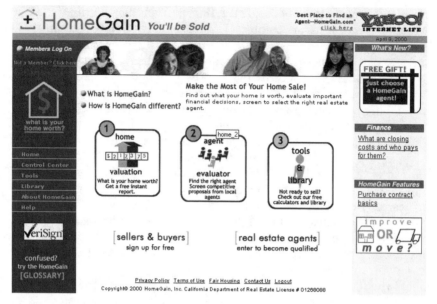

Figure 5.3   HomeGain, where buyers and sellers can sign up for agent proposals.   (Reprinted with permission. Copyright © 2000 HomeGain, Inc.)

eHome

eHome has a slightly different twist. Arguably, this type of selling transfers more of the responsibility for selling onto the shoulders of the seller. eHome will list the home on the local MLS, provide selling materials, and assist with closing the transaction. The fee charged for the listing service is a flat fee within a price range, but it is about 1 percent, not the 3 percent normally charged. You can check out a lively demonstration of the process at eHome's Web site at www.ehome.com, as shown in Figure 5.4.

Virtual Real Estate Store

Another service for sellers is at the Virtual Real Estate Store, whose Web address is www.virtualrealestatestore.com. Here, as at HomeGain, you can provide property profile information, which is then sent to pre-screened, registered agents in your area. You can also specify the level of service you desire and are able or willing to pay for. And don't bypass the educational materials at this site.

FSBOs

Absent a deal between friends, a relatively smaller percentage of people are successful in marketing and selling their homes themselves.

**Figure 5.4   eHome's web site.
(Courtesy of eHome.com.)**

The actual number depends on who you believe, but it is probably between 10 percent and 20 percent. That said, under the right conditions, a for-sale-by-owner property may be an advantage. For example, if you live in a tract where your "plan" home is highly desirable, it makes sense to take matters into your own hands: Find out whether one of your friends or neighbors has secretly been coveting your home. To that end, print up some flyers and distribute them throughout the neighborhood. I did this once and had two offers within 36 hours, one of which worked out.

Another time FSBOs make sense is during a seller's market. A seller's market is when there is minimal inventory, so when homes do come on the market, they sell within 24 to 48 hours, sometimes attracting multiple offers. However, selling your home and negotiating the sale in such a period requires considerable skill. If you are a businessperson who is used to dealing with people in this kind of an environment, you can certainly do it yourself. If, on the other hand, you do not have this type of skill set, I would think twice about it. But no matter how fortuitous the circumstance or how skilled a businessperson you are, as a rule of thumb, if your home does not attract an offer within a couple of weeks, take that as an indication that your marketing efforts—your ability to attract a buyer—are inadequate, and be prepared to offer to pay a 3 percent commission to an agent to bring a buyer. Distribute flyers to all the local real estate offices with these magic words: "Broker Cooperation." Also, check with your local Association of Realtors to see whether it will accept FSBO listings.

FSBO sellers underpricing their homes is so common it has become a real estate industry joke. For that reason, if you are going to list your own home without benefit of an agent, it is imperative that you get an appraisal and take advantage of the resources reviewed in Chapter 6, "Estimating What It's Worth," to determine the best selling price for your home. Then add a bit—say 5 percent—to allow for a little negotiating, and go for it.

Internet Help for the FSBO

Before e-commerce, the FSBO was limited to marketing his or her home to those within the same town or neighborhood. Advertising was limited to the local newspaper. At best, you could count on being able to expose the home to a small number of people. The Internet has changed all that. Resources now exist to enable you to "show" your home to a wider audience.

NOTE   The major real estate property search sites that we have discussed in these chapters do not currently accept FSBO listings. Almost certainly it is because they simply are not equipped to handhold sellers and deal with the myriad things that can go wrong between people and computers. The information on these sites comes directly from MLS computers, without much human intervention, and does not produce any revenue to the Web sites.

The best-known FSBO site is Owners.com. The site's home page, at www.owners.com, is shown in Figure 5.5.

At Owners.com, you can choose between three levels of service:

- A trial listing (free)
- The Standard package ($99)
- The Premiere package ($289)

Based on information supplied by Owners.com, those who choose the more expensive option have a higher success rate. Surprise! Again, this is not the time to be cheap. Owners.com is now including as a part of the Premiere package Ipix 360° pictures, discussed earlier. Figure 5.6 shows details of a typical listing at Owners.com.

Another recent addition is the Owner's Agent Network, where a seller who has been unsuccessful in marketing a home can be referred to a nearby agent. It is not clear what process is used to select those agents. The gimmick is that when the home is sold through such an agent, Owners.com will kick back 10 percent of the seller's portion of the commission to the seller. The Owners.com site is well organized and has lots of additional educational information available to both sellers and buyers.

Three other FSBO Web sites deserve mention, too. First is FSBO .net, at www.fsbo.net. Listing your property here costs $19.95; an optional

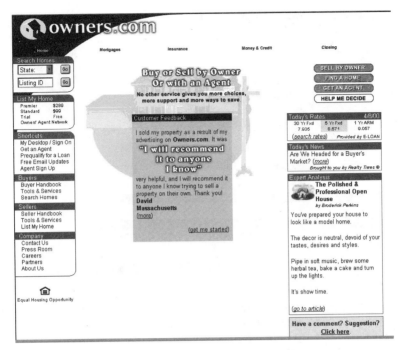

Figure 5.5 Owners.com, a haven for FSBOs on the Internet.
(© Owners.com, Inc. 2000. All Rights Reserved. *Copyright*
& Trademark Notices Privacy Policy & Security Statement
and *Terms and Conditions of Service and Use.*)

seller's toolkit comes complete with a yard sign, a book, and a pamphlet. Also check out www.fsbo-homes.com and www.fsbonetwork.com; the latter is a network of FSBO magazines. Though the number of listings at these sites is not in the same league with the other real estate sites, the advantage is that it will take just a minute to check them out. Who knows, you may find just what you are looking for.

 TIP I can't emphasize strongly enough the importance of establishing the right price for your home if you're going the FSBO route. See Chapter 6 for more information.

AUCTIONS

For those who must negotiate an immediate sale, there's the online auction option. However, this phenomenon is so new that very little information is available as to whether the various parties are satisfied with this method of buying and selling properties.

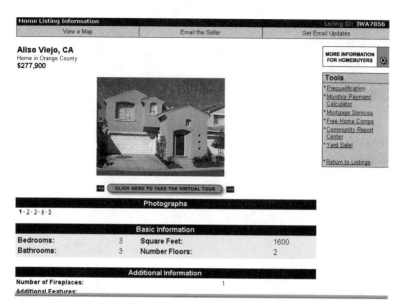

Figure 5.6   Presentation of a typical listing at Owners.com. (© Owners.com, Inc. 2000. All Rights Reserved. *Copyright & Trademark Notices Privacy Policy & Security Statement* and *Terms and Conditions of Service and Use.*)

Specifically, most auctions have focused on bulk sales, banks selling foreclosed properties, developers selling inventory, and other distress sales situations. In these cases, the sellers are typically more concerned about moving the properties than maximizing value. It is not clear to me, however, that many individual sellers are willing to compromise on value. Having said that, the success of other Internet auction sites would lead to the conclusion that this method of selling homes may well work for individual homesellers in the future.

Those interested in pursuing the method should go to www.homeauction.com. It will cost you $499 to list a home there. The other prominent home auction site is www.homebid.com. This site has just completed its first sale and may be accepting properties from individual brokers. Check the site to find current states.

SUMMARY

The purpose of using the Internet to sell homes is threefold:

- To make it easier for buyers and sellers to exchange information about properties

Additional Information	
Number of Fireplaces:	1
Additional Features:	

▷ This property has a **swimming pool** and/or **jaccuzzi**.

Year Constructed:	1998
Type of View:	None
Main Heating System:	Standard Gas
Main Cooling System:	Central A/C
Garage:	2 Car (Attached)
Sewer System:	City Provided

Price:	$277,900

Please Note the Following:

▷ The owner is willing to work with a real estate agent.

Property Description:

Spacious loft area w/ upgrades
Vaulted ceilings in living room
Upstairs laundry with maple cabinet
Gas burning fireplace
Central air conditioning
Gated community
Formal dining room
Prewired for surround sound in family rm
Upgrd Maple cabinets w/ lots of storage
Built in Sub Zero refer w/ maple fronts
Built in dishwasher w/ maple fronts
Custom stone flooring in kitchen
Built in Microwave
Nook area in kitchen
Giant built in stainless 48" DCS BBQ
Spacious jacuzzi w/ 2 motors & 40 jets
Exterior flagstone & colored concrete

Figure 5.6　*(Continued)*

- To help make it easier for both buyers and sellers to make decisions
- To streamline the process

For sellers it is important that as many people as possible know about their homes, and never before have sellers had so many tools available to spread the word. But just because it's easier doesn't mean it's less involved. It is important that sellers maintain an active role in the process and not rely on an agent to do all the work. I recommend several books on this topic in Appendix 1.

6

ESTIMATING WHAT
IT'S WORTH

Propositions arrived at by purely logical means are completely empty of reality, even if we could properly explain what reality means. Intuition is crucial to my thinking.
—ALBERT EINSTEIN

KEY POINTS

- Estimating market value is one of the most important tasks, both in listing a home and deciding what to offer.
- Most of the data on recent home sales are public information that has been available to agents and appraisers for years. Now it's accessible to the public.
- You can access recent sales in your neighborhood.
- Using the form appraisers use, you can better organize and understand the data.

The one nagging question always in the minds of those buying or selling a home is: "What is this property worth?" Valuing properties is an exercise in balancing the objective with the subjective. The objective factors obviously are the actual lot, the home constructed on it, and its specific characteristics. The subjective factors are less obvious: what people want—a wider lot, a more stylish home, one that is fixed up, one with a view, one with a swimming pool, and so forth—and what they are willing to pay. Although they are amateurs, all buyers and sellers go through a more informal valuation process as they put up their homes for sale, make offers, and negotiate the terms of sale. Appraisers tell lenders whether they were right.

Property valuation is the job of the real estate appraiser, a trained professional who goes through a formal process to arrive at a final estimate of market value. This process includes determining what is to be appraised and deciding how the market values the subject by finding, sifting, and reviewing public records and private sources. The appraiser then compares specific characteristics of the home in question against those of similar properties that have sold recently. First, the appraiser assesses economic trends, the stability of the job market, the availability of financing, community characteristics, and the specifics of the property. He or she then determines which characteristics of comparable properties are most relevant to the property being appraised, estimates the value of the differences in those characteristics, comes to a conclusion about the property's value, and summarizes the information in a formal report.

Ever since I entered the mortgage business, borrowers have been asking why an appraisal costs so much, typically $250 to $300. The answer is that arriving at an accurate, defendable value is difficult, time-consuming work, as you will see if you attempt to duplicate the work yourself. It is also vitally important that the report's conclusion be accurate. How much would you be willing to pay for an inaccurate appraisal? Appraisers maintain offices and staff; they subscribe to numerous, expensive data resources that are updated frequently; they have knowledge of their area; they have to be experienced in judging subtle market factors; and they must be knowledgeable about the rules established by the Uniform Standards of Professional Appraisal Practice as well as the requirements of the Federal National Mortgage Association (FNMA), the Federal Home Loan Mortgage Corporation (FHLMC), and other secondary market money sources. Appraisers usually drive from 2500 to 4000 miles every month inspecting properties. Moreover, in most areas, appraisers are now required to be licensed or certified, which requires passing a test, paying a license fee, and carrying errors and omission insurance in order to have some protection in case a client thinks they made a mistake and sues them. In short, I can assure you that a licensed appraiser's opinion of the value of a property you are about to buy is cheap at the price and very valuable to you.

If you are buying a home, I advise you to ask your lender to order the appraisal for you, even if you haven't made your offer yet but are just confirming value. If you hire an appraiser yourself, you may find the appraisal will not be acceptable to a lender. If, however, you do decide to hire an appraiser yourself, in some states you may be able to go to the appraisers' licensing authority to get a list of qualified professionals in your area. In California, for example, you can search the database at www.orea.ca.gov/html/licappraisers.html. Try plugging in the two-letter abbreviation of your state in place of CA to find a local listing.

A better source is the Appraisal Institute, whose site is located at www.appraisalinstitute.org. Members of this highly regarded organization can carry the designation Member of the Appraisal Institute (MAI) as well as other designations based on the member's experience in appraising different kinds of properties. MAIs have to pass rigid educational and experience criteria to be admitted, so if you find one in your area, you can be assured that he or she is one of the best in the profession. Note, however, that MAIs typically concentrate on complex commercial appraisals and do not normally do residential appraisals. Appraisers who specialize in residential properties have the SRA or RM designations.

A third alternative is to have an appraisal done by a network of professionals, which you can access at On-Line Appraisals, at www .ola.com. A unique feature of this service is that your appraisal will be posted on the Web site. Then, if your home is for sale, and after you have assured that it is listed on the real estate Web sites, you can establish a hyperlink from your Internet listing to the appraisal to enable a prospective buyer to see additional features of your home and the neighborhood. You may keep the appraised value confidential if you choose; or, if it is consistent with what you would accept for your home, you can post it for prospective buyers to see.

APPRAISAL FACTORS

During the appraisal process, appraisers look first at the various land factors:

- How big is the lot?
- Where is it located?
- What extra features does it have, such as a view?
- Is all of the lot usable?

In the middle of a homogeneous tract, lot valuation is fairly easy, but in areas where lot sizes vary, it is more difficult. It may not be easy to determine how much more a 9,500-square-foot lot is worth than a 7,500-square-foot lot.

When it comes to the structure on the land—the home—some aspects of the appraisal are easy, such as comparing the square footages and room counts. However, a number of other factors come into play as well:

- How old is the home?
- What is the quality of construction?
- What is its state of maintenance?
- Has it been upgraded recently?

And so forth. All of these questions have to be answered in one way or another, and you should realize that these issues can sometimes confound even professional appraisers who may have evaluated thousands of homes in their careers. You, with little or no experience in this process, are at a distinct disadvantage when it comes to deciding at what price to list the home, if you're a seller, or what to bid on it, if you're a buyer.

That is why buyers and sellers have traditionally relied on the evaluations of real estate agents to determine listing and offering prices and to develop negotiating strategies during the offer and counteroffer phase of homebuying and homeselling. This is still the wise way to go, but today, thanks to the Internet, other tools are readily available to help buyers and sellers alike make more informed decisions. Let's review the processes and then the tools.

Determining the Listing Price

A key function of the listing agent is to guide the seller in determining the appropriate price for the home. Obviously, the relative price must reflect the seller's needs, but ideally—and usually—it strikes a balance between being high enough to assure that the seller gets a fair price but not so high as to discourage prospective buyers. (In a game that can be played only in a very hot market, people with courage will use a perverse strategy: set the price a little low so as to attract multiple offers and then play the prospective buyers off one another, hoping to get more than the listing price they contemplate. Oddly enough, in the right market, that can work.) Of course, the determination of the ideal price is also a balance between the objective evidence—the recent sales prices of comparable homes—and the subjective valuations concerning other property characteristics.

A good agent will have a firm grip on values in his or her area of specialty, enabling him or her to make a price recommendation that is within 2 or 3 percent or so of what the home will end up selling for. From that, the seller can decide to add a little to allow for some negotiation. But—and this is a big but—a less experienced agent may not recognize some of the more subtle valuation factors and hence give misleading advice. An incompetent agent will leave a lot of money on the table because he or she is not familiar with the subtleties of the marketplace. And an unscrupulous agent knows that a lower-priced home is easier to sell than a high-priced one and that it takes a lot less work. With those distinctions in mind, I again stress the importance of finding a competent, ethical agent.

Until the advent of the Internet, sellers really had no way to validate the assessments of the value of a home unless they paid for a full appraisal, usually costing $250 to $300. And, for properties priced higher than $300,000 or so, I recommend that you pay for a full appraisal. Your buyer and his or her lender are going to get one anyway, so why not find out early in the process what they will be looking at later? Offers and counteroffers are usually in increments of $1000, and why some sellers will think nothing of giving away $1000 in negotiation, yet resist paying $300 for an appraisal that can help their negotiating position, is inexplicable. All that said, cheaper help is available on the Internet, and whether you use the information to get a ballpark figure before hiring a pro or use it "for real," going online for appraisal help is certainly a viable option today.

Determining an Offering Price

Needless to say, buyers have questions about value, too, especially if they are being relocated to a totally unfamiliar area. As a buyer, when you find a home whose characteristics you like, you have to ask yourself: How do I come up with a target price and an initial offering price? A seller's offering price may be low, realistic, or high, and it is important to know this before you start bidding. You don't want to offer 5 percent below an offering price and find that the seller determined the offering price by adding 10 percent to what he or she would accept!

Obviously, you should rely principally on your agent's assessments. But if you have been working with one agent, looking at a fairly widespread area, you have to consider that your agent can't be an expert in every corner of such a large area. A really good agent will recognize that and acknowledge to you his or her limitations and call on others in the office for assistance. Of course, the agent should also have ample comparable sales data gleaned from the local MLS database and from discussions with other agents who might have similar homes in escrow but not yet closed.

Regardless of your agent's experience and your confidence in the agent, you as principal *must* play a key role in controlling this process. It is, after all, your money and your decision.

APPRAISAL HELP ON THE INTERNET

Online help for valuing real estate property comes in two primary forms. First, there are services that can give you comparable sales data in your target neighborhood and price range, including houses being sold by their owners and those not appearing in the MLS. You'll also find automated valuation models (AVMs), which run comparable sales data through a computer program to predict a value and/or range of values for a property. Both are potentially useful, so I'll discuss them in detail.

Comparable Data Services

The foundation of the appraisal process is the analysis of prices at which other homes in the area have sold. If someone has paid $253,000 for the same model you have, they are not likely to pay $275,000 for your home unless you have a view, a pool, or a much larger lot. So the key to valuing your home or the one you are interested in buying lies in studying what others have paid for similar homes, making adjustments for all differences. Obviously, after a purchase contract is signed, the lender is going to have an appraisal done too, so you might as well start the process looking at the same data the lender will examine.

DataQuick. The grandparent of real estate data collection is Data-Quick, whose homepage at www.dataquick.com is shown in Figure 6.1. This company collects sales data from county assessors' offices and from public records, such as when deeds are recorded to transfer prop-erties. Its databases are generally searched by appraisers to develop a history of comparable sales that will be used when appraising a prop-erty for the buyer's lender.

DataQuick unfortunately does not cover the entire country, but it does contain data from some 800 political jurisdictions that include 75 percent of the population. If you live in a major metropolitan area, chances are that DataQuick has information on your property and com-parable sales data from your neighborhood.

NOTE DataQuick also offers a number of other useful links to real estate information. Be sure to follow them to increase your knowledge base. Begin by clicking on Consumer Services. For a fee, you can get

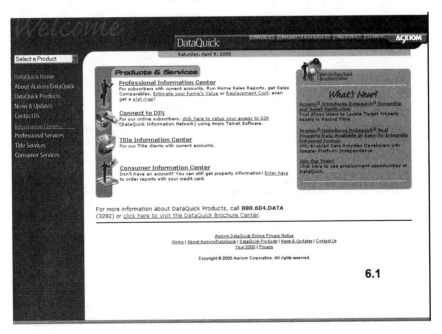

**Figure 6.1   The Homepage for DataQuick's services.
(Courtesy of DataQuick.)**

three types of reports here: Recent Sales ($9.95), Crime ($9.95), and Neighborhood Demographics ($5.00). The Recent Sales Report lists up to 30 comparable properties (note that you may not get 30 because the number depends on your neighborhood and the number of sales). There's also a Home Sales Price Trends (for the past 18 months) Report available free of charge. I found this report to be less useful than I anticipated, but not through any failing of DataQuick; median sales prices, stated on a monthly basis, vary so much that they are not helpful in determining the value of an individual property.

Figure 6.2 shows the first two pages of DataQuick's seven-page Home Sales Report for San Diego, which included a map showing the target property as well as locations of all comparable properties.

HomeSales Report

www.dataquick.com © 2000 DataQuick Information Systems.
This information is sourced from public documents and is not guaranteed.

CALIFORNIA

Geo Level: 0

Site Address:	*99 LEROY ST*
	SAN DIEGO, CA 92106
APN:	*533-238-16*
Census Tract:	*0071004*
Housing Tract Number:	*1448*
Lot Number:	*11*
Page Grid Old:	*64-C1*
Page Grid New:	*1288-B2*

Property Characteristics

Bedrooms: 2	*Year Built: 1968*	*Square Feet: 1,245*
Bathrooms: 1.0	*Garage: Y/2 space*	*Lot Size: 3,950*
Total Rooms:	*Fireplace:*	*Number of Units: 1*
Zoning: R1	*Pool/View: /Y*	*Use Code: SINGLE FAMILY RESIDENCE*

Sale & Assessment Information

Transfer Date: 05-24-1995	*Document #: 0000055435*	*Assessed Value: $336,005*
Transfer Value: $499,000	*Tax Amount: $3,688.36*	*Land Value: $245,755*
Cost/Sq Feet: $440.55	*Tax Rate Area: 8001*	*Improvement Value: $190,250*

Figure 6.2   A sample DataQuick Home Sales Report.
(Courtesy of DataQuick.)

Sales Comparables

1   **22 LEROY ST, SAN DIEGO CA 92106**

		APN: 531-240-20
		Ref APN:
Bed/Bath: 3/2.0	Lot Size: 10,563	Transfer Date: 03-26-2000
Square Feet: 1,663	Assessed Value: $205,673	Transfer Value: $400,000F
Year Built: 1935	Garage: Y/2 space	First Loan: $320,000
Use Code: RSFR	Number Of Units: 1	Cost/Sq Feet: $240.53

Quantity and Quality of comps will vary based on quality of recorded information in the respective county.

2   **33 LEROY ST, SAN DIEGO CA 92106**

		APN: 531-232-10
		Ref APN:
Bed/Bath: 2/1.0	Lot Size: 5,253	Transfer Date: 01-29-2000
Square Feet: 1,134	Assessed Value: $62,197	Transfer Value: $415,000F
Year Built: 1938	Garage: Y/2 space	First Loan: $290,500
Use Code: RSFR	Number Of Units: 1	Cost/Sq Feet: $365.96

3   **44 TALBOT ST, SAN DIEGO CA 92106**

		APN: 531-222-13
		Ref APN:
Bed/Bath: 2/1.0	Lot Size: 6,499	Transfer Date: 05-21-2000
Square Feet: 744	Assessed Value: $45,762	Transfer Value: $251,000F
Year Built: 1941	Garage: Y/1 space	First Loan: $200,800
Use Code: RSFR	Number Of Units: 1	Cost/Sq Feet: $337.37

4   **55 TRUMBULL ST, SAN DIEGO CA 92106**

		APN: 531-212-17
		Ref APN:
Bed/Bath: 3/2.0	Lot Size: 8,772	Transfer Date: 03-08-2000
Square Feet: 1,368	Assessed Value: $76,268	Transfer Value: $495,000F
Year Built: 1940	Garage: Y/2 space	First Loan: $395,000
Use Code: RSFR	Number Of Units: 1	Cost/Sq Feet: $361.84

Figure 6.2   *(Continued)*

DataQuick also has contracts to provide search capabilities to consumers through local newspapers. Check the Web site of your hometown newspaper to see whether this service is offered in your area. But a word of advice: You may find that the newspaper service is free, but I think it's worth paying $9.95 for the DataQuick report, because it will contain more information. I remind you again: When you are buying or selling a home, it's no time to be penny wise and pound foolish. In my area, the *Los Angeles Times,* at www.latimes.com/class/realestate/, offers sales data. When you click on Home Search, you go to a criteria page where you can enter in your data. Be sure to start with broader criteria and then narrow them down.

The *Los Angeles Times* output is in a summary format and has far less detail. On the other hand, it's free, and if a summary is all you need, go for it. You may want to use this report to initiate your search, assuming it's available in your area, then pay for more detailed information later, after you've narrowed your search criteria.

PropertyView.   Another source of comparable sales data is from First American Financial Corporation, parent of the large title company. Their PropertyView function can be found at www.propertyview.com/. Property sales in this database cover a nine-month period, and are limited to a half-mile radius from the target address. Do not be put off by those parameters. The result generated from a given search depends on the number of comparable sales, and in most urban areas a search will easily generate enough data to be useful. The report PropertyView produces includes a map showing the target property, as well as locations of all comparable properties. The format for this report is reproduced in Figure 6.3. Note that will you get only the barest information here; you have to pay $9.95 for the full report. It certainly may be worth it.

Others.   Two other sites to visit for comparable property sales data are Domania.com and iOwn.com.

Order Online for $9.95
Home Comparisons
Mortgage Calculators
Online Help Guide
Refinancing Tips

Home

BENNINGTON , IRVINE, CA 92620

Number of comparables found: **20**

This is a sample PropertyView report and map. All of the information contained in this report will be available for all comparables found when you order the full PropertyView report. Please refer to the Glossary under the Online Help Guide if you have any questions about the terms used on th s report. To order your full comparison, click the Order Full Comparison button on the bottom of this page.

Note: All fields that contain ***** will include detailed information on the actual report. This information has been removed from the sample for security purposes.

Target Property Profile

Site Address: 67 BENNINGTON , IRVINE , CA 92620

Year Built:	1978	Square Feet:	1538	Bedrooms:	2
Cost per sq ft:	*****************	Lot Size:	4590	Bathrooms:	2
Sales Amount:	*****************	Number of Units:	N/A	Parking:	ATTACHED
Sales Date:	08/03/1999	Zoning:	N/A	Fireplace:	No
Assessed Value:	*****************	Use Code:	SFR	Pool:	No
Annual Taxes:	*****************	Total Rooms:	6	Location Type:	N/A

Figure 6.3   A PropertyView comparable sales report format. (PropertyView is a registered trademark of The First American Corporation. © 2000 The First American Corporation. Used with permission.)

Domania.com offers Home Price Check, a home comparables search engine, at its Web site at www.domania.com. Initiate the search by entering a location, address, city, state, or zip code; then request sales data on that property, the entire street, or a neighborhood. You may also search by price. The site contains information for only about 75 percent of the United States and has plans to grow from there. The service is free, well organized, and useful. I particularly liked the ability to define the search parameters. Once delivered, these properties may all be mapped with one click.

Unique on the Web is domania.com's Property Tax Tool, which will be of help in assessing a property's annual tax burden. You can also get a list of the assessed values of properties in your neighborhood if you are arguing with the assessor's office about the assessed valuation of your home because you think it has been assigned too high a value. There is a lot more information at this site, which is transforming itself into an excellent full-service real estate Web site.

iOwn.com offers the HomeSales page at rhs.iown.com/buy/rhbuyindex.htm. The layout here is excellent, and, as is the case with other iOwn services, the report is somewhat easier to read and use than others. You can also access a map that will show you the location of comparable sales properties.

Automated Valuation Models

In an effort to simplify the mortgage process and reduce the cost to borrowers, the real estate industry has been trying to come up with ways to streamline the appraisal process. This is obviously a balancing act, because no one wants to compromise the accuracy and validity of the appraisal. The goal is to make it cheaper to get an appraisal while maintaining accuracy and thoroughness. As computers become more powerful and as the databases of property information become more reliable, clearly the appraiser's work can be made easier. The question is, can the appraiser be entirely removed from the process? Let's examine this question.

When it comes to properties in homogeneous neighborhoods—by which I mean, for example, tracts of newer homes with a small number of identical floor plans—the appraisal process can be fairly simple. In contrast, in higher-priced neighborhoods where homes are built to custom specifications (and so are all different) and where lot characteristics vary, it is more difficult. How can a computer figure out the value of a highly upgraded kitchen in a comparable property, even if it knew it was there, which it doesn't?

Nonetheless, many properties can be valued using automated valuation models (AVMs). Freddie Mac, which has data on the value of millions of homes, has developed an AVM that can be used, it is presumed, in connection with its Automated Underwriting System. When an application is submitted that, for example, purports to be on a $150,000 home, whether for purchase or refinance, it can quickly be cross-referenced against the value produced by the AVM with the known values of nearby homes recently financed by Freddie Mac. If that range were, say, $147,000 to $155,000, Freddie Mac would feel safe in requiring only a drive-by appraisal instead of a full appraisal. That saves you about $100.

> **NOTE** At the time of this writing, the Freddie Mac AVM is not available to consumers directly, only to their lenders after a consumer's loan has been approved.

Consumers have access to three AVM services on the Internet: Transamerica Intellitech, Inc., Solimar Inc., and domania.com. In the first two cases, the model is somewhat more simplified than the one used by industrial customers, lenders, advertisers, and market research firms. Domania.com's ValueCheck model, discussed in the following text, is available to consumers directly, but the other two models are only available through partners.

Transamerica Intellitech, Inc.'s model can be found through iOwn .com at http://secure.iown.com/secure/appraise.dll/start?center=buy& source=buy. Each report costs $14.95. The information here is pleasantly organized, well laid out, and easy to read.

Solimar Inc., at www.solimar.net, offers its AVM services through the HomeGain site, www.homegain.com. You have to register at Home-Gain to access the data, which is no big deal, but that gets you only one free report. This service will be of greatest value to those who have created a property profile of their homes, inviting proposals from real estate agents in their areas. I discussed that service in Chapter 5, "Selling a Home Online."

I would recommend these services to you only if I could verify the accuracy of these models, so I conducted a little survey. I took the addresses of some recent sales on transactions I was working on, properties in escrow but not yet closed. Obviously, the two companies did not yet have access to the prices at which those properties sold, but I did. I assumed that buyers and sellers had agreed on a fair market price. The results of my survey are shown in Table 6.1.

Let's establish a standard for evaluating these results. Typically, appraisers can fairly easily come within 5 percent of a home's market value as agreed on between buyer and seller. The variation demonstrated in Table 6.1 is just too great, so until AVMs can produce comparable results, they will not be as useful to consumers as appraisals done by experts—hand-crafted appraisals, if you will. In the meantime, work with a local expert.

Domania.com, at www.domania.com, has recently introduced its own valuation model, ValueCheck. This model requires that you enter

Table 6.1   Verifying Automated Valuation Methods

	Actual price	AVM#1	Value difference	AVM#2	Difference
Property 1	$750,000	$517,800	−31%		
Property 2	$360,000	$231,900	−36%	$330,603	−8%
Property 3	$225,000	$227,700	1%	$228,384	2%
Property 4	$238,000	$203,500	−14%	$214,216	−10%
Property 5	$465,000	$448,000	−4%	$342,321	−26%
Property 6	$279,900	$300,900	8%		
Property 7	$635,000			$552,938	−13%
Property 8	$475,000			$477,635	1%
Property 9	$735,000			$564,382	−23%

the address, purchase price, and date purchased. The model then extrapolates the figures using the appreciation rate of the median home in the property's neighborhood to arrive at a current estimate of value. I had no idea of the prices last paid for the properties in my analysis, so I could not test the accuracy of the model. I did use it for a few properties I did know about and found it to be reasonably accurate.

My assessment is that this model works best in homogeneous markets and where the length of time since acquisition is shorter. The results will be most accurate if the property in question has tracked closely with the path of the median value. Homes that are smaller or larger or in better or worse condition than average or that were purchased a long time ago will demonstrate wider variation from the norm. If a major improvement has been made to the property, this will have to be added onto the model's projected value.

NOTE I sincerely hope that AVM results improve, and I will be in communication with these companies as they work to improve these models. I will reexamine AVMs in future editions of this book and post interim updates at my Web site, www.loan-wolf.com.

In the meantime, it remains your responsibility to do your own evaluation using comparable sales data available and then work with your real estate agent on this task. To assist you in organizing and classifying the data you get, I know of no better tool than the standard appraisal form used by the industry. A portion is reproduced in Figure 6.4; the entire form is available in Adobe Acrobat .pdf format from my Web site at www.loan-wolf.com/forms.htm. You need to have the Adobe Acrobat Reader installed on your computer, but it can be downloaded for free from another link on that page.

ITEM	SUBJECT	COMPARABLE NO. 1		COMPARABLE NO. 2		COMPARABLE NO. 3	
Address							
Proximity to Subject							
Sales Price	$		$		$		$
Price/Gross Liv. Area	$	$		$		$	
Data and/or							
Verification Sources							
VALUE ADJUSTMENTS	DESCRIPTION	DESCRIPTION	+ (-) $ Adjustment	DESCRIPTION	+ (-) $ Adjustment	DESCRIPTION	+ (-) $ Adjustment
Sales or Financing Concessions							
Date of Sale/Time							
Location							
Leasehold/Fee Simple							
Site							
View							
Design and Appeal							
Quality of Construction							
Age							
Condition							
Above Grade	Total Bdrms Baths	Total Bdrms Baths		Total Bdrms Baths		Total Bdrms Baths	
Room Count							
Gross Living Area	Sq. Ft.	Sq. Ft.		Sq. Ft.		Sq. Ft.	
Basement & Finished Rooms Below Grade							
Functional Utility							
Heating/Cooling							
Energy Efficient Items							
Garage/Carport							
Porch, Patio, Deck, Fireplace(s), etc.							
Fence, Pool, etc.							
Net Adj. (total)		+ – $		+ – $		+ – $	
Adjusted Sales Price of Comparable			$		$		$

Comments on Sales Comparison (including the subject property's compatibility to the neighborhood, etc.): _____

Figure 6.4   A portion of the standard appraisal form.

SUMMARY

As I'm sure you discerned from what I said in this chapter, I hold in high regard experienced real estate agents who have the market knowledge and analytical ability to be able to help their clients with the tough task of valuation. Until recently, consumers had no choice but to call a local agent to get comparable sales data from the agent's MLS computer. Now, all those data are available to the public and can be accessed on the Internet. Having the data, though, is just the first step in the process. You need to know how to evaluate those data. Get the data, use a form to organize them, then go look at the properties, and you can be a lot more accurate in estimating the current value of any property, whether it's a home you are selling or one you are interested in buying.

7

FINDING AND WORKING WITH A REAL ESTATE AGENT

The world is under no obligation to make sense to us. We stumble along as best we can, subject to correction from anyone who knows better.
—FRIEDRICH SCHILLER

Experience is one thing you can get for nothing.
—OSCAR WILDE

KEY POINTS

- Most real estate transactions, including yours, will be consummated with the assistance of a real estate professional.
- What agents do and why they do it will not always obvious to you. You need to learn what to look for—and what to look out for—in an agent. The Internet will enable you to do a lot of preliminary work yourself, but the time will come when you need an agent, so you need to learn how to choose wisely so that you get someone who will work to advance your best interests.

As a mortgage lender, I do many more property transactions than most real estate agents. I have had the benefit of observing more than 1000 families interact with their real estate agents, more than most agents will be involved with throughout their careers. It is from this in-depth experience that I have gleaned the following advice for both homesellers and homebuyers. My goal by sharing it with you is to make your real estate transactions more productive and enjoyable.

111

TAKE MY ADVICE

We've all heard someone say that to us at one time or another, and more often than not, the last thing we wanted to do was take the advice being offered. But, because you're reading this book, I assume that you trust I know what I'm talking about and that you bought this book for my expertise. Nowhere is this more important than regarding the topic of finding good agent representation, whether real estate agent or mortgage loan agent. Incorporating the advice I offer here in your search for an agent will prove essential to ensuring a positive experience in the real estate marketplace.

Face the Facts

When you decide to sell your home, before you take any practical steps, my first piece of advice is to acknowledge that selling your home is like saying good-bye to an old friend. Sure, to some people, particularly the analytical types, selling a home is just another business process; but for most of us it's an emotional experience. So take the time to become aware of your feelings, then relegate them to their proper place so that you can make good and clear-headed decisions. Don't let your feelings cloud your judgment.

The Sensitivity Factor

That leads to my second piece of advice: It will be helpful to have a partner—your agent—who is going to be sensitive to your needs, particularly if the move is an emotional one for you. Fortunately, most agents are sensitive to their clients' feelings; the good ones know it's a prerequisite to success. Of course, you will run into those agents who are all business and no heart. However, as you interview prospective agents, these qualities should become readily apparent, as will your ability to communicate with each other.

The Respect Factor

My third piece of advice also stems logically from the preceding, and it is predicated on a real estate industry truism I want to share with you:

> *It is not your agent's job to sell your home.*

I know that sounds contradictory, but it's true. In fact, your agent's job is to sell another agent on selling your home.

This is a critical distinction. Sure, you may luck out; your agent might have a buyer who wants a home like yours, and as soon as you list your home, the deal follows in short order. It is also possible that a buyer without an agent can find out about your home and call your agent and work with him or her in making an offer. Neither is likely, however.

NOTE It's called *dual agency* when one real estate agent represents both the buyer and the seller. We'll talk more about this later in the chapter.

What *is* likely is that some other agent will have a buyer who will purchase your home, so two agents will be involved in the transaction. So here's piece of advice number three: It is important to hire an agent who is well respected by other agents—not always the case, I can tell you! I know agents in my area who are jerks (there's no kinder way to put it), and the other agents know it. No reputable agent wants to get in a deal with a jerk, so they easily avoid it by not showing properties listed by troublesome agents.

The Experience Factor

Obviously, no one can be an expert in everything. This is true for real estate professionals, too. All good real estate salespeople are experts somewhere, but no good real estate salesperson can claim to be an expert everywhere. Unfortunately, there is a certain sales mind-set that prevents some salespeople from admitting to themselves—and hence to you—"Gee, I'm really not that familiar with this area." You also need to be alert to "newbie" agents who are faking it while earning their stripes. The only thing that saves them is that their clients know even less than they do! Don't be one of those clients. Let the inexperienced real estate agent practice on someone else. You want a pro handling your property.

To give you a little more insight into this process, and to stress the value of experience and a good reputation, I'm going to share some personal experiences with you. In our town, my wife Carole (also a real estate professional) and I live in a small enclave composed of 324 homes, of which about 100 homes are still in the hands of the original owners, who bought from the developer over 25 years ago. Naturally, that means that approximately 200 of the homes in the development have changed hands. And in her 20 years in the business, my wife has been involved in the sale of almost half of them. Pride aside, plain and simple, Carole really knows the properties in our area. She knows what they are worth and how to market them. But most important is that all the other real estate agents in town know this, too! So when they have a potential buyer for our area, who are they gonna call? Carole. "I've got a buyer for your area, Carole. I've shown them the few properties that are listed and none of them is right. Do you know of any single-story homes that might be coming on the market soon?" You bet she does. Why? Because she knows about properties not yet on the market, but that will soon be available, because someone has called to say, "I'm not quite ready to put my home on the market yet, but if you hear of someone who might be interested, let me know." Bingo! I hear a deal about to be made.

Carole also gets calls from other agents who tell her, for example, "A dear friend of mine who lives in your area is moving and I'm going to be listing her property. Can you help me a little with valuation? (Read, "I haven't a clue what property is worth there, but I'm sure not going to turn the listing down.") So Carole helps the outside agent, and in that way, too, maintains a fair and orderly market. The alternative is that some agent ignorant of our area lists a home too low, and it sells in four hours because a buyer and his or her agent know more than the seller or the seller's agent. True, the buyer gets a deal, but this inaccurate low-priced sale becomes a comparable sale for those who come afterward. Thus, it misrepresents the valuations and marketing plans for everyone else in the community.

Here's another example of the importance of truth in expertise. Carole had a listing and was showing it to a client and his agent. The client, who has three children, asked his agent, "Are there many children in this neighborhood?" Fair question. That agent should have said, "I don't know," because he didn't. Instead, he said, "Oh, there are lots of children here." Wrong! The average age of homeowners in our area is over 65. It is practically a retirement community; in fact, in over 300 homes, there are probably fewer than 25 children. What if you were that buyer and relied on the agent's counsel and bought the home? I emphasize that you want to deal with an expert in the area of your search, because the expert will know the right answers to your questions. At the very least, you want to deal with an agent who is not afraid to say he or she doesn't know something and who is willing to find someone who does.

To summarize my advice so far: List your home with the best person you can find. This is not necessarily the person with the highest visibility—which leads me to the next issue: types of agents.

DISTINGUISHING AGENTS

The Superagent

Every city and town has them, the agents who sell 100 homes or more every year. I hear tell of a guy in Michigan who sold 600 homes in a year. I doubt he had a chance to say, "Thank you," because—do the math—selling that many homes per year means he sold two-plus homes every working day of the year, one sale every four hours. That allows one hour to take the listing, one hour to negotiate the transaction, and two hours to handle all the details of closing. Who is kidding whom? It doesn't work that way, folks.

You don't want a superagent. What you want is someone who will pay attention to you and your needs and concentrate on selling your home. Listing your home with someone who already has 15 listings translates to this: You are going to get two days of that person's attention every month. Not enough. In those two days, all you'll get is your home listed in MLS databases and responses to agent inquiries. You should get more attention than that from your agent. How much more?

Well, it probably varies, if for no other reasons than the changing nature of the real estate market—whether there are too many or too few homes listed and how fast they are selling—and how much your agent works. A workhorse who regularly puts in 60 hours per week can obviously do more than someone who only works 30 hours. It also depends on whether your agent works with buyers. Some agents only list properties, and eight listings for such an agent may not be too many. Alternatively, if an agent works with both buyers and sellers, you should be wary if he or she has five listings and is also juggling five buyers. Therefore, one of the questions you should ask when you're interviewing agents is about their workload. If your agent has more than, say, five listings, I'd be concerned about the amount of time he or she will be able to devote to you.

One problem, of course, is that agents may not tell you the truth, I'm sorry to say. Like the agents who refuse to admit they are unfamiliar with a neighborhood, there are agents who will assure you that they're not too busy because they do not want to turn down business. How serious is this? Let me share another story with you. There is a superagent in my hometown who probably sells around 100 homes every year. She is very presentable, works hard, and has several assistants to help her manage scheduling and details, allowing her, in the main, to make listing presentations and get more business. How does this work? We know one couple who listed their home with her, and after the deal was closed, they said, "After she took the listing, we didn't see her or hear from her for 45 days. We just talked with her assistants who gave us canned speeches about what was going on. Then we got an offer and, although we thought it was too low, she pressured and hammered us to accept it. We finally got a slightly higher price, but it was still less than what we thought our home was worth. We thought she should have spent more time working to get the buyer's price up than ours down." Do you want to be telling that kind of story after your house sells?

The Part-Time Agent

The agent at the opposite end of the spectrum is the part-timer. Every time the market picks up, the number of real estate people renewing their licenses and paying dues to their local boards increases dramatically. Who are these people? They are the homemakers with licenses, the semiretired folks, and other part-timers. These people do not earn their livelihood selling homes; they just do it when the pickings are easy—when, frankly, anyone can do it. The part-timers may sell only two or three homes a year, to make a little extra spending money or enough for a nice vacation.

What's wrong with part-time agents? In general, they do not—cannot—provide good, consistent service. They do not know the market because they haven't invested the necessary time to learn it and keep up with changes. Thus, they do not have a good grasp of values, and their negotiating skills are usually a little rusty. These skills must be in top shape if you are to drive the best bargain.

The Up-Desk

Every real estate office is staffed during business hours by agents who spend four-hour shifts answering calls from other agents and, most importantly, prospective buyers. A fair number of buyers will see a newspaper ad or an Internet listing and call the office to inquire about seeing the property. The person on the "up-desk" has the right to try to convert those prospects into clients.

This is a poor way to get an agent. All you know about these agents is that they know how to answer a phone. While it is not universally true, more often than not the real pros have moved past the point in their careers where they will even take "up time." That leaves the new agents—those without any business or experience—to handle up-desk duties. I repeat: Let these agents practice on someone else, and go find an agent using one of the other methods I describe in this chapter.

Full-Time Professionals

That leaves the full-timers. Simply, by almost every measure, full-time professionals—those who spend all their time in the business—will serve you better. So if your neighbor or someone you play bridge with wants to represent you in selling your home, politely decline the offer and go get a pro.

AGENT MISCELLANY

There are just a few more topics I want to delve into regarding agents before we get down to the nitty-gritty of how to find an agent: commissions, showings, and the open house.

Commissions

The subject of commissions can be a touchy one. This is another area where consumers have a tendency to be penny wise and pound foolish. And they're encouraged in this in other real estate books, which say an agent's commission is negotiable. This is true, but keep in mind that you get what you pay for, so I want to issue a word of warning about negotiating too hard up front.

The standard commission in most areas of the country is 6 percent, and every buyer's agent wants to earn 3 percent on his or her side of the transaction, not 2.5 percent (the split on a 5 percent commission). So when they see a home listed with a 5 percent commission, they simply do not show it; they show their clients homes where there is a 6 percent commission. Yes, this is unethical, and most agents will show their clients homes without regard to the commission structure, but I challenge anyone in the industry to say that this commission prejudice does not exist. You must keep this in mind when you discuss commission rates.

If, however, the market is strong, you can discuss with your agent the possibility of a lower commission rate if your home sells quickly and the agent doesn't have to spend much time or invest a lot in advertising. While agents routinely pay a 20 percent referral fee to an out-of-area agent who refers a client to them, almost universally, they will resent it if you want to cut that same 20 percent out of their 3 percent commission. In part this is due to the fact that, unlike the referral from someone out of the area they have never met, they will have spent considerable time and money over the last 5, 10, or 20 years to attract you. Naturally, the experienced agent will be unwilling to agree to a commission cut when she or she has no idea how much work is going to have to be done and how much advertising money will have to be spent to attract a buyer. The better time to discuss a lower commission rate is when you get an offer shortly after listing the home. There isn't an agent in the Western Hemisphere who hasn't had to kick in part of a commission once in a while to make a deal "go" after everyone else has given all that they can give; and, if circumstances are right, you might benefit from it.

Overall, my advice is, do not enter a transaction expecting to get a lower commission rate. You want your agent to work his or her heart out for you, and ensuring good pay is the way to earn his or her loyalty to you and to guarantee the successful sale of your property.

Showings

Every real estate expert I have ever known has admonished sellers to "get out of the home when prospective buyers are viewing your property." That is good advice. Frankly, buyers are hesitant to say what they think and feel if they know the owner is in the next room and can overhear them. As a seller, you do not want this. My wife recently had a listing where the seller demanded to be present at all showings, and it really made things difficult. In addition to the obvious discomfort, it also made arranging appointments more difficult because the seller's schedule had to be accommodated as well as the buyer's and the agent's. Bad idea!

However, as a seller, you have a reasonable right to a response, within 24 hours, from the buyer's agent as to clients' reaction to the property, even if the response is, "It doesn't meet their needs." Knowing this, even if it is not good news for you, is better than sitting at home wondering. So ask your agent to follow up with the other party's agent after each showing.

The Open House

Most sellers do not understand the purpose of an open house. They think it is to give prospective buyers the opportunity to see their lovely home. Some sellers even pressure their agents to hold open houses to expose their homes to buyers. Let me dispel the myth of open houses here and now. Most professionals agree that fewer than 10 percent of homes are sold to a buyer who first sees the property while it is open for inspection during a Saturday or Sunday afternoon.

The purpose of an open house is to enable the real estate agent to find buyers, people who are cruising around on weekends looking at properties. They play a game called, "What's your name? What are you interested in? Will you work with me?" Actually, this is a fairly successful way of finding clients. This does not mean that an open house doesn't play a role in the marketing of your property; it does, but it's just a part. You want your home open so that your neighbors can come and see it, perhaps to call a friend and say, "You know, Joyce, a really nice home down the street has just come on the market. You should come see it." Remember that *agents* sell most homes and those agents should be seeing your property. Typically, all of the agents in your agent's office will tour recently listed properties during office previews. Later in the week, agents in the other real estate offices in town will tour those properties. That *is* important!

FINDING AN AGENT

Okay, I've described what to look for and what to look out for in an agent, and I've explained how the agenting process works. Now let's find you an agent! As an overview, let me say this: Most real estate agents are multipurpose professionals who can represent either party in a transaction. If you follow my advice, you will be working with someone like this too. If you already live in the area in which you're looking at properties, the best way to find an agent is by talking with other folks who have recently bought a home in the area. Then interview the agent(s) recommended, get another reference or two, and check those out. Then and only then, make a decision.

To List Your Home

Most sellers find an agent through local advertising. Real estate is a very competitive business, and agents in every major office in town will want your listing. These agents will mail flyers, notepads, calendars, and just-listed and just-sold flyers to everyone in their farm on a regular basis. Agents who have been selling real estate long enough will really know their farms. Like my wife, there will be at least a couple of agents who are equally knowledgeable about your neighborhood.

Therefore, when you're ready to sell, call your neighbors to get feedback about their experiences with agents who work your area. Rely on their experiences.

Next, invite the two or three most highly recommended agents to make a *listing presentation* to you, telling you about their experience, perhaps a comparative market analysis, and a description of their services. These presentations will be remarkably similar. After all, what can they say? What you really need from them is a list of references. This is an important step, but one that is followed by very few people. Any qualified agent can easily give you the names of his or her three or four most recent clients. Yes, those clients probably have already moved somewhere else, but that shouldn't make a difference. They have a phone wherever they've gone, and you should call each one of them and ask about the relationship they had with the agent you're considering.

Checking references is probably the most important step you can take to assure a smooth transaction.

$\boxed{\textbf{NOTE}}$ At this time, refer back to Chapter 5, "Selling a Home Online," for further thoughts on this process.

To Buy a Home

Buyers sometimes overlook one of the most important functions of a real estate salesperson. This has to do with the word *salesperson.* It's not *representative,* not *consultant,* not *customer service rep,* but *salesperson.* The reason this is so important has to do with buyers'—and sellers'—unfamiliarity with the homeselling-homebuying process, their hesitancy about proceeding with such a major transaction, and their lack of urgency when it is necessary, all of which are part of human nature. Thus, the only way many real estate transactions are consummated is through the actions the salespeople take.

There are times when the principals in a deal simply will not act or will not do things that are in their best interest. It is the job of the salesperson to get them to see the light, to show them what needs to be done, to show them the merits of a course of action, to help them make an intelligent decision, and to compel them to act. I hope that you will recognize that ethical salespeople motivate their clients in this way all the time—to their credit and to the ultimate advantage of their clients. I'm not talking here about obnoxious salespeople. No one likes the high-pressure sales tactics practiced by some, but there is a difference between exerting pressure and helping a client understand what is in his or her best interest. So when you are evaluating agents, take into account your own personality. If you have trouble making decisions and taking action, I can't stress strongly enough the importance of choosing an agent who can and will help you overcome that inclination.

Sole Representation

It is important to establish a relationship with one agent and only one agent. If this seems obvious to you, you are one of the wise ones, but I can assure you it is not so obvious to many others.

Don't misunderstand; I'm not saying that you should do business with the first agent you meet. What I am saying is that once you have selected an agent, make it clear that you are using him or her solely and ask for a similar commitment to you. Every agent can tell you stories about spending a week driving a prospect around and then finding out the client is working with someone else, too. You want 100 percent dedication from your agent; why should he or she want anything less from you? If you are only 50 percent committed to an agent, he or she is more likely to show a hot property to a client who is 100 percent committed, rather than to you. Is that what you want?

$\boxed{\textit{TIP}}$ As a part of your commitment to the process, it also makes sense at this time to get preapproved by a lender. That way you can assure your agent and the seller that you will be able to consummate the transaction quickly.

Honesty Is the Best Policy.   Except when you might be considering two totally different communities that cannot reasonably be covered by the same agent, in my view it is not ethical to work with more than one agent. If this is your situation, I recommend you be up front with the second agent, saying, for example, "I'm also considering Springdale, and am working with an agent there." That way, the second agent can choose to work with you or not.

You should also tell your agent if you need to sell your current residence *before* closing on a home in the new location. Be aware also that in a hot market, many agents will not work with buyers who still have to sell their homes, because, frankly, it can be a waste of their time to show you properties on which you are unable to make an offer. Unless you are shopping during a really slow market, most sellers won't take a *contingency offer,* one in which performance is contingent on selling your current home.

Assuming you are using the Internet to help you in your search for appropriate properties (as described in Chapter 4, "Finding and Buying a Home"), you should tell your agent this, too, to better enable you to work together. For example, if you have been unable to find the right home among those homes currently on the market, your agent can e-mail you when a new possibility comes on the market. And, if the listing agent is on the ball, he or she will be able to tell you on which Web site the property will be listed so you can check it out and move quickly if it looks like a good prospect.

| NOTE | One downside to being able to list homes almost immediately on the Internet is that, in a hot market, your competitors—those whose criteria are similar to yours—in all likelihood have the same capabilities. If they find out about a great property at noon and you don't check new listings until 8:00 P.M., you're too late. Moreover, most astute real estate agents will know about homes soon to come on the market, and if they have a motivated buyer, they may get their client in to see a home even before the listing is put into the MLS computer. Though you may see that home when it pops up on the Internet only hours later, you are already too late. So I remind you: In a hot market, zero in on an area and the type of home you want, then form a relationship with a real estate agent so that you are the one to beat out your competitors.

Dual Agency

Laws that govern real estate agents vary widely from state to state, so before you begin agent hunting, I advise you to check with an attorney or other reliable source about the applicable laws in your state. In most jurisdictions, the seller has an agent and the buyer has an agent. In those states where the buyer's agent is the subagent of the seller's agent, the rule of thumb is that the parties involved should not be represented by agents who work for the same company. In practice, however, regardless of their employer, agents will do their utmost to represent each party fairly, even when the buyer's agent is a subagent of the seller.

With greater numbers of consumers finding desirable properties on the Internet before they even think about finding an agent, the number of unattached buyers is likely to increase. That's the opposite of the way it has worked historically. Thus, it is more likely in the future that a buyer will contact the listing agent directly to find out about, and perhaps make an offer on, a property, rather than working through his or her own agent. In these cases, if both buyer and seller agree, one agent can represent both parties. Of course, in this situation, the agent gets the full 6 percent commission, instead of just 3 percent—and what agent would not like to double his or her income?

The question sellers must ask themselves is whether they believe they can be assured of an agent's loyalty if he or she is attempting to represent someone else's interests, in particular as it relates to price. This is a very important issue, and not an easy one to answer. But over the years, watching agents acting in a dual agency role, I can only conclude that it takes someone with an uncommonly strong sense of ethics to maintain a 50-50 position all the time. That said, if you have confidence in the person listing your home, or he or she was referred by someone you trust, perhaps it is possible. Then, if the buyer agrees, go for it. Still, it might make sense to ask the office manager at the real estate brokerage or other objective party to act as "referee" during the negotiating so as to assure fairness. In general, however, I strongly suggest that you tell the buyer to get his or her own agent.

[*TIP*] You can find a 12-page explanation of the law concerning the relationships between principals and their agents at www.homeauction.com/seller/agency_law.asp?x=svb.

The Buyer's Agent

In those states where such representation is legal, homebuyers have another choice. Some real estate agents choose to work only with buyers; they do not accept listings from sellers. They may even work for a company that represents buyers only. If you are concerned about the ramifications of dual agency, which I just described, seeking and working with a buyer's agent might be the way to go.

Before you choose this alternative, however, you need to know that buyers' agencies are typically not full-service companies that have spent millions developing a strong, nationwide brand identity, so you are going to have to work a little harder to find one. Fortunately, there are a couple of Web sites you can go to for help:

- The National Association of Exclusive Buyers Agents, at www .naeba.org
- The Real Estate Buyers Agent Council, at www.rebac.net

As is common in listing a property, a buyer's agent may want you to sign an exclusivity agreement saying that you will work only with him or her. There is nothing wrong with this, assuming you have done your research. Remember the 100 percent commitment rule!

FINDING AN AGENT ON THE WEB

Most sellers are able to find an agent on their own, largely because they are already located in the farm of 10 or 20 agents in their hometown. After years of receiving gift calendars, notepads, refrigerator magnets, and countless just-listed and just-sold flyers, you'd have to be from Mars not to know some of their names. On the other hand, you may know enough about these people to know that you do not want to do business with any of them. So how else can you find an agent?

First, realize that almost every real estate Web site has an agent search area. All you have to do to get a list of names is to type in your town or zip code. Those agents who are Realtors will be listed at both the state association and the national Web site at www.realtor.com. Sounds easy enough, right? Well, yes and no. You'll find that many real estate Web site agent search tools are not as effective as they might seem—and as you need!

For example, when I searched for a realtor by city and state for my area, I was given the option to get more information about each agent listed. However, the search for my hometown turned up only nine agents, including several from 5 to 10 miles away—too far to be of much use. Then I did a white-pages search, and I got 26 agents, all from the same office. A similar search at the California Association of Realtors Web site listed only 5 agents of the 1000-plus in town. Based on my research, at the time of this writing, I cannot recommend this approach (that is, city–state–zip code) as a reliable way to find a real estate agent.

In contrast, when I searched via the map, going to my state, then to my area, then to my county, and then to the local association, I was rewarded with a more inclusive list of over 1000 agents. However, though the list was more comprehensive, the amount of information about each agent was minimal—name, company, phone number—and did not include any hyperlinks to agents' Web sites, assuming they had Web sites. By the time you read this, that may well have changed. In the meantime, when you do an agent search, be very concerned about the reliability of the information you get.

If you are relocating from another area, your task will be more difficult because you will not have those same resources at your fingertips. If your company is moving you, perhaps you can get some helpful information from other employees. Frequently, corporate human resources departments maintain lists of agents who have worked with other employees.

In general, at this time, I would not without qualification recommend any of the agent search functions at prominent real estate Web sites. Of course, it's only fair to point out that agents who have registered at these sites are clearly making a commitment to Web-based real estate transactions, which may mean they're more ambitious than other agents. These are probably qualities you are seeking, so don't dismiss agent searching on the Web entirely.

Also be sure to check out individual agent Web sites. It's easy enough to do: Go to one of the major search engines, such as AltaVista or Yahoo!, and type in *real estate agent* and the location you are interested in. I think you'll find that the personalities of most agents are accurately reflected in their Web sites, enabling you to pick up useful information. Just don't forget to check references, no matter how slick the Web site.

You can also find agents by going to real estate company Web sites. Probably you already know several company names from advertisements and from yard signs; if not, simply pick up a phone book, where you'll find not only names, but Web addresses as well. Make a note of them, then go to their Web sites. Or log on to HomeGain at www.homegain.com, where you can register and "invite" proposals from interested agents in your area. You might also visit American Most Referred Real Estate Agents, www.amrr.com, which takes a unique approach. It selects three "top" agents for various areas based on referrals from other agents. Sounds good, but again, take care. The results for my area were not too good, as only one of the three was actually from my town; the others were from nearby towns. The results may be better in the area you are searching, and certainly it's worth a try. You can follow a hyperlink to the agents' Web sites and dig deeper.

Finally, agents who have signed up for the service can be found at Realty Times Agent Locator, www.realtytimes.com/rtnews/rtapages/agentlocator.htm.

Interviewing Agents

To get the best agent, you must interview several, and ask specific questions, some you might not think of on your own. A good list of 11 questions can be found at www.homegain.com/articles/interview.htm. To that list, I would add the most vital question: "May I have three references of recent clients you have worked with?" The good agents will be pleased that you asked, and be proud to give you a list. Be sure to call the references and ask them how they felt about the agent's representation.

SUMMARY

The money you pay for commissions earned by agents in the purchase and sale of real estate property will probably be many more dollars than you are used to writing checks for. So be sure to get value for those dollars. Do some research to find an agent who can best represent you. Agents vary widely in their experience and abilities, and it will both save you money and make the process more pleasant when you deal with an expert. My purpose in this chapter is to educate you briefly on the agenting process and profession and to give you some guidelines for finding a highly qualified person to work with you. However, comprehensive coverage of this topic is beyond the scope of this book, so in Appendix 1 I recommend several other books you might want to use as additional resources.

8

UNDERSTANDING AND CONTROLLING THE CLOSING PROCESS

Things themselves don't hurt or hinder us. Nor do other people. It is our attitudes and reactions that give us trouble. . . . We cannot choose our external circumstances, but we can choose how we respond to them.
—EPICTETUS

KEY POINTS

- A lot happens during the closing process. It can be confusing because so many things happen in a short period of time, and it is easy to become overwhelmed.
- If you and the other parties are prepared, the closing will go smoothly.
- Make sure you understand the form in which you are to bring in closing funds, usually a cashier's check or wire transfer.
- If you are a seller, do all the repair work early on in the process; don't wait until the last minute.
- If you are a buyer, set a specific date for occupancy, then schedule the closing to meet that occupancy date.

Settlement or *closing* is the final step in the process: You show up with your down payment and closing costs, the lender sends in the loan proceeds, and the seller signs the deed transferring the property to the buyer. In many states, this is accomplished around a *closing table,* sometimes in an attorney's office. In others, escrow companies handle the closing; after each party has done his or her part separately, the escrow company and title company close the transaction when instructed to do so. Whether it is the custom to close with an attorney, title company, or escrow company, each is a *settlement agent*. Their charges are detailed on your good faith estimate, and, after the deal closes, on the settlement statement, prepared on the HUD-1 form.

This ought to be a simple process, but often it is stressful. The secret—indeed the key—to a smooth, satisfactory closing is preparation. Let me state it another way. The primary reason closings are delayed is that there is some problem. With some exceptions, most problems are solvable, especially if everyone involved knows what the problems are early on in the process. Too frequently, however, no one actually does whatever it takes to solve the problem in a timely manner, so there it is 30 days later, still a problem. I hate to have to say this, but while some real estate agents and/or escrow officers stay on top of problems, there are others who seem to go blindly along in a deal hoping that someone else will solve problems. With this in mind, my advice is that if you want a smooth closing, remember that you are the principal and you must take responsibility for assuring that any and all problems are solved. Don't rely on others to solve these problems.

THE BUYER'S RESPONSIBILITIES

The most important responsibilities a buyer has in ensuring a smooth and timely closing relate to getting loan approval. If you have not gotten loan approval prior to making an offer—which I strongly recommend you do—you will have to move quickly. Even though you may not close for 30 or 45 days, it is common for most sales contracts to require that you have loan approval within 10 or 15 days of opening the transaction. The seller wants to ascertain whether you have the financial strength and backing to go through with the deal. I discuss loans in greater depth later in the book, but for the purposes of this chapter I want to alert you that if you get a loan through an out-of-state Internet lender, remember that every state has its peculiarities, so allow a few extra days for everything in the transaction.

Here are a few other issues to keep in mind if you're the buyer:

- The buyer is responsible for checking the preliminary title report, usually referred to as the *prelim*. Unless you're comfortable with the terminology in this document, I recommend you review it with your agent or attorney. One purpose of this process is to establish liens and other claims against the property. If, for example, the seller has two loans on the property and a tax lien, the title company will assure that these are paid off so that the property is transferred to you without these encumbrances. The report will also show easements, such as the one given to your power company so it can run electricity to the home. If the title company does not require a survey to check the physical size of the lot, I'd do a little work on my own, pacing off the lot to assure that it is the size showing on the plat map that is part of the prelim.

- Make sure that the property is in salable condition and that any repairs are completed. Almost assuredly, your agent will arrange for a home inspection. I think that it is a good idea to accompany the inspector. He or she will likely find some corrections that are needed, and this may result in further negotiations with the seller. Obviously, the seller doesn't want to spend any money he or she doesn't absolutely have to, so be prepared to negotiate what you want, as long as it is reasonable. Refer to my further comments about this in the next section. When the repair work detailed on the property inspection report and the termite report are reported as completed, review them to verify that all deficiencies have been corrected. One more thing: Do this as soon in the process as you can.

- Plan a walk-through a day or so prior to the closing to assure that nothing untoward has happened to the property. This is your last chance to confirm that everything you and the seller have agreed on has been taken care of. Also, if the seller has agreed to leave certain items as part of the sale, such as a chandelier, make sure they're there. Sometimes these things "get legs" and disappear.

- Review the loan documents a day or two before closing. If a lender is going to pull a funny one on you—and that happens all too often—they may delay getting the loan documents to you until the last minute. If you find something wrong, you will be under tremendous pressure to close anyway. The seller will feel, correctly, that you chose the lender and that it is irresponsible to delay the closing because of some misunderstanding about loan terms. However, once you sign the documents, you won't be able to change anything. The solution is to have the lender give you a copy of your loan documents several days earlier. That gives you plenty of time to review them. Typically, there are more than 40 documents, but most are boilerplate and easy to understand. The important one is the promissory note that shows the loan terms—the interest rate; the monthly payment; the term; and, if it's an adjustable-rate mortgage (ARM), the mechanism for interest rate changes.

⬜ *TIP* ⬜ Toward the end of the promissory note will be a paragraph that states either that there is a prepayment penalty or that you have the right to make prepayments without penalty. Make sure this is what you want, because sometimes unscrupulous lenders sneak in a prepayment penalty clause, hoping you won't notice.

- Most states have laws governing payments made to settlement agents to make sure that all funds deposited are "good funds." This means you can't write a personal check except for the initial deposit, because it may take a week or more for your check to clear and you can't close until it does. You will need to bring a cashier's check or make arrangements to wire transfer money into the settlement agent's trust account. Review with the closer in advance how you intend to make payments. If by wire, get wiring instructions, including the closer or title company's bank's ABA number and account number. Line this money up well ahead of time, especially if it is in a stock brokerage account. The brokerage company might want to issue a cashier's check drawn on its bank in New York, which is an out-of-state bank for the other 49 states. In some states, if you show up with such a check, you may have to wait 24 hours before you can close, and then everyone will be mad. My advice? Almost every settlement agent is set up to accept wire transfers today, so I suggest that you use this method.

  NOTE Purchasing a new home requires much less work, because the builder is a professional seller whose staff has closed probably hundreds of transactions. They also nag buyers about their responsibilities. You obviously will not need to worry about termite reports and such, but property inspection is still important. Notwithstanding the builder's responsibility and obligations under whatever warranties are required by your state, your best opportunity to get builders to fix things is before the closing—do not close until they have. Most companies have excellent customer service people to follow up on problems that arise later. But they have a greater incentive to correct problems if you are going to delay closing until they are done. Some experts suggest hiring an independent inspector to accompany you. That will cost around $200, but it may save you a lot of headaches.

THE SELLER'S RESPONSIBILITIES

The seller's primary responsibility is to make sure that the property is in salable condition. Most buyers will require an inspection of the home by a property inspector. Indeed, both real estate agents will require this too, because they want to dodge liability. But there are property inspectors and property inspectors. I have seen nitpickers who noted even small holes in the window screens and chipped paint on the doors, both normal wear-and-tear items in my view. You, the seller, do not need this type of inspector, and, frankly, neither does the buyer. All this type of inspection does is to inflame both parties, because the buyer will probably want all kinds of repairs done, which under normal circumstances would not require fixing. After all, it is not a new home. My point is, find a reputable—and reasonable—property inspector. Your real estate agent will be able to recommend such a company and dodge the nitpickers. The inspection company will also provide a home warranty policy, usually paid for by the seller.

    TIP   You can also find inspectors online now. Members of the American Society of Home Inspectors, Inc. are listed at www.ashi.com. State associations are now on the Web, too, such as California Real Estate Inspection Association at www.creia.com.

    The buyer is also going to want a termite report that states that the property is free from infestation. Termites have been here for about 100 million years, and it is not likely that you have scared them off your property for good. Of course, the likelihood of insect damage varies geographically, but if you have to have damage repaired, or if the house has to be tented, do it now, before a buyer even shows up. You're going to have to do it sooner or later, so don't wait until two days before closing! Lenders will want to see a "clear" termite report too, and will not fund the loan until they check the report. If you wait until the day of closing to give them the report, they aren't going to drop what they are doing just to accommodate you, and you will delay the closing.

    I don't recommend that you rely on the buyer to choose a termite company. Even though all of these companies are licensed by the same state law, they vary in ethics and competence, just as in any other business. The buyer will want a thorough inspection, so he may choose a company that finds a lot of problems and produces a "make work" report that assures that they will get a lot of work. You may get a $1500 invoice although $700 of it isn't really necessary. But at that point, you've lost your ability to control the situation, such as by getting a second opinion. The buyer will naturally want all the work accomplished as described on the worst report. This is not what you want. Last, it is important to note that most lenders will require that a licensed contractor do the work. This means that if you choose an independent contractor—not the termite company—to do the repairs, you will need to get license information to submit with the termite company's final report. Note, too, that the termite company usually will not warrant the work of independents; likewise, the buyer may be concerned about accepting unwarranted work, especially if he or she finds this out 24 hours before closing. I hope it's clear now why it is a good idea to do this work first.

As a lender, it always astonishes me how the repair of items discovered in the home inspection, including the repair of termite damage and tenting of a home, becomes such a big deal in so many transactions. Why? Probably just procrastination. But who is served by delaying? No one. What can you do to prevent this? I'm going to give you some advice that you've probably never heard before: When you list your home, immediately have your agent order a title report, a preliminary commitment to ensure the sale. Next, have your agent order a property inspection, and when you get the report, immediately make arrangements to fix the deficiencies noted. That way, you can show the buyer that all deficiencies have already been corrected. The buyer may choose to get his or her own report, but then it ought to be at his or her cost. If this happens, though, you'll have to deal with any additional items that the new inspector comes up with. Most buyers won't bother, especially if you've been conscientious about your role.

SCHEDULING THE CLOSING

Most transactions merely specify a number of days until closing, typically 30 days or 45 days. There is a better way. Get out a calendar and figure out which day of the week the thirtieth day falls on. If it falls on a Saturday or Sunday, pick a specific date, such as the preceding Friday. Monday is not a good day because, depending on the custom, a lender might have to fund on Friday and then the buyer has to pay interest over the weekend.

Better yet, figure out on what day possession is to occur, and then plan the closing date accordingly. Here's what that can help you avoid. Recently, one of my clients was scheduled to close a deal on Tuesday, with the contract specifying that the buyer would take possession of the property three days later. The buyer wanted to move in on Saturday, his day off, and had rented a truck and lined up some friends to help with the move. Unfortunately, however, the seller found out that he wasn't going to be able to take possession of his new house until Monday of the following week. He didn't want to move out on Friday and not be able to move into his new place until Monday. In spite of the agreed-on closing date, the seller just delayed the closing, which thus delayed the buyer's possession date too. My buyer got possession on Monday but couldn't move until the following weekend. The carrying costs for this delay totaled about $300, not to mention the considerable inconvenience.

Accordingly, some words to the wise: If you want to take possession on Saturday, but the deal is supposed to close several days earlier, fix the possession day in your purchase contract, not on the closing day. Then, even if the seller delays the closing, he or she is playing with his or her own time, not yours.

THE FUTURE

The technology exists today to have documents signed electronically. I have already started working with appraisers who send me the appraisal, along with color photographs, via e-mail. The appraisal is attached in Adobe .pdf format, and I print it out on my laser printer. It is identical in every respect to the one the appraiser would print on his printer and would send me in the mail, except for the appraiser's signature, which is electronic. Some lenders (but not all) accept electronic signatures, and someday everyone will. For a peek into the future, go to the VeriSign Web site at www.verisign.com/enterprise/ins/index.html.

At issue is the ability of a lender, for example, to go to court five years later and prove that you signed loan documents five years earlier and are thus on the hook for the mortgage. As of June 30, 2000, the law provides that electronic signatures on contracts are as valid and binding as traditional signatures. To become widely accepted, however, technology and authentication will have to be improved until government agencies, title companies, and lenders are more comfortable than they are now.

SUMMARY

I want you to imagine a world in which every buyer is preapproved for a loan, in which every seller already has a preliminary title report; imagine, too, that the home inspection is complete and all repairs have been made, and a clear termite report has been filed. Today, thanks to faster appraisal service and the ability to send loan documents directly to the settlement agent via e-mail, you won't need 30 days, or 45 days, or 60 days to close an escrow. You can close in a week or 10 days, and this is not a fantasy.

So, now that we've fleshed out the basics of how the transactions work, in the next chapters we'll deal with how to finance your home.

9

GETTING A MORTGAGE ON THE INTERNET: PART ONE

Assumption is the mother of mistakes.
—ANGELO DONGHIA

KEY POINTS

- Lenders are using the Internet in record numbers, but is it progress?
- Leaders in various industries have been characterized by technological leadership, low cost, or exemplary customer service. Can Internet lenders measure up?
- Many Internet lenders are still searching for their first dollar of profit, and that is not an environment in which they are looking for ways of providing additional services.
- There are many kinds of lenders: banks, mortgage bankers, mortgage brokers, and other new forms spawned by the Internet.
- Each has different regulators and different cost structures, and may provide different approaches to the consumer.
- The newest development is the call center, what you get when you dial 1-800-anything.

In my first book, *How to Save Thousands of Dollars on Your Home Mortgage,* written in late 1997, I devoted only one chapter to the topic of mortgages on the Internet. After all, the Internet was relatively new back then. The changes that have occurred in the real estate industry as it relates to the Internet amaze even me, a seasoned veteran. More changes will occur between my writing and your reading this book, too. The sweeping advances in technology—in particular, the Internet—offer consumers and professionals alike a number of advantages. But they also make it almost impossible to stay up to date and difficult to know whom to trust. The number of real estate lending sites alone is astounding—perhaps over 50,000, far too many to cover in this book. What I can do is to give you guidelines and examples that will help you to navigate not only the mortgage process, but the related Web sites as well.

To begin this chapter, I want to spend some time exploring the state of lending today, to ensure that you understand the complexities of the business and the ways Internet lenders approach serving their market. My concern is that too many consumers will be tempted to think, "Oh, I'll just go to all the lender Web sites, find the one with the lowest rates, and apply there." That may be a good strategy for buying books online, but we are talking about what is for many the largest and most complicated financial transaction in their life, clearly calling for a more sophisticated strategy!

 $\boxed{\textit{TIP}}$ Take the time to go through this chapter carefully before going on to the next one, which contains information on how to find and use the lender Web sites. As I've said before, preparation is essential to a successful homebuying/homeselling experience.

ADDING VALUE

A relevant strategic question for any business at any time is, "Who is adding value to the process?" When you look at any successful business, you will most likely find that it has at least one of the following characteristics at the core of its operation:

- Technological leadership
- Low cost
- Exemplary customer service

Note that having a gimmick is not on the list—although I will be the first to acknowledge that in the mortgage business, having a gimmick, such as offering "free" loans and financing homes to 125 percent of their value, can be phenomenally successful in the short run. This raises a second important question: Is Internet lending a gimmick? Not in the slightest. That said, it is important to recognize that the rapid growth in Internet lending from 1997 through mid-1999 occurred during a time of absolute euphoria for the real estate industry, which recorded the highest volume in its history. The lowest interest rates in 30 years, coupled with 7-plus years of a strong economy and the resultant rise in personal income, have meant success—at least in terms of volume—for everyone in the business. Thus emerges question number three: How will e-lenders who have been successful in these boom times fare when the inevitable slump occurs? With those issues in mind, let's explore how the e-channel mortgage business stacks up against the three criteria we just stated.

Technological Leadership

Are e-lenders technological leaders? Certainly, just establishing an Internet presence, is a step in the right direction. For customers who rate shopping, having rates displayed online means they don't have to make phone calls, making the process faster, more convenient, and confidential. Moreover, enabling customers to fill out loan applications online saves lenders money compared with having a clerk type in the data.

Today, lenders can access credit reports in five minutes. They can submit loan applications directly to the Federal National Mortgage Association (FNMA) or the Federal Home Loan Mortgage Corporation (FHLMC) for automated underwriting—a topic we'll cover shortly—and get an approval in a matter of minutes. They can give customers the option of going online to check out the progress of a loan at any time. And, though we're still a long way from being a paperless society, lenders can now receive appraisals from appraisers and send loan documents directly to a settlement agent via e-mail. The other side of the coin is that most forward-thinking lenders, still a small minority, have adopted these procedures for their non-Internet customers as well.

The true advantage of the Internet to lenders—and thus to their customers—is that the lenders can bundle all of these services together, thereby streamlining some of the processes, to offer faster service than traditional lenders. How fast? I have taken an application and have funded loans eight days later—still a difficult task for most lenders today and impossible even for me just a year ago. Luckily, most people don't need their loans in eight days. Still, I can envision a future in which most Internet lenders can reduce the processing time from the standard 30 to 45 days to half that.

FNMA and FHLMC have introduced automated underwriting systems, a significant leap forward to streamlining the process. FNMA's system, Desktop Underwriter, and FHLMC's system, Loan Prospector, allow lenders to input the significant data from the borrower's application, order an instant credit report, and obtain loan approval or denial in minutes. Although this process is more efficient than traditional underwriting, easy loans—those for credit-worthy, well-qualified borrowers with money in the bank—do not take all that long at most lenders these days. It's just that most lenders will not allow the file to be given to the underwriter until everything is ready in the file. With Desktop Underwriter and Loan Prospector, a lender can submit an application immediately on receipt of the application. That means the lender knows within minutes exactly what documentation is going to be required for complete approval, and that is a significant advantage.

Both FNMA and FHLMC are now accepting less expensive and faster "drive-by" appraisals on some transactions; and for loans on properties in homogeneous neighborhoods, computerized appraisals will be possible some day soon.

Further streamlining of the processes is probably limited for the moment, as the rest of the industry is going to have to catch up with FNMA and FHLMC. In part this is because so many people and companies—appraisers, title and escrow representatives, lawyers (in some states), home and termite inspectors, as well as processors, underwriters, coordinators, document preparers, funders, shippers, and many more—must be involved in every transaction. A loan package is still on paper—a lot of paper—and most of it just isn't going away. A compelling reason for maintaining this paper documentation is that there are crooks out there who will steal money from lenders if they get a chance. Making sure that everything is in order—that no security walls have been breached—is important so that when someone tries to circumvent the precautions built into the system, that person is going to get nailed. Of course, there are technological developments on the horizon that promise secure paperless transactions, but until the money sources are confident about the security of these transactions, in the main the processes will remain pretty much the same.

If it seems I've essentially dismissed the impact of technology on the real estate industry, don't misunderstand. Technologically, we have come far in this business in a very short time, and more innovations are in the offing. I think it's safe to say that the Internet will hasten the adoption of more capabilities that will streamline the process. As for efficiency, the Internet certainly has had an impact there. Most Internet borrowers—73 percent in one survey—are very price conscious, and in the very near future, a lender with a traditional cost structure simply is going to face a more daunting task of convincing customers that they are being given value-added services that are worth the additional fees charged. Specifically, Internet lenders are establishing new pricing standards that are going to cause them to gain market share. Even if those gains are modest, the very presence of more efficient lenders will cause the rest of the industry to modernize so as to be able to compete effectively. Let's take a look now at the effect on costs and pricing.

Low Cost

At the time of this writing, Internet lending faces a major challenge having to do with income and expenses. Successful businesses are those that have more revenue than costs, meaning they make a profit. Being the low-cost producer means that your costs are $.80 when others' costs are $.90, which allows you, theoretically, to reduce your price from $1 to $.89 and make money when others are losing money. As a businessman, it is hard for me to talk about the concept of being a low-cost producer when every e-lender that has made its profit and loss statement public seems to spend about $3 for every $1 it generates in revenue. Reducing costs from $.95 to $.90 is ambitious enough, but how to reduce them from $3.00 to $.90? I don't see how that can ever work out, but I guess when a company has $50 million of public capital to go through and is only losing it at the rate of $10 million per year, the accountants have several years to figure it out.

A common claim of Internet lenders is that they are "cutting out the middleman." Are they, or is this just marketing hype? In Chapter 1, "Decision Making and Salesmanship," we discussed advertising and salesmanship and we learned that along with words like *discount, free,* and *having an in-law in the business,* Americans just love the idea of cutting out all those nasty middlemen. The fact is that lenders are middlemen too. Except for portfolio lenders, who account for perhaps 10 percent of the business, all lenders are middlemen because they sell their loans to FNMA, FHLMC, and others. Until FNMA and FHLMC start doing business directly with the public (highly unlikely in my view), there will always be middlemen.

In a traditional lender's organization, typically a loan officer makes from one-fourth to one-half of the total amount of markup charged to the customer. So if you eliminate the loan officer, you can reduce costs by 25 to 50 percent. When you look at the pricing of some Internet lenders, sure enough, it seems as if they have cut their prices by about that amount. In effect, that passes the savings on to the customer. On a $100,000 loan, we're talking about $250 to $500.

The other side of the coin is reduced benefit to the consumer by ¼ to ½ point, too. In short, the Internet lenders haven't cut out the middlemen; they have just eliminated the knowledgeable people who were there to help the customer. In place of the loan officer, consumers get low-paid telemarketer/customer service representatives; instead of professionals making $50,000 per year, consumers get inexperienced staff making $7 per hour. (And don't think I'm kidding about the $7 per hour!)

Let's explore this in the context of another industry: discount retailers, specifically low-cost warehouse giant Costco. Costco's business approach involves establishing huge, low-cost warehouses in industrial areas; selling products primarily in large quantities; and keeping staffing to a minimum. In this way, Costco lowers the costs of handling, displaying, and selling merchandise, and inventory turnover is faster than at more traditional stores. But what about customer service? I challenge you to find an employee in any of Costco's stores who can do anything more than tell you which aisle you need to go to—and sometimes they can't even do that! Is that bad? Certainly not, but when my wife and I shop at Costco, we know we're on our own. In short, Costco has found that millions of people are willing to accept the trade-off of less service for lower price.

The same kind of dynamic is catching on in the stock brokerage industry, as full-service brokerage companies have been forced to compete with upstart companies (usually Web based) that charge substantially lower prices for executing trades. Without a doubt, these companies are a boon for the knowledgeable investor who spends hours every day doing his or her own research; lower transaction costs mean higher profits. But for the increasing number of amateurs doing the same thing, lower cost may simply mean saving money buying the wrong stocks. Indeed, a recent study showed that online investors' portfolio performance fell significantly when they stopped seeking professional help. Whatever they saved in execution costs was more than offset by the reduced performance. Is that really saving? Another study showed that 70 percent of day traders lost money.

Which brings us back to the subject at hand. Can Internet lenders attract enough customers with that same kind of kind of business plan? Specifically, are people willing to settle for a low-service business model when searching for a loan? For a while at least, I don't see a low-cost producer emerging among the Internet lenders. In fact, the opposite seems to be happening. To attract customers, Internet lenders are spending large amounts on advertising, as you will see when you start surfing. You will be confronted with so many banner ads from lenders that you may even be put off by the clutter they create. In some cases, these banners are the result of exclusive arrangements under which a lender has paid $200,000 or $500,000 or more to have its name in front of visitors. In fact, it's rare when a real estate–oriented site doesn't have a link to one of the brand-name lenders. These arrangements are called *strategic partnerships*—contracts with high-volume related Web sites—which means that the partner shares in the revenue in one way or another. These associations are not cheap. In contrast, the traditional lender has an ad budget, but it is a relatively small budget item, nothing like the costs of advertising on the Internet. An Internet lender may spend $1 million in advertising to attract 1000 customers. That's $1000 per customer. If the Internet lender has cut out the commission loan officer who was going make $500, and replaced him or her with an advertising program that costs $1000, how does that benefit the consumer? For the moment, it means that these companies are just losing money—which is not the same as being a low cost producer, the topic of this section.

Internet lenders are also facing a steep learning curve in regard to converting prospects to customers. Readers of my first book will remember that I talked about the cost of denying loans. Some 35 percent of all loan applications are denied; applicants whose loans are denied do not have to pay any money for the process. In effect, then, one-third of the people in the mortgage business are engaged in an activity—denying loans—that produces no revenue. Who pays their salaries? You do, if your loan is approved; you pay for the cost of processing your loan plus one-half the cost of processing the loan of the person whose loan was denied. Wait, there's more.

As with any retailer, not every customer who comes into the lender's "store" buys. And the ratio of actual buyer to shopper is a lot lower on the Web, where only some 1 percent of the visitors take the next step and initiate an application. That 99 percent doesn't cost the lender anything; only when someone makes an application does the meter start running. But one e-lender has acknowledged that it has to take more than 400 applications to fund 100 loans. That is a 75 percent fallout rate, which has horrendous long-term implications for the possibility of Internet lending being profitable for the lenders.

Of the 300 fallouts, perhaps 50 were not qualified or had poor credit. Maybe 100 others had applications in progress at several lenders, were unable to make a decision up front, or were taking advantage of the fact that Internet lenders do not require much of a commitment. Still others may just have been playing the free interactive game called "Apply for a Mortgage." All of this leads to our next topic: relationships.

The job of the loan officer/salesperson is not just to provide information to the customer and get information from him or her. It is to establish a relationship with the customer. The results of such relationships are better decisions, and that's why I work so hard to form relationships of trust with my clients. But in the Internet environment, those relationship builders have largely been taken out of the equation, to be replaced by a new equation:

$$\text{Low Relationship} = \text{Low Commitment} = \text{Low Conversion Rate}$$

$$= \text{High Cost Structure} = \text{Failure}$$

Granted, this is speculation on my part, but I don't think I'm far off the mark. Frankly, to understand the Internet lending phenomenon and predict its future, we're going to need some in-depth studies of the Internet borrower, what he or she does and why, and, perhaps more important, why he or she *doesn't* do certain things.

In summary, the way borrowers and Internet lenders are interacting currently does not bode well for the cost structure. Of course, some lenders are prepared to lose money on each transaction, but they will be able to do that only as long as the capital lasts. Companies that are bleeding venture capital like a jet on afterburners raise the question, "Will they be able to reach a sustainable orbital velocity before the fuel runs out?"

Exemplary Customer Service

Outstanding customer service is so uncommon today that when the words are spoken, one company name comes to everyone's mind: Nordstrom. Ever wonder why we can't name 10 other such companies? Can you name even one more? Frankly, as big companies grow bigger and bigger, they always seem to downgrade the importance of their customer contact people. If a company has 100,000 or 1 million customers, how can it demonstrate that it cares about them? Obviously, it can't.

The mortgage industry grew out of the banking and savings and loan industries that dominated the lending business until the financial crisis that ravaged them both in the 1980s. In those days, the institutions were customer oriented. Customers knew the manager at their bank and the tellers knew their customers by name. The loan officer was the same person, year after year; he or she raised a family in your neighborhood, and likely was a member of a service organization or church with you, and his or her children went to school with yours. So when you wanted a mortgage, that's who you called. You were confident you would receive terrific service from someone who knew you, who cared about you.

Today, that is seldom, if ever, the case. At many large companies, the loan officer's job has been designated as—downgraded to, really—an entry-level position; at others, the job is just one stop in the company training program. Loan officers may be 20-something young adults who live in apartments and have not personally experienced home ownership. So just how is it they are going to help you? This is prevalent in industries other than the one under discussion, but it is so common that I have come to the conclusion that some companies believe the easiest way to meet customer expectations is to lower the level of those expectations.

Sad to say, the mortgage industry has done a pretty good job of lowering the customers' expectations. It is notorious for being insensitive and unresponsive to customers, for having dumb rules, for requiring too much paperwork and too many documents, and for being way too costly. We have treated our customers pretty shabbily. But they keep coming back! But really, what's the alternative? A rich uncle, maybe—but what rich uncle wants to lend you money at a rate competitive with the mortgage industry? The fact is that until more borrowers start demanding better service and demonstrate that they are willing to pay for it, the movement to lower-service, lower-cost models will continue to grow, led, perhaps, by Internet lenders.

Will Internet lenders be able to find enough customers to take the lower level of service? In these buoyant times the answer is probably yes. More than 10 million people are going to get loans this year, and something like 300,000 will do so on the Internet. On the other hand, that's only about 3 percent, which must mean that 97 percent are choosing to do business with the industry in the more traditional way.

As a potential loan customer, by now you may be thinking I've painted a bleak picture. My purpose is not to discourage you, but to prepare you. I want you to succeed at getting your loan, whether over the Internet or through traditional means, perhaps using online services to educate yourself, and to be powerful enough to exert more control over the process. If you choose to go the Internet lending route, you will have to accept more of the responsibility for the success of the transaction, and the best way to do that is to prepare. Reading this book is a good first step in that preparation.

TYPES OF LENDERS AND THEIR NET PRESENCES

The next step in preparing to use the Net to fund a loan is to understand who the lenders are and how they're using the Web to conduct business.

Large National Banks

Most of the large national banks have only recently established an Internet presence, and none has capabilities that enable you to do much more than send in your name and phone number and wait for a response. These companies have built dominant market positions with their own mix of *retail lending* (dealing directly with borrowers), *wholesale lending* (funding loans for mortgage brokers), and *correspondent lending* (buying loans from mortgage bankers), and they are doing just fine, thank you. Were they to establish a Web site to directly solicit clients, they would be competing against one of these other mature, and, most important, already profitable business channels. Thus, the potential of competing against themselves might be a deterrent to aggressive development of this channel.

As you'll learn in the next chapter, mortgages are just one of many services that mega-banks offer to consumers. Therefore, their Internet strategy should encompass the entire breadth of their relationship with consumers. From their perspective, moving services to the Internet— account access and transfer, bill paying, as well as loan applications— makes sense. If the customer wants to come into a branch, they have those; if the customer wants to interact with them on the Internet, they'll meet him or her there too.

Nonbank Lenders

One of the largest lenders in the country is Countrywide Credit Industries, Inc., which, though not a bank, was an early Internet presence. Apparently the earlier plans, which involved centralized processing, did not meet the company's goals, as it has continued to experiment with a number of different approaches. The most recent model first interacts with client and takes the application on the Internet, then offers the customer the choice of continuing to deal online or transferring to one of the company's 400 branches for processing and funding. I talk more about Countrywide in the next chapter.

Remember that because of the global scope of the Internet, a lender does not have to *be* a national company to *look* like a national company. The only requirement is that the lender have the license to lend legally where it does business. This has allowed smaller regional lenders that have traditionally acquired customers by direct mail and telemarketing techniques to establish Web sites as a new way of attracting customers.

Most of these operate as mortgage bankers, funding the loans themselves and selling them to FNMA, FHLMC, and others. These lenders also emphasize lending to the credit-impaired borrower, so-called subprime lending, because it is far more profitable than "A" lending.

Regional lenders, those who have not had national aspirations, are working to increase visibility in their core markets and expand their reach, efforts made easier thanks to the Web. Even a small company can look substantial and professional on the Web. Many smaller lenders have survived—indeed, some have prospered—over the years by concentrating on a high level of customer service. Others are vultures and can damage your wallet. Let's examine how various local lenders operate, in general and in conjunction with online services.

Traditional Lenders.   Some fairly large mortgage banking companies have found success in their own market areas. Usually they have traditional retail branches as well as wholesale operations that deal with mortgage brokers. There are some excellent mortgage brokerage companies too. After all, mortgage brokers originate more than 60 percent of all loans. Most of these companies have established Web sites, although from my research, it appears as if many of these sites, especially those of the smaller companies, are dormant.

Mega-Advertisers.   Several regional companies established their market positions by spending huge sums on telemarketing, direct mail, and radio, television, and billboard advertising. For them, moving to the Internet was a logical progression, another way to get the phone to ring.

Aggregators.   Aggregators are not lenders at all, but high-traffic Web sites that offer a package of services to attract customers, who are then funneled to lenders that have partnered with the aggregators and pay the aggregators to find customers for them.

Internet-Only Companies.   These companies have little or no previous history in the mortgage business. Free of the baggage of "this is how we've always done it," which can plague established industry leaders, they are comfortable experimenting with new techniques and procedures.

LEGAL FORMS OF ORGANIZATION

The mortgage industry has a number of different forms of organization, and it is important for consumers to understand how all of these operate, particularly the work they do and what they get paid for it. Each type is subject to regulation by different authorities.

Banks, Savings and Loan Associations (S&Ls), and Savings Banks. Monitored by state or national regulators, depending on their charters, these organizations offer a broad array of consumer services and often have their own loan programs and fund their own "portfolio" loans, usually adjustable rate mortgages (ARMs) as well as loans that can be sold to FNMA and FHLMC. These companies process your loan themselves and make their own decisions. Income for these entities comes from the spread between the cost of funds and the yield on their loan portfolios of loans they keep, as well as from fee income on loans they sell. They also get servicing income for handling the monthly payments on loans they have sold.

Mortgage Bankers. These are independent mortgage-only companies that originate loans and sell them immediately to FNMA, FHLMC, or other secondary market conduits. Regulation varies significantly from state to state. Mortgage bankers borrow money from a bank—say $20 million. They draw on this line of credit and fund loans as necessary, borrowing and paying interest only when they need to fund a loan. Several days later, they sell the loans to FNMA, FHLMC, or other purchasers of loans. Although they are technically direct lenders because they fund loans themselves, and they make the underwriting decisions, in fact mortgage bankers will follow the rules of the entity to which they are selling the loans. Their income is derived from fees that are a combination of what the customer pays and profit made from selling the loan. Like banks, they usually like to retain the servicing of loans—a profitable business.

Mortgage Brokers. These companies act as independent sales organizations for sources of money, typically the wholesale loan departments of banks, S&Ls, or mortgage bankers. In most cases, they are supervised by state government departments, such as the Department of Real Estate in California. Mortgage brokers process loans, submit the loan packages to a lender that approves and funds them, and pay a commission to the broker. Brokers are free to direct loans to the lender that has the most favorable loan package for the borrower, but they neither approve nor fund the loans themselves. Income to a mortgage broker comes solely from the commissions earned from loan origination. The obligations of a broker to the customer vary from state to state. In California, brokers are legally agents of the customer and owe him or her fiduciary loyalty. That kind of relationship is good for consumers—but it does not relieve customers of the need to research the character of the individuals with whom they choose to do business.

Mega-Advertisers. These typically operate as mortgage bankers, which gives them one additional advantage. In my state, mortgage bankers are licensed by the Department of Corporations under a different law from that under which mortgage brokers are licensed. Importantly, the law allows them to operate with employees who are not licensed. This is fine when the licensee is the mortgage subsidiary of a huge bank used to operating under intense regulatory scrutiny, but not all lenders are like that. In California, more than $140 billion in loans was originated by companies operating with licenses issued by the Department of Corporations, the agency charged with regulating them. The agency has fewer than a dozen auditors—hardly enough to supervise that tremendous volume of transactions.

Worse, in California, the recent passage of a law removed the prohibition against mortgage bankers brokering loans, an activity that requires individuals be licensed by the Department of Real Estate. Thus, a mortgage banker can broker loans exactly the same way that the mortgage broker next door is doing, but with unlicensed people. Experienced, licensed people will not work for minimum wages under sweatshop conditions—but inexperienced, unlicensed people will.

Aggregators.   As mentioned in the previous section, aggregators typically do little more than take an application from the borrower and direct it to a lender. They do not process, approve, or fund loans, but they may operate a communication channel whereby the client can check on the progress of his or her loan at the aggregator's Web site. On funding, the aggregator makes a small fee, on the order of $250 to $500, for its service.

Other Forms of Organization

In addition to the forms of organization for the various types of lenders, you also must be aware that lenders of the same type may be organized in different ways. This will help you know how to interact most effectively. The loan officer in a branch of a large bank may well be someone in the bank's training program who has spent several months as a teller and is now preparing for his or her next job in a commercial loan office. In most banks, neither this person nor the branch manager has any authority to approve or disapprove your loan. His or her job is simply to hand out material prepared by the marketing department, take your application, and send it off to a centralized office for processing. Such a centralized office in a large bank may be working on a thousand loans at any given point in time. Yours is one of them. Your loan officer will surely be paid a modest salary commensurate with his or her status as a trainee whether you get your loan or not.

Other lenders have loan offices that are totally separate from their "retail" branches. In these organizations, it is more likely that the loan officer will have substantially more experience. Indeed, the loan officer will likely be a career employee in the company. Also, it is likely that his or her income will be a combination of salary plus a commission on each loan funded. And this loan officer may or may not have the ability to adjust pricing based on competitive situations—or on your gullibility. The ethically managed organizations will not allow loan officers to tweak pricing. Mortgage bankers are typically organized in this fashion, though in my experience most mortgage bankers will allow their loan officers to change pricing from the company's base price. In some cases, the loan officer will be given a base price, and his or her commission is everything he or she can get above that base.

Here's a good rule of thumb to follow: Before dealing with any organization, find out what authority the loan officer has. More specifically, come to an understanding with your loan officer about the level of his or her compensation so that he or she does not try to increase it when you're 90 percent of the way through the process.

CALL CENTERS

The most recent phenomenon of mortgage lending is the *call center.* When you call almost any 800 number these days, you are likely to reach a call center and be connected to a customer service representative. Or maybe you first get a message saying, "All of our representatives are busy helping other customers. Please continue to hold and someone will be with you shortly." E-lenders operate call centers too, and after you fill out an application, someone at a call center will contact you.

Perhaps the most benign of these are operated by the megabanks that are trying to support their loyal customer base. In those cases, the employee you're dealing with is not much different from the employee you talk with when you want to check your account balance. Of course, all the lenders promise that their people are well trained and experienced, but my research shows that most of them are working for modest incomes in the $8 to $10 per hour range. At the reputable companies, additional compensation—bonuses—may be based on the quality of customer service rather than on the number of loans originated—a good move.

The more insidious manifestation of the call center concept has recently been created by the mega-advertisers, whose employees can more appropriately be called telemarketers rather than loan reps. A company can hire unlicensed, part-time, inexperienced students, for example, run them through a quick training program, equip them with scripted answers to frequently asked questions, stick them in a cubicle, and put them on a phone. One person I interviewed at one of these operations described some of his fellow employees as "morons." Yet an aggressive lender's combination of advertising, direct marketing, and an Internet presence can generate hundreds, even thousands of phone calls a day, and those people—morons or not—will talk someone into doing business with them. Will it be you?

It is likely that you will run across some of these lenders as you cruise the Internet. If you consider getting your loan from of them, be very careful. A call center run by your bank is likely to be ethically managed, but that run by a lender you've never heard of, offering terrific prices, may be one of those that employs 500 people at a call center. Unfortunately, because of the gullibility of consumers, these call centers are quite profitable for lenders, so it is not likely that they will go away anytime soon.

SUMMARY

Lender is a generic term for what is in practice a widely diverse mixture of financial sources. Each may have a different cost structure and a different approach to the mortgage process. As a consumer, to get your needs met, it is vitally important to link up with a lender that matches closely with who you are and the resources you bring to the table. In particular, if you are inexperienced in seeking financial assistance, do not deal with a low-service operator, regardless of how attractive the price you are quoted. You'll ultimately save more by finding someone qualified and sensitive to your situation and your needs. In the next chapter, I'm going to explain how to do just that.

GETTING A MORTGAGE ON THE INTERNET: PART TWO

Obstacles in a hard journey are the work of demons, anxious to test the sincerity of the pilgrims and eliminate the faint-hearted among them.

—TIBETAN SAYING

Liars can mask their lies, but no man can put on the look of simple honesty.

—JOHN GARDNER

KEY POINTS

- Different lenders have different objectives, and their Web sites reflect their needs more than your needs.
- Most banks, savings and loan associations (S&Ls), mortgage bankers, aggregators, and mortgage brokers have Web sites, which vary significantly in terms of what they offer to borrowers.
- Reading this book will go a long way toward preparing you to successfully complete your real estate transactions. In addition, taking advantage of the tools available at various sites described here will give you greater insight into the market and help you get your needs met.
- Even after you have chosen a lender, it will continue to be important to track economic data and mortgage rates in order to determine when to lock in your rate. A number of financial services Web sites can help you here.
- Whether you choose to get a loan on the Internet or via traditional methods will depend more on your needs, resources,

and preferences than on pricing. But, whichever route you take, be aware that Web sites offer a wealth of data to make the process more productive and efficient.

FINDING AND USING LENDER WEB SITES

Research from Yahoo! indicates that 138,968 Web sites use the word *mortgage* to describe what they do, so you will have no problem finding one of these sites. What may be more difficult is finding one that suits your individual needs.

Before guiding you to individual Web sites, I want to establish a baseline for our discussion of Internet lending. There are only so many things that you can do on and from a Web site, and as you become familiar with a number of sites, you'll find they have more in common than they have differences. Most post rates, most offer educational tools, most have an array of calculators, and most give you the opportunity to fill out a mini-application of one sort or another. Rather than delving into these characteristics at each site, therefore, my focus will be on highlighting those characteristics that differentiate one site from similar sites.

BANKS AND S&LS

Early in 1999, most of the large national banks still had not established an Internet presence for their mortgage operations. By late that year, however, all that had changed. Most had finally come to the party, and no doubt more will have arrived after this book is published.

There is a fundamental difference in the approach the big banks take on the Internet compared to that of other, more specialized lenders that only originate loans. Big banks have millions of customers. Citigroup, for example, with a host of financial services, boasts that it has 100 million customers worldwide. My bank alone has more than 1 million customers who have signed up for online services, such as the ability to check balances, move money between accounts, or print out an interim statement. Like so many of us, I find this service far more convenient than going into a branch or calling some 800 number and wading through a tedious voice menu system to accomplish the same tasks. Many banks now offer their customers the ability to pay bills online securely. Of course, getting a mortgage is much more complicated than checking your account balance.

If, say, you are a Chase depositor and you want to find out about mortgages at its Web site, Chase is going to place at your fingertips (literally) the type of information its managers think that you are likely to want. They want to capitalize on an existing customer's propensity to do business with his or her own bank by making its portal easy to use, thereby encouraging the customer to take the next step online. That next step probably is to fill out a mini-application that will provide the information necessary for a bank employee to better help you when he or she calls you the next business day. In some cases, however, don't be surprised to find only an 800 number to call. This level of interface is not true Internet lending, because it does not tap into the many capabilities of the Internet. As I said in the introduction to this section, most banks do post rates, so getting rate information is easier to do online than by phoning or visiting a local branch. And, as mentioned, most major lenders offer calculators (which, by the way, often fall more in the toy classification than useful tool classification; for a list of Web sites that have more useful calculators, refer to Appendix 1). At some sites, the educational tools are quite rudimentary, while at others they are very useful, especially to the first-time borrower who is just learning to navigate the sometimes rough homebuying waters.

Most of the major lender sites also have interactive loan advisors designed to help you determine which loans might be more suitable to you. Unfortunately, I cannot recommend any of those I surveyed, as the answers they gave were misleading or worse—although many or most consumers could not know that. For example, at one site, I indicated I wanted a fixed-rate mortgage, but when I shortened the contemplated ownership period, the "advisor" recommended a 30-year fixed-rate loan, even when I indicated I was only going to be in the house for one year. Other sites ask how many points you want to pay, rather than recommending a rate versus fee choice most suited to you. Better to use the tools in this book.

Most large banks and S&Ls don't offer much more on their sites than plain vanilla products. For example, I know that certain banks, through their wholesale channels, offer pricing incentives of one sort or another to brokers. These niche, or promotional, offerings might include a ¼ point ($250 on a $100,000 loan) reduction in fees for loans where the credit scores are above 700. Such a deal was not offered online, probably due to the assumption that consumers either wouldn't understand what it meant or, if they did, how good a deal it really might be. In contrast, the mortgage brokers would quickly respond to such offers, thereby creating an incentive to send more loans to these lenders. Thus, the borrower who deals directly with a lender's retail—that is, online—channel may not find out about these specials.

In contrast, a useful tool at one bank's Web site is a fairly extensive section titled "Community Home Buying Programs." Under such programs, banks have typically loosened down payment requirements, credit standards, and underwriting criteria so as to expand home ownership opportunities for those who have traditionally been underserved by the mortgage industry, including minorities and those at or below the median income level in their area. This type of information on a Web site can go a long way toward making a lender's interface more inviting to those borrowers who might otherwise feel intimidated by large institutions and apprehensive about applying for a loan in the first place. I applaud that outreach effort and hope that other banks follow suit.

Here are the Web sites of the major banks and S&Ls:

Chase Manhattan	mortgage02.chase.com/noframes/ frameset5.html
Citicorp/Citibank	www.citibank.com/mortgage/
Bank of America/ NationsBank/	www.bankofamerica.com/ mortgage/
Dime/North American	www.dime.com/—click on Home Financing
Flagstar Bank	www.flagstar.com/dhtml/lending .htm
Wells Fargo Bank/ Norwest	wellsfargo.com/mortgage
Fleet Bank/BankBoston	www.fleet.com/mg.html
Washington Mutual	www.wamumortgage.com/
Cal Fed/First Nationwide	www.calfed.com/mortgage/index .htm
LaSalle/InterFirst	www.lasallehomemortgage.com/top
World Savings	www.worldloan.com/

Keep in mind that some of these banks have nationwide operations, while others may operate only in a few states or certain areas of the country. If you are contacting your own bank, obviously you know it's located in your area. But before you get involved with one of the others, be sure it does business in your state.

NOTE The banks listed here almost invariably do business with the public through a mortgage banking subsidiary. That means the banks seldom lend their own funds; they originate mortgages, which will be sold in the secondary market just like loans originated by mortgage bankers. So although I make a distinction between banks and mortgage bankers, the difference is largely in the fact that mortgage bankers do not offer the broad range of other services that we expect from banks. That can also make the mortgage bankers more efficient.

MORTGAGE BANKERS

Recall from the preceding chapter and from the previous section that mortgage bankers are in the business of originating mortgage loans, then selling them into the secondary market and servicing the loans. Let's look at one mortgage banker in greater detail.

NOTE | The Web site for the Mortgage Bankers Association of America is www.mbaa.org. You will find a good array of consumer tips and tools there. You'll even find my first book, *How to Save Thousands of Dollars on Your Home Mortgage,* in the online bookstore at the site.

Countrywide

One of the largest lenders in the country is Countrywide Credit Industries, Inc., whose home page at www.countrywide.com can be seen in Figure 10.1. Countrywide has a nationwide network of branch offices, currently over 400—not quite one on every street corner, but certainly enough to service people all across the country. From my point of view, Countrywide's online model has an excellent chance of success because it takes advantage of the strength of the organization already in place. You might argue, "All it has done is substitute one method of acquiring customers for another. That isn't anything revolutionary!" True, but now customers have a choice: to deal 100 percent electronically or to interact with the company on a more personal level. Countrywide's system is a preferable alternative to the call center model adopted by so many other lenders, which I described in the previous chapter.

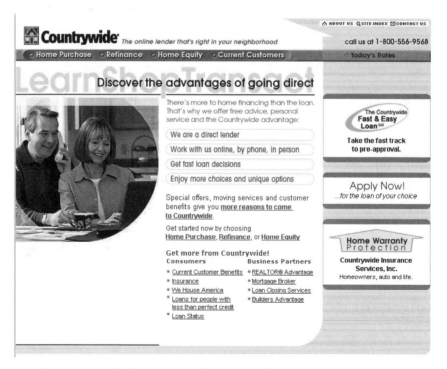

Figure 10.1   The home page of Countrywide, a leading online lender.

In my view, Countrywide made a wise decision to use the strength of its 400-plus branch offices to process and fund consumer loans. From customers' perspective, dealing with a professional in their area offers convenience as well as personal service, a real plus for those who prefer face-to-face contact. The other advantage of this system is that the customer gets the benefit of dealing with people who have years of experience doing business in their area, or at least in their state—a real advantage when the inevitable problems arise. They can also communicate by e-mail.

Countrywide's most attractive feature for online customers is the Gold Credit Home Loan, a fee discount service for A+ borrowers—those with squeaky-clean credit, long-term job stability, and a lot of equity in property. As you probably deduced, these are the borrowers who will be quickly and easily approved by one of the automated underwriting programs, a program that costs less to administer. Clearly, Countrywide is attempting to attract the easy loan with lower pricing made possible by the lower cost structure.

OTHER MORTGAGE BANKING COMPANIES

Companies like GMAC and General Electric are household names, but you may be unaware of their extensive involvement in the mortgage industry. GE, for example, claims to make more than 1 million loans annually, many of which are loans bought from other lenders. Like Countrywide, these firms generally have substantial wholesale and correspondent business, originating loans for brokers and purchasing loans from other mortgage bankers and banks. In some cases, they may have only recently established an online retail presence, and most do business through a call center. Here are the Web sites of three large mortgage banking concerns:

GMAC	www.gmacmortgage.com/
HomeSide Lending	www.homeside.com/cd/main.htm
GE Capital	www1.gemortgageservices.com/
	loans_homemortgages.asp

HOMEADVISOR

The financing section at HomeAdvisor has gone through a substantial change with the creation of HomeAdvisor Technologies, owned by Microsoft and four of the nation's largest lenders. HomeAdvisor acts as a mortgage broker and earns a fee for referring the applications to a variety of lenders, not just those with an ownership stake in the company. Indeed, it is technology that separates this site from its competitors, and you should understand its unique style of operation, the early phases of which are accomplished without human intervention.

At the heart of the process is a new software platform called MortgageDirect, which ties borrowers, HomeAdvisor, and lenders together. Affiliated lenders post the types of loans they are interested in internally on the HomeAdvisor platform. When you complete a mini-application form at the Web site and authorize a credit check, your characteristics—income, LTV, creditworthiness, and desired loan type—are compared with the offerings of the lenders and your information is sent electronically to those lenders that are most suitable. At this point, the lenders' own automated underwriting programs swing into action and, assuming they preapprove your loan, you are notified, usually within a matter of a few minutes. If a lender needs more information from you, you will be asked to call the lender's toll-free number.

If the terms of your preapproved loan appeal to you, you initiate a real application with one of the lenders, giving them contact information and paying an up-front fee, and the humans take over. You may lock in the terms at that point, but the rate is guaranteed only for an hour. As of this writing, the platform is too new to get feedback from users, so I hope that those who use the site will send me an e-mail at feedback@loan-wolf.com to share their experiences. The following evaluation of this site is based on my judgment and conjecture.

The advantage of this system is that it gives you an instant indication that if the information you presented is corroborated, your loan will fund. For those who are at the margin of qualifying, this can be reassuring. For the highly qualified borrowers—probably you—it is of less value because you already know that you will be qualified, especially if you have used some of the tools I recommend, such as the Qualify spreadsheet available at my Web site.

That said, any lender using the automated underwriting systems provided by the Federal National Mortgage Association (FNMA) or the Federal Home Loan Mortgage Corporation (FHLMC) can offer approval within a matter of an hour or two. It is not clear to me that in a 30-day escrow a 5-minute approval has significant merit over a 2-hour approval. The market will tell us. The major benefit will be to the people who just plain do not want to contact a lender and complete the real application yet, but who will be comforted by a quick preapproval without having to make any commitment whatever. The key question, as I see it, is whether HomeAdvisor's lenders can create enough "glue" to cause the preapproved borrowers to stick with the process and fund their loans.

The lenders find this process attractive because they do not have to make any expenditure—save a $6 credit report and a little computer time—to get a good preapproved lead. Compare that with the hundreds of dollars the average lender pays to get applications from borrowers or the $1000 in marketing costs that some Internet lenders are paying to attract customers!

Pricing

In order to dispense with consumer worries about pricing, HomeAdvisor lenders offer the following guarantee to their customers:

> *If a HomeAdvisor lender has approved you for a loan with MortgageDirect technology and you obtain a comparable underwritten approved loan from another lender the same day, we will meet the other lender's pricing or, at our discretion, we may choose to pay you $250 upon the closing of your loan with the other lender.*

My perception is that the main purpose of this type of guarantee is to put the customer at ease about the pricing issue, to get him or her to stop shopping. It is going to sound appealing to some borrowers, at which point they will turn off their sense of reason and stop thinking about the other decisions they need to make. I can think of a number of good reasons to use HomeAdvisor, but this isn't one of them. For openers, to initiate the guarantee, you basically have to get pretty well into the process with another lender, in all likelihood more trouble than it's worth.

As to competitiveness, my assessment is that the pricing is competitive with that of other legitimate, efficient lenders that are trying to be competitive. In my evaluation of pricing available at the site, I determined that using other lenders I do business with, I would have been able to offer my clients more attractive pricing than most lenders at HomeAdvisor. The site's lenders do not seem to offer any pricing enhancements from their normal retail pricing, meaning I could go to the same lenders' wholesale sites, add my typical 1 point markup, and the pricing would be identical. Why? Let's say you are a manager at Chase and 99 percent of your business comes from non-Internet channels. What is the incentive for you to offer cut-rate pricing through this one channel that provides only 1 percent of your business? None that I can see. The few exceptions were the pricing posted at HomeAdvisor from newer lenders, perhaps those that are not defending some other marketing turf, who had decided to use this method and offer more aggressive pricing. The conclusion I come to is consistent with the theme I emphasize throughout this book: Assume that pricing is going to be almost the same at any legitimate, efficient lender, and choose your lender based on various aspects of service offered. On this basis, HomeAdvisor has a unique offering that will appeal to some borrowers more than the combination of services available at other sources, both Internet-based and traditional.

How to Navigate the Site

The financing section can be accessed from the home page (see Figure 10.2) by clicking on Financing. At the subsequent page you have a number of options. You can immediately check rates by selecting a loan amount in the drop box and hitting Go. Otherwise you choose the channel, Purchase or Refinance. The Get Pre-Approved button seems to go to the same screens as the Home Purchase button. You start the six-part interview process with a description of the loan purpose. You then go to the Background page, as shown as Figure 10.3.

As you work through the rest of the pages, you'll find that the context-sensitive advisor moves along with your cursor, so help is right there. At the Income & Debt page, a feature unique to HomeAdvisor is the very useful embedded worksheets for income, debt, and cash available. As you enter data, the summary totals carry over to the main screen.

When you get to the last step, you have to give some personal information before you get your recommendation. You can make up your own mind about whether you want to do that based on where you are in the process and how committed you want to be to HomeAdvisor. I omitted giving my Social Security number because I felt it was an unnecessary step, given that I was interacting with a computer. The recommendations I received are shown in Figure 10.4.

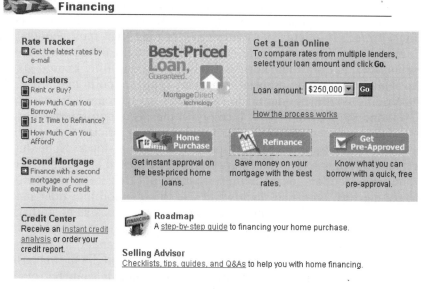

Figure 10.2   HomeAdvisor home page.
(Courtesy of HomeAdvisor.)

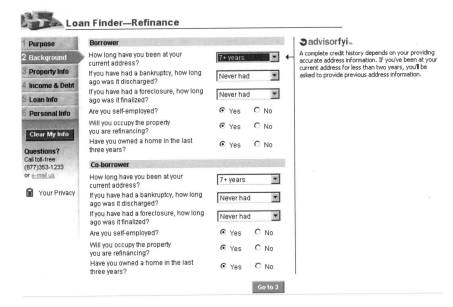

**Figure 10.3   Loan Finder Background page.
(Courtesy of HomeAdvisor.)**

I was prompted several times that I wasn't getting the best prices because I hadn't given my Social Security number, so I finally did. The result? I got one offer of slightly better pricing, probably because that lender was trying to "cherry-pick" the applicants, giving preferred pricing to the ones with low loan-to-value (LTV) ratios and high credit scores. There is nothing wrong with that as a business strategy, except that I question the competency of the lender in question. Its history is that lenders and mortgage servicers outsource some of their back-office functions to this company. My question relates to how a company like this, with no history of experience in dealing with thousands of individual borrowers, can possibly get up to speed in providing the kind of service that I believe applicants deserve. Time will tell.

Another feature of HomeAdvisor is Rate Tracker, which will notify you about current rates as frequently as you like. It can also send you an alert when the market gets to the particular rate you specify. A word of caution here, though. Doing this too often keeps the emphasis on rate shopping—not that rates aren't important, but when you become too concerned about rates, you tend not to look at more important factors that impact on your decisions. I also found that I could not always correlate the e-mail notices with rates posted at the site.

While at HomeAdvisor, I also tried to get information about which of its dozen or so lenders ended up getting the referrals. The answer I got suggested that the inclusion of various lenders was based not just

Loan Finder Results

◄ Back to Loan Finder Interview

Loans for Your Review
These loans match the information you've provided, but they don't offer the best customized prices, instant approval or online locking because you didn't authorize lenders to review your credit online. By completing the **Personal Info** tab and clicking **Get Results**, you'll allow lenders to find you loans with the best prices.

🔒 Your Privacy

Questions?
Call toll-free
(877)353-1233
or e-mail us

Your Top Recommended Loans

	Lender	Loan Type	Rate (APR)	Points ($Total)	Monthly Payment*	Lock Period	Closing Costs*	Loan Amount
1	HomeSide Lending, Inc.	5Yr/1Yr Treas ARM	7.75% (8.231%)	1.187 ($2,968)	$1,791	25 Days	$7,981	$250,000
								See Details
2	First Mortgage Network	5Yr/1Yr Treas ARM	7.625% (8.299%)	0.99 ($2,475)	$1,769	30 Days	$7,462	$250,000
								See Details
3	LaSalle Home (ABN AMRO) Mortgage	5Yr/1Yr Treas ARM	7.625% (8.526%)	1.375 ($3,438)	$1,769	15 Days	$7,871	$250,000
								See Details
4	Chase Manhattan Mortgage Corp	5Yr/1Yr Treas ARM	7.625% (8.599%)	1.875 ($4,688)	$1,769	15 Days	$9,573	$250,000
								See Details
5	HomeComings Financial Network, A GMAC Company	5/1 ARM	7.875% (8.633%)	1 ($2,500)	$1,813	30 Days	$7,851	$250,000
								See Details

Loan Finder Results

◄ Back to Loan Finder Interview

Congratulations—customized, lockable loans are waiting for you!
Choose the one you want and you'll be instantly approved. These loans offer lockable rates and points. They're the best-priced loans for you. You're ready to go!

🔒 Your Privacy

Questions?
Call toll-free
(877)353-1233
or e-mail us

Review your choices, then choose the loan you want and click **Apply Now**.

Your Top Recommended Loans

	Lender	Loan Type	Rate (APR)	Points ($Total)	Monthly Payment*	Lock Period	Closing Costs*	Loan Amount
1	Wendover Financial Services Corporation	5 Year Balloon	7.375% (7.695%)	1.108 ($2,770)	$1,727	30 Days	$8,120	$250,000
							See Details	Apply Now
2	HomeComings Financial Network, A GMAC Company	5/1 ARM	7.875% (8.633%)	1 ($2,500)	$1,813	30 Days	$7,851	$250,000
							See Details	Apply Now

These rates are valid until 07/09/2000 5:46:50 PM Pacific time. Refresh rates.

Tell Me More
Since you care most about **paying minimum total interest** and expect to hold the loan for **four to five years**, you can consider the loan with the lowest available rate for that time period. In this situation, Loan Finder recommends a 3-year/6-month adjustable-rate mortgage (ARM) (which offers a fixed rate for three years, followed by rate adjustments every six months), a 5/1-year ARM (a fixed rate for five years, followed by annual rate adjustments) or a five-year balloon (a fixed rate for five years, followed by an extension at a new rate or a single repayment of the remaining principal). Because these loans typically have low initial interest rates and their initial rates will be in effect for all or most of the time you plan to keep your loan, they offer the lowest interest payments for the time period you are considering.

Figure 10.4   Sample loan recommendation at Microsoft's HomeAdvisor. (Courtesy of HomeAdvisor.)

on rate competitiveness, but on feedback from customers about the quality of service they received—an enlightened policy in such a rate-sensitive market. Remember that even though Microsoft earns a broker fee, it does not process loans, but passes you off to a participating lender that is likely to be processing loans through a centralized office that most likely is clerical in its approach to customer service. Nevertheless, remember that, as a mortgage broker, the company's fee is earned only when the loan funds, so it has a vested interest in monitoring customer satisfaction with the process and wants to assure that its chosen lenders keep customers happy.

In conclusion, HomeAdvisor offers several advantages to borrowers. For the most part, you are dealing with leading nationally recognized lenders. You will be paying the same retail price that you would if you dealt with the same companies through some other channel, the process is obviously going to be faster here. Perhaps more important, HomeAdvisor offers a level playing field where every borrower, whether a tough negotiator or newcomer, gets the same deal. You won't be treated unfairly.

QUICKEN LOANS

Like its larger software competitor, Intuit, the publisher of the deservedly popular Quicken and TurboTax personal finance software, is attempting to parlay its position as a trusted advisor to its clients into being a full-service financial powerhouse. This recently upgraded site contains access to a full array of services that are available at many other sites as well. Advice is offered on investing, insurance, taxes, banking, and retirement, as well as an array of home loan products.

Quicken Loans used to operate as an independent aggregator, sending loans to banks and other lenders but it recently acquired Rock Financial Corporation (www.rockloans.com), a Michigan-based mortgage banker. The objective of the acquisition was to exert more control over the loan process by bringing the processing in house. You should be aware that as a mortgage banker, Quicken Loans' role is different than when it was just a referral service, portraying the products of a multitude of lenders.

I found the educational tools somewhat inferior to those at other sites, but other unique features are worth pursuing. Take a look at Quicken Loans' home page at quickenloans.quicken.com, shown in Figure 10.5.

I'll begin the discussion of this site with its credit assessment program, which allows you to enter data about your credit history, after which you are given an evaluation ranging from Needs Improvement to Fair to Good. Unfortunately, entering more than one derogatory report—say, the admission of a 60-day late payment—in any field seems to downgrade you to Fair; entering two derogs drops you to Needs Improvement. As it stands, this is so simple a tool as to be trivial to consumers, and it needs improvement. You really need to get your credit report, which you can do at the sites discussed in Chapter 13, "Checking Credit."

On the assets side, Quicken Loans has the only rate versus fee calculator I have found anywhere, and you know how important I think

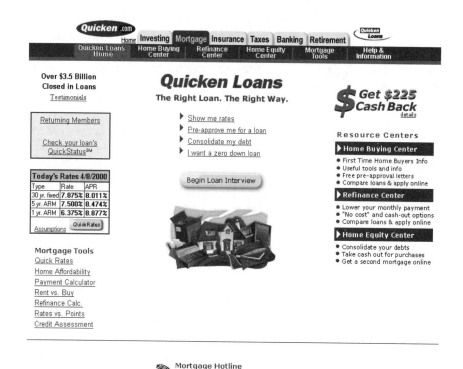

Figure 10.5   The Quicken Loans home page. (Reprinted with permission of Quicken Loans, Inc. All rights reserved.)

that is. The program evaluates any two different rate versus fee alternatives. However, for this to be relevant, you have to have been keeping written notes as you were checking rates so you know what to enter. The program displays the answers both graphically and in text form. I entered some different interest rates and points as a test, and the answers I got, given in terms of break-even periods, appeared to be based on the difference between payments. I believe my methodology, which is based upon differences between interest rates rather than payments, is easier to use and is more helpful to consumers trying to make this decision. The Excel spreadsheet I recommend can be downloaded from my Web site at www.loan-wolf.com/download.htm. This entire topic is discussed in Chapter 14, "Understanding APR, Buy-Downs, and Discount Points."

I also tried out the Quicken Loan interview process to see what kind of a loan it would recommend. Composed of 14 screens, it was thorough but a little tedious. Note that you have to set your browser to accept cookies so your choices can be stored, making it easier for you when you revisit the site. (A cookie is a small identifying file that a Web site places on your computer. It stays there, and when you revisit the site, the cookie identifies you to the site, enabling you to do things like more quickly reenter a program in midstream. Some people are paranoid about invasion of privacy; if you're one, you'll have to start from scratch. Most sites will place a cookie on your computer unless you set your browser not to accept them.) In my trial, even though I set my browser according to the instructions, I was unable to get past the initial page in Internet Explorer 5.0, so I accessed the interview through Netscape. I entered personal data and preferences and finally got the results shown in Figure 10.6. Note that the program recommended a 4-point loan, something no human would have recommended and few customers would have accepted. However confusing it is to get there

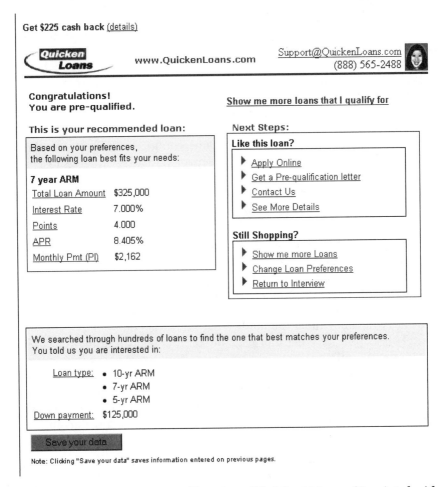

Get **$225 cash back** (details)

Quicken Loans   www.QuickenLoans.com   Support@QuickenLoans.com
(888) 565-2488

Congratulations!
You are pre-qualified.

This is your recommended loan:

Based on your preferences,
the following loan best fits your needs:

7 year ARM

Total Loan Amount	$325,000
Interest Rate	7.000%
Points	4.000
APR	8.405%
Monthly Pmt (PI)	$2,162

Show me more loans that I qualify for

Next Steps:

Like this loan?

▶ Apply Online
▶ Get a Pre-qualification letter
▶ Contact Us
▶ See More Details

Still Shopping?

▶ Show me more Loans
▶ Change Loan Preferences
▶ Return to Interview

We searched through hundreds of loans to find the one that best matches your preferences. You told us you are interested in:

Loan type: • 10-yr ARM
             • 7-yr ARM
             • 5-yr ARM

Down payment: $125,000

Save your data

Note: Clicking "Save your data" saves information entered on previous pages.

Figure 10.6   Quicken Loans told me I qualified for 20 loans. (Reprinted with permission of Quicken Loans, Inc. All rights reserved.)

though, this information is presented in a useful manner. I found inconsistencies between the pricing shown here and that displayed in the Quick Rates section of the site.

In summary, I think the Quicken Loans site is less useful and somewhat more cumbersome than others such as HomeAdvisor and iOwn .com. That said, I have a high regard for Intuit's management and believe that the site is ethically and efficiently managed. If Intuit can marry its consumer orientation with mortgage smarts, the result will be an effectual competitor and a value to consumers. As with other sites, as a consumer, you need to evaluate your needs and compare them with the benefits offered by proposed lenders.

Computerized Loan Originators

Computerized loan originators (CLOs) are a hybrid, though they operate much like aggregators. Keystroke.com, at www.keystroke.com, is one of the few with national reach. It provides a free prequalification service (no credit report necessary) and refers applicants to one of a large number of lenders. My assessment of this site would be higher if somewhere consumers were told the company's precise role in this process, what it does to earn a fee, and who its lenders are. None of this information is spelled out. After filling out a rate quote sheet, you get to a listing of rates and fees—but if, for example, 200 lenders are compared, it is not at all obvious whose rates you are looking at. Are they the best of the 200? For Keystroke.com to be truly valuable to consumers, it needs to be more forthcoming.

LET LENDERS COMPETE FOR YOUR LOAN

A more recent phenomenon are the Web sites that invite you to apply for a loan, then send the application to a number of lenders that then post a bid, a rate, and fee at which they will process your loan. (Your name, Social Security number, address, and phone number are kept confidential.) These offers are sent to you via e-mail; if you like what you see, you can contact the lender that interests you.

This is exactly what mortgage brokers have been doing for years, but they only tell you about the best rate. Whether this lending system will become viable among borrowers and/or lenders remains to be seen. At the time of this writing, it is too early to tell. The leader of this pack is Lending Tree, at www.lendingtree.com. If you try one of these services, please let me know your results via e-mail at randy@loan-wolf.com.

INTERNET-ONLY LENDERS

Internet-only companies (meaning they are only "clicks-and-mortar" companies) for the most part are very new, having been established in the past few years for the purpose of originating loans solely or largely on the Internet; they do not have bricks-and-mortar branches to handle walk-in customers. If you've done any Web surfing at all, probably you've seen the ads for these companies, which display (and sometimes distract) at every real estate Web site. There are three that are of the most interest to us: Quicken Loans, already discussed; and E-LOAN and iOwn.com. Let's look at the latter two to give you an idea how they work.

E-LOAN

The Internet-only company with perhaps the greatest visibility is E-LOAN, at www.eloan.com. Backed by the sale of over $50 million of stock in its initial public offering, E-LOAN has been able to establish the strongest brand identity among lenders on the Internet. It has established strategic partnerships with a large number of Internet portals, and is also using other, more traditional media—radio and print—to promote itself. Take a look at some of E-LOAN's offerings in Figure 10.7.

Is E-LOAN a broker or a direct lender? Good question. In its advertisements, E-LOAN promises to "scour the planet" for the best rates; at its Web site it boasts, "Our rate database contains over 50,000 mortgage loans from 70 leading lenders." However, the company has negotiated warehouse lines of credit for more than $100 million, giving it the capability of funding most of its loan origination volume as a mortgage banker. Indeed, in a report filed with the Securities and Exchange Commission on September 30, 1999, the company stated, "E-LOAN's loan origination and sale operations, initiated June 1998, represented 85 percent of total mortgage loans closed for the quarter ended September 30th 1999."

Thus, these statistics would seem to demonstrate that the company is determining its own rates for 85 percent of its loans, funding them, and selling them through conduits, rather than acting as a mortgage broker and forwarding your application to one of those 70 lenders. That said, even in the world of mortgage banking, companies like E-LOAN sell their loans to other companies—Chase, Countrywide, and the other giants of the business. In a perfect world, the "scour the planet" promise would suggest that these companies would always pass on to the consumer any below-market deals they find at these sources of funds. Getting back to reality, the truth is mortgage bankers almost always pocket the difference. The profit margin is higher for a mortgage banker than a mortgage broker and, perhaps more importantly, the mortgage banker has to disclose neither the source of funds nor its profit margin, as brokers do. That is not necessarily bad; it just means that consumers need to judge E-LOAN as a company with something for sale, not as an ally like a true broker acting as the customer's legal agent.

Regardless of where the money comes from, the E-LOAN Web site is operationally well organized. In addition to the obligatory online

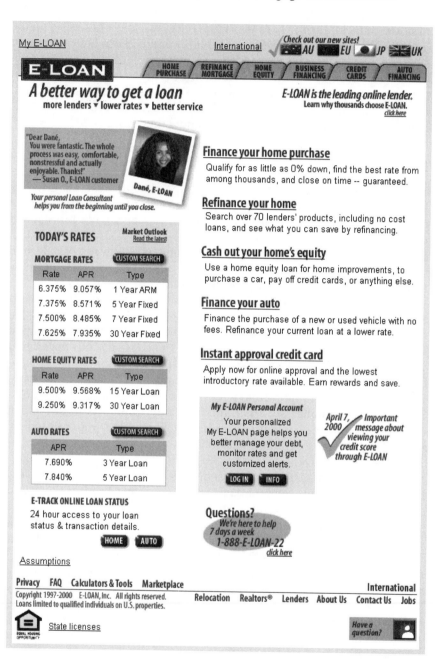

Figure 10.7   E-LOAN is a strong presence among Web-based mortgage
companies. (Courtesy of E-LOAN.)

qualification, the site provides comprehensive custom rate quotations on a broad variety of loans; it also offers E-TRACK, a feature that enables customers to check loan status 24 hours a day, 7 days a week, and a single-point-of-contact loan consultant. I did, however, think the educational area was inadequate.

E-LOAN has also expanded into the home equity, small business loan, credit card, and car financing markets as well as setting up subsidiary operations in several foreign countries. These ventures can provide additional profit opportunities that can insulate the company from the vagaries of the ever cyclical mortgage business. Through its Marketplace, E-LOAN has partnered with a large number of companies providing real estate–related services such as homeowners' insurance, home inspection services, moving companies, pest control services, and a very handy service for sending out change of address notifications (www.changemyaddress.com). Presumably, E-LOAN earns a fee when the loan customer uses one of these ancillary services. E-LOAN's partners appear to be sound, and you should consider using these services should you need them. Finally, the company has just introduced an excellent new feature, My E-LOAN, a personalized account where you can order a credit report, and through the related E-TRACK service, keep track of changes in the market. The company says that over 85,000 people have signed up for these services. This novel approach may cure the transaction orientation, the curse of the mortgage business. Building more lasting relationships and selling other services traditionally purchased at traditional banks, E-LOAN may find the greatest hope for the future profit. A point that I have made throughout this book is that for you as a consumer, it is important not just to look at pricing, but to assess the value of the services you get for your money. This may be an important step in the value-added process that I think the industry will have to find.

Because E-LOAN is a public company, it has to make its financial performance a matter of public record. Like most other e-commerce ventures, it is losing a staggering amount of money. Whether it will continue to be a dominant player in the Internet mortgage marketplace will hinge largely on its ability to step judiciously through the financial minefield ahead and beat out the other e-commerce giants.

iOwn.com

Another significant Web-based player in this market is iOwn.com, at www.iown.com. Formerly known as homeshark.com, the company has one of the most comprehensive and best-organized Web sites on the Internet, a page of which is shown in Figure 10.8. The information here is presented in a pleasing, easy-to-read format. The site also has the most comprehensive coverage of closing costs of any site I visited.

Operating as a true broker, iOwn lists the actual rate sheets from its participating lenders in addition to a summary price quote. More helpfully, and perhaps uniquely among large Internet lenders, iOwn shows all of the rate versus fee options—a half-dozen or more—that each lender offers. As a broker, I see these same options when these same lenders send me their rate sheets. Sadly, no methodology was available to help the consumer differentiate between one option and another—although you, dear reader, have all of the tools necessary to do your own analysis. Check out Chapter 14.

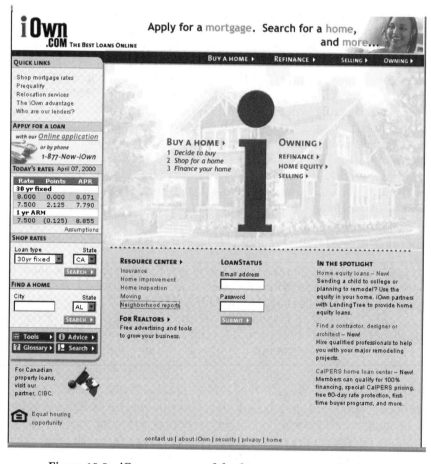

Figure 10.8   iOwn.com, one of the few true mortgage brokers.
(© iOwn Holdings, Inc. 2000.)

Less impressive was the Choose the Right Mortgage tool, which gave only obvious answers. For example, when I said I was willing to take a loan that was fixed initially and adjustable thereafter, and that I was going to be in the home for five years, sure enough, it recommended a 5/1 adjustable-rate mortgage (ARM). (The 5/1 refers to the fact that this loan is fixed for five years, then adjusted annually for the next 25 years.) I suppose if I had said 3 years, it would have recommended a 3/1 ARM. My advice? Forget it. Look at Chapter 11, "Choosing the Right Loan."

In addition to the typical services offered by other mortgage sites, iOwn has more far-reaching resources for the consumer, which I discuss in the chapters relating to them. But to whet your appetite, I'll mention HomeScout, iOwn's home listing site, which links to HomeSeekers.com. The information about homes for sale is displayed very professionally—even better than at the HomeSeekers.com site. Real estate brokers can also enter listing data.

Furthermore, iOwn's recent acquisition of Genesis2000, a successful mortgage processing software company, demonstrates that the company intends to push the technology boundary, conceivably creating an interface that enables the customer to fill out the loan application, which is then directly entered into one of the automated underwriting models without much human intervention. Although this reduces costs, it also reduces interaction with a real estate professional. As to pricing, iOwn.com's stated loan origination fee is only ½ point, or $1,000 on a $200,000 loan. This compares with a fee from 1 point to 1.5 points charged by conventional lenders, online or not. Assuming that a customer can choose to deal with a particular lender at its retail branch or online, it is probably going to be cheaper to deal with that lender through iOwn.com. Again, the question you have to ask is whether the service level—read help—is discounted more than the price. As with other Internet lenders, iOwn.com has assembled a package of services relating to all other aspects of the homebuying process.

Other Internet-Only Sites

There are thousands of other mortgage Web sites. The following are better than average and worth checking out:

www.mortgage.com

www.interloan.com/

www.mortgagebot.com/

www.mortgageit.com

www.finet.com

www.loanz.com

www.loanworks.com

You might stop by Gomez.com mortgage scorecard at www.gomez
.com/scorecards/index.cfm?topcat_id=39. This company rates the services of a huge number of industries. Before you settle on a lender, you
might find it useful to check out Gomez.com's ratings, which are based
not only on independent evaluations but on feedback from customers
as well.

MORTGAGE BROKERS AND MORTGAGE DIRECTORIES

It seems that every one of the 20,000 mortgage brokers in the country
has a Web site. Of those, 11,000 belong to the National Association of
Mortgage Brokers (NAMB), which also has its own Web site at www
.namb.org. If you are interested in a mortgage broker (and as a broker, of
course I hope that you consider some of the benefits of hiring one), you
may enter your zip or area code and get the names of NAMB members
in your area. Unfortunately, this listing contains minimal information
and does not as yet have hyperlinks to member Web sites. Until it does,
you'll have to type in the Web addresses yourself. Many of the states
also have their own associations, which may be more useful. You can
find a list at www.namb.org/mortgage/statechapters.htm.

Probably in an effort to become competitive online quickly, many
of the 20,000 mortgage brokers have Web sites, although most seem to
have been quickly assembled and a number are not updated conscientiously (for example, I found pricing data on many sites that was
months old). Happily, other sites are well monitored and very useful,
offering a number of services and tools and links to other services.

To find a mortgage broker in your area, probably the best place to
start is a mortgage directory, essentially a lenders' Yellow Pages. If you
prefer a lender closer to home, check out the following Web sites. Most
are organized so that you can search by area.

www.loanpage.com/finder.htm, the Web site of ComCity, claims
to have the largest searchable list of mortgage brokers on the Internet—
over 2000. You can search a number of ways, a useful feature. When
you narrow down the search, you can review lender profiles and then
click on a hyperlink to go to that lender's Web site.

www.amo-mortgage.com, the Web site of America Mortgage
Online, contains more educational material than most sites, along with
a searchable database of lenders, including hyperlinks.

www.interest.com, the Web site of Mortgage Market Information
Services, Inc., is a very valuable educational site for homebuyers. In
addition to a broad array of other tools, it has a database of lenders,

many of which you can get to via hyperlinks. In addition, there is a large number of educational articles.

www.mortgage-net.com is sponsored by Myers Internet Services. It has an extensive listing of lenders displayed very professionally, in part because lenders pay to be listed here. The site has sections for various types of loan needs, such as for those with imperfect credit. Each company's listing contains a hyperlink to its Web site, so you will find it easier to cruise among them to find a company that appeals to you.

www.newhomesale.com, the Web site of NewHomeSale, has a mortgage broker directory in addition to directories of architects, builders, and many others in the broader real estate industry. Rather than just listing sites, this site evaluates them too. You may find it easier just to cruise those sites that have been awarded the Gold Site Award, as mine was.

www.realtor.com is the site of the National Association of Realtors. It has a Find a Lender section on its home page that contains a listing of 38,000 lenders. To use it, go to the site search engine, type in a city and state, and you'll get a list of lenders in that locale. Beware: You may get too much help. I got 17 pages of lenders listed in my hometown. Moreover, you will not get any information about the companies or hyperlinks to their Web sites.

You can also use the search engines to find lenders. If you just type in a simple phrase such as mortgage lender, I warn you, the results can be overwhelming. Don't be surprised to receive a page that says "1 to 10 of 138,000." The problem is, that just means there were 138,000 mentions of the phrase you typed in, not that there are 138,000 mortgage lenders to check out. To prevent that kind of deluge, I recommend that on Yahoo!, for example, you access relevant information in the sequence Business & Economy, Real Estate, Regional, State, City, to find companies in your area, some of which will be lenders. Or go to lenders at Yahoo! via Real Estate, Legal and Financial, Financing, Real Estate. But don't be tempted by Yahoo! Loan Center, which seems to be nothing more than an ad for its sponsor, a prominent lender.

Sadly, the same thing is true at the otherwise highly useful GO Network. The GO Network Real Estate and Loans directory leads you to a page that has been purchased by one lender, not a directory of lenders. What I do like is that the giant search engine GO Network is my preferred search tool. In effect, you can specify the use of all engines, not just one at one site. So a better choice is to go to the GO Network search engine and type in *mortgage* and then your hometown and state in the request so you don't get too many answers.

THE NETWORK

In 1996, shortly after I had started my Internet Web site, a writer asked about my thoughts on Internet lending. At the time, many of the mortgage Web sites had been hastily assembled, and none was particularly notable by today's standards. Most lenders seemed to be using the Internet as a lead generator to develop prospects for their bricks-and-mortar-based businesses. A lot of people expected that the lenders dominating traditional lending would dominate Internet lending, too. I didn't agree, and I still don't. As I told the writer, "I think that the paradigm for success in lending is going to be far different from what anyone imagines today. The great strength of the Internet is not going to be in reducing the cost of acquisition to the megalender but in dramatically increasing the ability of the best people in the business to serve customers who cannot find them now."

Today, I am more convinced than ever that there are a large number of homebuyers and homeowners who will never use the Internet for these purposes if it means dealing with the low-service model that most of the recognized Internet lenders have adopted. This formula is not, and probably never will be, right for everyone. After 20 years in the business, and 2000-plus loans, one thing has become absolutely clear to me: Most borrowers do not give a hoot where the money comes from. Given that it may be from FNMA or FHLMC, it has that organization's brand on it, regardless of the originator. You know my philosophy from this book, and I think that many customers care about dealing with a person who cares about them. At some point in time, brokers may band together in a network, referring loans to counterparts in other states. Perhaps a step in that direction has been taken by Jack Guttenberg, The Mortgage Professor, at www.mortgageprofessor.com. Jack has developed the idea of the Upfront Mortgage Broker (UMB). UMBs, of which I am proud to be one of the first, pledge to treat their customers fairly and to disclose all fees and costs up front and not change them. For a list of UMBs, go to www.mortgageprofessor.com.

OTHER MORTGAGE INFORMATION WEB SITES

Perhaps the best source of rate information is at www.hsh.com, the Web site of HSH Associates, which claims, probably correctly, to be the world's leading publisher of mortgage and consumer loan information. You'll find lots of free information at the site, along with an inexpensive service for more detailed information about lenders and rates in your area. There is also a nifty calculator you can download from www.hsh.com/hbcalc.html. This site is also useful after you have chosen a lender, to keep informed of mortgage rates.

The Web site of *International Real Estate Digest* at www.ired.com is also worth visiting. Billed as "the world's foremost online real estate magazine," it was the Internet's first of its kind. Browse this site for its extraordinary amount of helpful educational information for borrowers and homebuyers.

At the home page of Microsurf, Inc., www.mortgagequotes.com, you'll find the rates of more than 1000 lenders posted. You select a state and program and go to a screen where you select points. If, for example, you choose 1 point, you'll get a screen that shows the rates at or about 1 point; from there you can go via hyperlink to the page of a lender you are interested in. Though I am in favor of service shopping rather than rate shopping, this site can be a handy source for checking on lenders in your area you may have otherwise missed. Note that some lenders here may be a little tardy in posting rates and thus might not appear to be competitive, when in fact they are.

FINANCIAL SERVICES WEB SITES

Though I advise you throughout this book to stay focused on service, not just rates, when you are in the market for a loan, you must keep track of mortgage rates, because they vary daily. You should also track the yield on the 30-year Treasury Bond, the so-called long bond, because when it rises, so will mortgage rates—and quickly. Conversely, when yield falls, mortgage rates will follow, although not as quickly. For this, the Internet is invaluable. If your loan is floating and you're within 30 days of closing, you can—and should—go online several times a day to check the yields. If you see the bond market tanking, call your lender and lock—fast! Don't wait until tomorrow because you will probably pay ¼ point more, $500 on a $200,000 loan.

The following are sites that carry financial information. Become familiar with them as a prelude to taking a more active role in your financial future and your real estate transactions. I would be somewhat wary of pricing shown at these Web sites. You can get some idea of pricing, but you may not be able to find any lender offering these rates.

Briefing.com at www.briefing.com is my favorite in this category. The service costs $6.95 per month, but it will save you much more in the long run. You'll also like the stock quote page. I like it more than others, particularly the charting choices.

Bloomberg.com at www.bloomberg.com, then click on U.S. Treasuries to go to a Treasury Bond page where you can see the treasury yield curve and much more data than most people can assimilate. It's helpful, nonetheless, in improving your understanding of the forces at work, forces that *will* have an effect on your mortgage rate.

www.bankrate.com, the Web site of ilife.com, provides all manner of financial data, research, and editorial information on noninvestment financial products, as the site correctly claims. You have access to financial data not just on mortgages, but also on credit cards, banking, and a host of other financial products. Because it's not just mortgage info here, this topic is not covered as comprehensively as at other dedicated sites, but I like its unbiased approach, and it is well worth checking out. I applaud the site also for having a hyperlink to www.consejero .com/esp/usa_home.asp, a Spanish-language site.

The Motley Fool, at www.fool.com, is one of the Web's most popular financial sites. Its irreverent approach is a like a breath of fresh air in the financial world. Though the site doesn't have much bond information of import to mortgage borrowers, you may want to become a permanent subscriber to the site just to help yourself get organized and to keep your head filled with fresh, original thinking.

PRICING

There has been very little research done on the motivation of borrowers as it relates to the Internet. One study, a survey at Gomez.com, mentioned earlier, indicated that 73 percent of borrowers were seeking a loan online because they thought they could get a lower rate and/or lower fees. That is, their most important criterion was to save money, as opposed to seeking reliable professional service. Because saving money is the number one concern of so many consumers, I will end this chapter with a discussion of pricing and then the effect of all this on the mortgage industry.

To begin, let me establish some rules of the game. You can measure the performance of an investment portfolio compared with some benchmark, such as the Dow Jones industrial average. Mortgage rates cannot be compared in the same way. The only public data we know are the average rates and points quoted by about 125 lenders in Freddie Mac's Primary Mortgage Market Survey (available at www.freddiemac.com/ pmms/rate0217.htm). This survey does not actually tell what loans people *actually get,* only what these lenders were quoting. Although it could happen, I have never heard of a borrower bragging to his neighbors saying, "I beat the Freddie Mac averages by 0.135 percent." That actually may be a valid method of comparison, but no one ever does it.

If 20 families all move into the same block during the same week, wouldn't it be nice to know that your interest rate was lower than everyone else's? But how are you going to find out? You can't, and neither can anyone else. Consequently, homebuyers feel as if they are competing with the industry for the best rates, not against their fellow homebuyers. Importantly, in that environment, a lender does not have to have the best deal; the loan rep just has to convince the borrower that he or she is close enough so that the borrower stops shopping. The borrowers' universe is composed of the half-dozen other lenders they talk with, and, to the extent that they use the online tools described here, whatever the Internet lenders are offering. If it were possible to find out the rates at which various borrowers were able to borrow money, and we plotted those figures, we'd get a bell-shaped curve like the one shown in Figure 10.9.

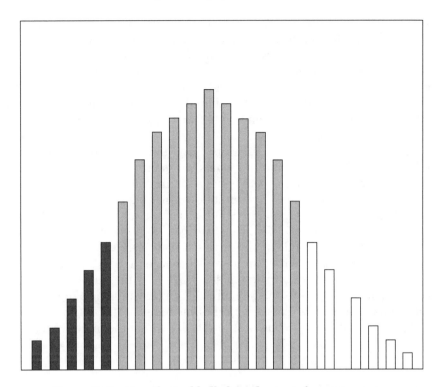

Figure 10.9   Hypothetical bell-shaped curve of mortgage rates.

Three items are important here. First, it's impossible for all borrowers to get a deal that is better than average, regardless of what they believe; nor can 50 percent of the people be in the top 5 percent. Second, exactly half the borrowers get a deal that is below average and the other half get a deal that is better than average; the majority of borrowers—in the middle—get about the same deal, typically from one of the largest lenders, which is how those lenders got to be so large. Third, only 5 percent of borrowers really get a great deal, one that is better than those that 95 percent of their neighbors get.

Approximately 10 million families got mortgages in this country last year—a staggering 40,000 every day. If you were to interview all 40,000, most would probably say, "I got a really good deal." The fact is that 50 percent of the people thought that the pricing at Norwest or Countrywide or Chase or Bank of America or Washington Mutual and the handful of other lenders that have 50 percent of the market was perfectly acceptable: 20,000 got a deal in the top half, and only 2,000 were in the top 5 percent. Therein lies the problem. How do you find those who were in the top 5 or 10 percent?

A lender that has a 5 percent market share has to sell 800 loans a day, loans that they originate at their retail branches, fund through brokers, or buy from their correspondents. I have friends who are pros in the secondary marketing department in charge of selling those loans—the guys who really know what's going on. When I asked them, "You buy loans from lenders who are doing loans on the Internet. Do you see their customers getting a better deal?" they answered, "The average Internet borrower gets a better deal than the average borrower gets from a traditional lender, but not any better than those borrowers who deal with the best of the traditional lenders." The conclusion that I have come to is that the Internet offers just one more service versus price model, one of the same kind of models we see in businesses all across the American economic scene. I believe the Internet has great promise, and personally, I am highly committed to making sure that my company is automated, computerized, and efficient; but I never forget that my clients want me to know them and be 100 percent committed to their success. Other lenders who have similar objectives will also continue to be successful with their clients because they will do an excellent job of meeting their customers' needs. Will the current Internet lenders succeed too? I think they will if they can find ways of meeting the needs of a broader cross-section of customers, not just those customers who will only do business at rates at which the lenders are losing money.

THE EFFECT OF INTERNET LENDING ON THE MORTGAGE INDUSTRY

What Internet lenders *are* doing is setting up one standard against which other providers are measured. To the extent that most Internet lenders offer pricing that is slightly better than the average in the industry, and that they are now highly visible to millions of consumers, they are a force the rest of the industry has to deal with. Does that mean that every lender has to adopt a low-service model to compete? I think not. In this book, it is natural to concentrate on those lenders with the largest share of the Internet market. What is more difficult is to remember that there is a far broader spectrum of companies available to consumers, some of which may offer a package of convenience, intelligence, experience, and caring service that might better meet the needs of consumers than the ones we have covered.

For comparison, there is no doubt that Wal-Mart, Kmart, Costco, and Sears have large market positions in the retail business. Yet an analysis of the retail industry that concentrated only on those companies would miss the point. Many more customers, in total, choose to do business with retailers other than those four companies. Similarly, about 97 percent of borrowers are currently choosing to do business with traditional lenders, even though a large number—perhaps as many as 40 percent—have visited lender Web sites in the process of getting information. The good news for the industry is that I think consumers are going to be much more astute when they ask questions like, "OK, you cost a little more. What am I going to get for that?" Those are questions that Nordstrom, Neiman Marcus, Bloomingdale's, and tens of thousands of other successful retailers have to answer every day, and they do it very successfully. I perceive that this process, instigated by the Internet lending phenomenon, is going to be an extraordinarily useful exercise for the health of the mortgage industry, too, and ultimately its customers.

SUMMARY

The single most important task for any borrower is to find a lender that matches his or her unique needs. Diligent, prepared borrowers can certainly get a better deal than those who do not spend the time and effort to prepare themselves.

What role should the Web play in your preparations? It all depends. As you have no doubt deduced from reading this chapter, the levels of service and the quality and quantity of helpful features at the various sites vary widely. Some borrowers—particularly those with clean credit profiles and experience in the homeselling/homebuying process—certainly may take advantage of the convenience of dealing online. In contrast, the person who is, shall we say, credit impaired or who needs a lot of handholding is probably going to be disappointed trying to get a loan in the low-service environment that currently exists online. As I've admonished repeatedly, assess your needs and resources carefully and then choose the channel that offers you the service that best matches those needs and resources.

Any business will move in the direction in which consumers drive it. As Internet lending develops as we enter the twenty-first century, it will be a potent force if it meets the needs of a greater percentage of customers. It is my fervent hope that customers will drive the mortgage business in the direction of more service, broader education, and greater customer care.

11

CHOOSING THE RIGHT LOAN

Mistrust the obvious.
—ARTHUR HAILEY

KEY POINTS

- The decision that will have the most significant impact on your long-term cost of home ownership is the type of loan you choose.
- The more risk protection you want, the more you'll have to pay.
- Everyone has a different propensity for risk.
- The ideal loan is the one that balances these factors in your household.

FITTING THE LOAN INTO A FINANCIAL PLAN

Whoever said, "Everyone is going to end up somewhere. If you have a plan, you'll end up where you want to be," was right. Rarely, I have clients referred to me by a financial planner who has laid the groundwork for the mortgage process. Such clients have a well-thought-out idea about what they want, something that fits into their overall financial plan. These clients are all too few. But you can be one of them. If you haven't already done so, I strongly recommend that you hire a professional who can help you plan for your financial future. If the professional is astute about mortgages, such counseling should include mortgage planning, because it is such a large part of everyone's financial picture. I talk about that topic in detail in Chapter 18, "Managing Your Mortgage." If you know more about mortgages than your financial planner, have him or her buy my books too, and have mortgage management be a part of your planning process.

In my experience, people go through the following phases in their economic lives:

Age 20 to 30	Young people, first-time homebuyers
Age 30 to 40	Maturing adults, often with growing families
Age 40 to 50	Approaching middle age, perhaps with children in college
Age 50 to 60	Approaching retirement; building equity and investments
Age 60-plus	Retired or close to it, in their last home

Each of these groups has different considerations when seeking a loan. Furthermore, people at every stage of life suffer the ups and downs of the economic cycle. Finally, in the world in general, at any given time things are either getting better or worse; rates are either up or down and are heading one way or another. Those factors, too, influence what constitutes the proper type of loan for people at any given point in time. Perhaps that sounds obvious to you, but let me remind you:

Most people get the wrong loan or pay too much for their loan.

People tend to go to one kind of institution or another based on marketing hype or past experience or because they don't know about or understand the alternatives. A friend of mine runs the conduit through which a lot of credit unions sell their loans. Credit unions are pretty much fixed-rate stores, and most do not have employees who are adept at explaining complex loans to the members. Typically, regardless of where we are in the business cycle, between 90 and 95 percent of the loans made by credit unions are 30-year fixed-rate loans. When you go into a big savings and loan association (S&L) that is probably a portfolio lender, you'll find that it has one-size-fits-all adjustable-rate mortgages. "Our loan is perfect for you!" the rep will say; and, in fact, many people will choose that loan, because they heard a well-crafted sales pitch. Do the members of a credit union and the customers of an S&L really have different needs or come from communities with different characteristics? Not at all; they just buy what they are sold. Though it may be easier to train the sales staff to sell a single product, in my view that's a patently absurd approach to the market from the consumer's perspective.

While reading this chapter, therefore, you should be particularly sensitive to your personal needs and goals so you can select the exact type of loan that will suit you precisely.

TYPES OF LOANS

The following are broad categories of generic loans currently available.

Conforming FNMA/FHLMC, Currently Less than $252,700

- 30-year fixed, 20-year fixed, and 15-year fixed loans, fully amortized

- 5/25 loans; fixed for 5 years, then fixed for another 25 years
- 7/23 loans; fixed for 7 years, then fixed for another 23 years
- A wide variety of adjustable-rate mortgages (ARMs)

Jumbo Loans, Greater than $252,700

- Thirty-year fixed, 20-year fixed, 15-year fixed, and 10-year fixed loans, fully amortized
- Interim fixed 3/1, 5/1, 7/1, and 10/1 ARMs (also called FIRMs) fixed for the first listed number of years, then turning into ARMs tied to the one-year Treasury bill (T-bill) index
- ARMs tied to T-bills, certificates of deposit (CDs), London Inter-Bank Offered Rates (LIBORs), 11th District cost of funds, and the prime rate

Again, these are just the broad categories. With specific differences, there are probably 300 or 500 different loans. Let's look at loans from the lender's perspective to understand why the industry offers so many choices.

THE PRICE OF MONEY PLUS THE PRICE OF INSURANCE

Lenders are really concerned about three things: money, insurance, and risk. On any given day there is a basic price for money, which is related to what lenders have to pay their depositors or the price at which a conduit can sell loans in the secondary market. That determines the lowest base cost to the consumer.

The insurance part of the price is what you pay for long-term rate protection. If you ask the lender to guarantee your rate for one year, you'll get one price. If you ask for 15 years of protection, you'll pay more—a premium based on how risky the market perceives the additional 15 years of rate protection to be. You can rightly conclude that the 30-year fixed-rate mortgage would have to be the most expensive product the industry offers.

Finally, lenders assess the more obvious risk factors. The more risk the lender perceives, the more you pay. If a prospective borrower has a poor credit history, the lender perceives that it has a greater risk of not getting its money back, so the risk part of the price goes up. At higher loan-to-value (LTV) ratios, there is less equity to protect the lender's interest, so the rate goes up.

Here's the first lesson in choosing a loan: Buy rate protection only for the length of time you'll be in the property. If you select a 30-year fixed-rate loan and you are in your home for only 7 years, you paid a lot of extra money for 23 years of rate protection that you didn't need. How much is that? Well, the industry offers loans that are fixed for just 7 years, and they are priced approximately ½ percent below 30-year fixed-rate loans. On a $200,000 loan, that ½ percent amounts to $1,000 per year. Choosing a 30-year loan initially instead of a 7-year loan would cost you $7000. Can you afford that? To easily dodge one of those expensive "risk adjustments," buy rate insurance only for the amount of time you are going to be in the house. Not every homebuyer knows this in advance, but many people do, and I just gave you 7000 reasons to consider this carefully. Millions of people make this mistake simply because they don't have someone like me to explain it to them.

The Yield Curve

People in financial circles talk about the yield curve because it is a very important concept in the management of large sums of money. Basically, it shows how the market values the yields on government obligations with varying maturities. Other financial instruments, such as mortgage loans, vary along with Treasury bills, notes, and bonds. This curve can be of value to borrowers in determining the general tenor of the times; it reflects how the market values the premium you might pay for longer-term rate protection. For example, the yield curve in Figure 11.1 is relatively steep, reflecting a large difference between short- and long-term rates. By comparison, the curve in Figure 11.2 shows that the market differentials are low, making the cost of long-term borrowing not much more expensive than that of short-term borrowing.

Finally, Figure 11.3 shows a comparison between the yields on Trea-

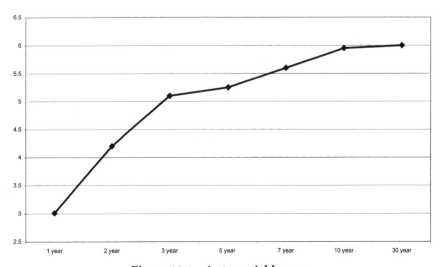

Figure 11.1   A steep yield curve.

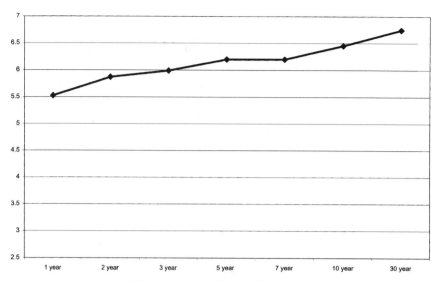

Figure 11.2   A flat yield curve.

sury instruments and the aggregated cost to a borrower of a one-year ARM (index plus margin; not start rate), various FIRMs (loans such as 3/1, 5/1, 7/1, and 10/1 ARMs), and finally, a 30-year fixed-rate mortgage.

We look at these data to see how expensive—or cheap—various loans are at a given point in time. If you make the assumption that

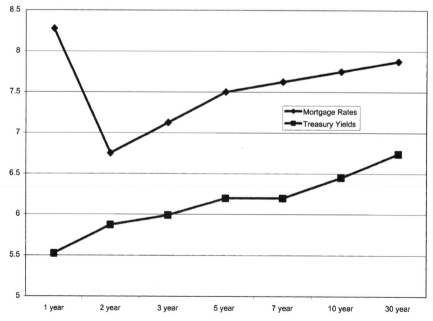

Figure 11.3   Mortgage rates versus Treasury yields.

lenders could invest in Treasury bonds if they wanted to, it follows that they will invest in (fund) mortgages only if they feel that the yields they can obtain on mortgages are enough higher than the yields on Treasury obligations of comparable maturity to warrant the risk. If the lender offered to make loans at the prices reflected in the higher curve, the difference between that curve and the Treasury yield curve could be interpreted as the markup, or profit margin, of that particular mortgage loan. You want a loan with the lowest profit margin (I hope!). Analysis like this helps you understand the opportunities more easily.

As you can see, Figure 11.3 shows that the largest markup is on the one-year T-bill ARM, which, by definition, has a markup equal to its margin of 2.75, making it a very expensive alternative. (Note that index plus margin—the rate after the first year—is seldom quoted, only the much lower teaser rate.) The markup for the FIRMs is lower, which is another reason I am so fond of them. This kind of analysis is a little obtuse for many people, I know, but the data are not hard to get. The Treasury yield curve is printed in many newspapers on a weekly basis, but an easier way to get it is to go (where else?) to the Internet. To see what the yield curve looks like today, go to www.bloomberg.com, then click on U.S. Treasuries.

Fixed Rate versus Adjustable Rate

The first question many people shopping for loans ask is, "Am I better off with a fixed-rate loan or an adjustable-rate mortgage?" The answer is twofold:

- If you are in a period of rising interest rates, get a fixed-rate mortgage. Even though you'll pay a higher rate initially, you'll save in the long run when the rates move higher.

- If rates are falling, get an adjustable-rate mortgage. You can refinance when rates are bottoming out.

That may sound too simple, but it's true. Anyway, it's the first issue to deal with. I can hear someone asking, "How do I know whether rates are rising or falling?" Well, I can't predict the future any more than you can, and if you find someone who claims he or she can, run, do not walk, in the other direction! However, I will point out that this is a cyclical world—the tide comes in and the tide goes out. If rates are or have been high, the next move will probably be down. Conversely, when rates have been down for a while, the next move will probably be up. Whether you are reading this book in 2000 or 2008, you probably have a pretty good feel for where rates have been and where they are going. Trust your intuition, but try to avoid making an emotional decision that leads to an unwise choice. Let's leave it at that.

Real Risk versus Perceived Risk

Next we need to evaluate risk factors—*your* risk, not the lender's risk. There are two types of risks: real and perceived. Real risk factors include being on a fixed income, having limited liquid assets, and so forth. People who work as ministers, teachers, or government employees have very little ability to change their income. (It's unlikely that a minister whose mortgage payment goes up $500 per month is going to start moonlighting by tending bar on Friday nights.) With some rare exceptions, my view is that ARMs are totally inappropriate for anyone on a fixed income.

I define perceived risk as the propensity to accept risk. Over the years, I can't think of anything I have done that is more important than helping people identify their propensity to accept risk. According to the people I interview, about 90 percent describe themselves as being "more conservative than average." That's a little silly when you think about it, because, by definition, exactly 50 percent of people are more conservative than average and the other 50 percent are less so. Let's call the first group "less willing to take risk than average" and the second group "more willing to take risk than average."

Most people in the first group are going to be predisposed to get a fixed-rate loan. They are more cautious, probably have more cash and investments, and probably have less credit card debt than average. In terms of their employment, more of these people gravitate toward jobs that are more secure. The people in the second group, to varying degrees, have the opposite characteristics.

Unfortunately, most people don't know which group they belong to. They become indecisive and uncomfortable even talking about risk. Let me tell you a funny story. A firefighter came into my office one day. Rates were moving favorably downward, and most people were interested in ARMs. So we talked about ARMs. His initial reaction to the ARM loan was, "That sounds scary!" I responded, "Wait a minute. You're a guy who runs into burning buildings, and you think *this* is scary?" He quickly added, "Well, I won't run into just *any* burning building." The point is that he knew enough about burning buildings to be able to tell which ones he could safely run into and which ones to stay out of. He had found a comfort zone about burning buildings. My job was to explain ARMs to him so that he could find a similar comfort zone about them. Once he felt comfortable, we proceeded to obtain an ARM for him.

Risk Wrap-Up

It may be stating the obvious, I know, but the ultimate protection against financial woes is wealth. But very few people—even those who have wealth—think of themselves as wealthy. Of course, everything is relative. Someone making $50,000 may think that a person making $500,000 doesn't have any worries. Well, people who make $500,000 worry, too; they just worry about different things. At every level in our economy, there are people who are comfortable and those who are stretched all the time, which is another facet of my propensity-to-accept-risk factor. A person's income or the amount of money a person has accumulated has very little to do with this factor.

I'll end this section with an illustration that demonstrates how you can use common sense to work through the decision-making process. With certain exceptions, people on fixed incomes should not have adjustable-rate mortgages. Here's a true example of one such exception. A teacher has inherited about $200,000, which she has invested in CDs and T-bills. She wants a loan, but fixed rates are unfavorable and ARMs are priced attractively. I analyze her situation with her. I point out that if rates go up 1 percent, her $100,000 mortgage will get more expensive by $1,000 annually. She is worried about this until I point out that the interest income on her investments goes up by $2000 for every 1 percent increase. That's twice as much. Because the increase in her interest income exceeds the increase in the cost of her mortgage, an ARM actually can't possibly hurt her. She is actually one of those people who should pray that rates increase. This sounds like a commonsense deduction, but it is not intuitively obvious when you first start thinking about it.

Risk Assessment Calculator

To assist in determining where you stand with regard to risk, get out a pencil and paper and start making notes based on the categories in Table 11.1. Give yourself 1, 3, or 5 points depending on how closely you fit the description.

You can see that if you are young and moderately advanced in your career, even though you may not have a lot of financial strength, your potential for rising income puts you in a position to take some risks. On the other hand, if you are approaching retirement, you are past the point of wanting to bet the farm on whether interest rates will go up or down. I hope you'll agree that it is worthwhile to think about these factors and to put them down on paper. Refer to this exercise as you continue to read.

CASE HISTORIES

I find that people can relate to individual experiences better than to generalities. Some of the following examples are composites, but the basic facts have been taken from my case files. I hope you find a case that mirrors your situation and helps clarify your thinking.

Young Couple

Joe and Alice Freeman are typical of many first-time homebuyers. They graduated from school a few years ago and have begun to build their

Table 11.1   Calculate Your Risk Tolerance

	1 Point	3 Points	5 Points
Age	Over 50	30–50	Under 30
Employment	Looking	Okay or uncertain	Very stable
Income	Scraping by	Okay	Very comfortable
Income potential	Stable	Growing	The sky's the limit
Resources	Little or no savings	Doing okay	Numerous investments
Credit balances	I was afraid you'd ask	Under control	Pay in full each month
Future burdens	Children in college	Under control	None
Insurance	Employer provided	Some	Plenty or no need
Investment profile	CDs at my bank	Mutual funds	Stocks, bonds, others
Return expected	2–5%	5–10%	More than 10%

Now add up your score.

	10–20 Points	20–35 Points	>35 Points
Profile	Risk intolerant	Can take some risk	Can take more risk
Alternative term	Cautious	Moderate	Aggressive

careers. They both have secure jobs. Joe and Alice want to start implementing their financial plan by purchasing a home; they want to feel secure before they consider starting their family in a few more years. Here are some of the variables they should consider when selecting a loan.

Federal Housing Administration (FHA) and Department of Veterans Affairs (VA) loans have historically been the best loans for people with low down payments, and though they are the loan of choice for some, the interest rates on these loans have been higher than comparable conventional mortgages. This, in my view, makes them the loan of last resort—to be sought only after other choices have been explored and rejected.

A common requirement of many low-down-payment loans is that the borrowers must have saved 5 percent themselves. After they have saved their 5 percent, they should try to get gifts from their parents to increase the down payment to 10 percent or even 20 percent. They could pay their parents 14 percent tax deductible and it would be about the same as paying non-tax-deductible premium payments to a private mortgage insurance (PMI) company. (Remember that lenders who provide loans for people putting less than 20 percent down almost always are required to get PMI coverage. The borrower pays for this policy at rates that generally vary from about one-third to one full percent of the loan amount annually, or $300 to $1000 per year on a $100,000 loan.) You should also investigate the so-called piggyback loans, in which an 80 percent-LTV loan is combined with a second mortgage for 10 or 15 percent of the price. This avoids PMI and can be cheaper.

Recently there has been a dramatic increase in first-time-buyer programs designed to accommodate people with 5 or 3 percent down payments or even none at all; for some programs the down payment can be a gift, even from a community housing assistance program. The cost of private mortgage insurance is high, but how else are you going to get into a home with a small down payment? Check www.fanniemae.com and www.freddiemac.com to see what is being offered currently. Many states also offer special programs. In California, the Public Employees Retirement System (PERS) and the State Teachers Retirement System (STRS) both offer attractive financing to those who are contributing to these funds for their own retirement.

Many of the first-time-buyer programs are set up only for 30-year fixed-rate loans. In contrast, studies show that most first-time buyers own their homes for only about seven years. For many people, a two-step loan will meet their needs. As of this writing, the Federal National Mortgage Association (FNMA) and the Federal Home Loan Mortgage Corporation (FHLMC) will make 7/23 loans at 90 percent LTV—but not 5/25 loans. However, there are many lenders who will do interim fixed-rate loans, such as 5/1 or 7/1 ARMs, at LTVs of 95 percent for loan amounts up to $300,000. Joe and Alice should ask themselves serious questions about how long they are likely to be in the property. If it's for five years or so, they should opt for an interim fixed-rate or two-step loan.

The following steps will prepare anyone in Joe and Alice's situation for home ownership.

- Live in a modest apartment or small home. Don't squander down payment money on expensive temporary housing.
- Start putting money aside every payday. If possible, live on one paycheck and save the other.
- Defer buying a new car.
- Don't allow credit card debt to build up.
- Eat at home and enjoy inexpensive entertainment and vacations.

- Discuss the possibility of financial help with parents and other family members who are in a position to help.
- Check your credit report, and correct errors you find in it.
- Find a good lender and get preapproved.

Single Mother

Jane Roberts is a recently divorced mother with a young child. She has a good job, and the divorce settlement awarded her both spousal support and child support payments. The previous family home was sold, and Jane's share of the proceeds will be used as the down payment on a new home for herself and her child.

Jane should evaluate how long she is likely to be in the home, but I would probably recommend that she stick with a 30-year fixed-rate mortgage. In my view, single mothers fall into the same category as ministers, teachers, and others who are not in a position to take much risk. Jane should choose a risk-free loan.

Many lenders offer loan programs through the Community Reinvestment Act (CRA), available only to people who make less than a designated percentage of the average income in a particular county. Since hers is a single-income household, Jane may very well qualify for such a program, which has more flexible underwriting guidelines.

Several other considerations are unique to Jane's situation:

- She will have to give the lender a copy of the interlocutory decree she received from the court, showing the mandated support payments. Many lenders also require evidence (via copies of checks from the ex-spouse) that she actually *receives* the support payments. You may wonder who bothers to keep them. That's my point! Keep them or provide bank statements that show those regular deposits.
- Jane should establish credit in her own name—get her own credit card account and close all joint accounts she has with her ex-spouse. That way, if her ex-husband is (or becomes) a flake, his behavior won't damage her credit. Though creditors for which she has an outstanding balance may not release her liability on the existing account, she can require that the card be closed to further purchases; when the existing balance is finally paid off, the account can be closed.
- Because child support payments are not taxable income, many lenders will increase them through a process known as *grossing up.* That will increase the income used in the calculations and thus the loan amount for which Jane qualifies.
- If she is paying child care costs, such as for a day care center, Jane should not put this information on the application unless

the lender requires it. If she does state it, lenders will count it as a negative, thereby reducing her ability to qualify for a loan. If she doesn't mention it, most lenders don't ask and don't care.

Middle-Aged Couple Buying a New Home

John and Brenda Francis have just celebrated their youngest child's college graduation. They no longer need their large family home and have decided to move to a smaller home. The significant financial characteristics are as follows:

- Because they will no longer be paying college expenses, John and Brenda have more disposable income.
- They probably have significant equity in their current residence.
- They are close to retirement.

Fifteen-year loans are ideal for people in this situation. John and Brenda probably do not want to make mortgage payments for the next 30 years, because they will not be working for 30 more years. For a home that is smaller and less expensive, they can get a 15-year loan for which the monthly payment is actually less than the one on their current home. Even if the payment were larger, they could accommodate a larger payment in their budget. As a retirement plan, owning a home free and clear is a great first step for many people. Just think about what your budget would be like without a mortgage payment!

Although biweekly payment plans have gotten a lot of publicity lately, when you read Chapter 17, "Understanding Fifteen-Year Loans and Accelerated Payoffs," you will learn that there is very little difference between a 15-year loan paid monthly and biweekly payments on a 30-year loan—except that the 15-year loan is typically ⅜ percent cheaper! That ⅜ percent makes the 15-year loan a much better choice.

Couple Moving to a Higher-Cost Market

Peter and Nancy Grant have just sold their home in Omaha for $200,000 and are moving to San Francisco. The Grants have discovered that comparable housing in California costs $500,000. They are experiencing the housing industry's equivalent of sticker shock! Even if Peter gets an immediate raise, it might not be enough for them to comfortably make a mortgage payment that is more than twice the amount of their payment in Omaha.

Their first step is to inquire about Peter's employer's relocation policy. Many companies have a mortgage differential payment program that pays some of the increased mortgage payment, based on regional cost of housing variations, phased out over a five-year period of time. We are presuming here that Peter's income will be rising, because in general only employees who are advancing are candidates for a job-related move. That means they have the ability to take greater financial risk than other people. They are also more likely to be transferred again. Consequently, this is one of those cases where a pure ARM with a low introductory rate or an interim fixed-rate loan such as a 3/1 ARM or 5/1 ARM would be the best choice.

If 30-year loans are at 8 percent, ARMs might have a start rate of only 6 percent, and a 3/1 ARM might be at 7 percent. An ARM with the potential for negative amortization might have a start rate even lower, perhaps 4 or 5 percent. Peter and Nancy can ease their payment shock significantly with these loans; for them, the future risk is almost certainly within acceptable boundaries. By the time the payment gets higher, Peter's bonuses will have started to kick in, making the mortgage payments more affordable.

Elderly Couple Selling Home and Downsizing

Bill and Fran Jensen are retired and have decided to sell their home to move to a retirement community. Let's assume the following:

- They have developed significant equity in their current home.
- Their income will be modest compared with that of their pre-retirement years.

Their first decision is whether to have *any* loan on the new property. With the tax law changes in 1997, most people will no longer incur a capital gains tax on the sale of their current residence. Therefore, there is no need to get a loan to save cash for paying taxes on the sale of their current residence. This decision depends on the tax situation of the borrowers and the availability of investments that earn a return higher than the cost of the mortgage. Let's review these issues.

If Bill and Fran's income is mostly from Social Security and pension benefit payments, it is likely that their marginal income tax rate is low. Everyone gets a standard deduction on their tax returns even if they rent. So if Bill and Fran's Schedule C expenses are not going to be as high as the standard deduction, the mortgage interest deduction has no value to them, effectively increasing the cost of borrowing. Thus they should consider paying cash for their new home.

A couple with investment income or income from rental properties in addition to Social Security would be in a higher tax bracket, and the deductions would be correspondingly larger. Other things being equal, they should get a mortgage. If they are experienced at investments, they will be earning significantly more than the cost of financing. If the cost of borrowing is 7 percent, and if Bill and Fran have a portfolio of stocks and mutual funds that yields 12 percent, they would be better off having a mortgage and adding to their investments. There are even situations where the after-tax cost of borrowing—4.5 or 5 percent—may be such that they can invest in tax-free investments such as municipal bonds and still come out ahead.

For people who do not have significant savings or who are used to the 3 or 4 percent the banks pay on savings deposits, it makes no sense to borrow at 7 percent and put the money into investments that yield only 4 percent.

As for the type of mortgage, 30-year fixed or 15-year fixed mortgages are appropriate loans for people who are not in a position to take any risks.

Single Woman Who Doesn't Plan to Get Married

Sheila Fisher is a single woman who does not plan to get married. She is secure in her career, has made maximum contributions to her company's 401(k) plan, and has developed a portfolio of investments. She is thinking about cashing in some of her portfolio for a down payment on a home.

First, she should carefully plan which assets to liquidate. If she sells stock to get the down payment, she should remember to set aside enough to pay any capital gains tax that might be due as a result of the sale. As discussed earlier, she should attempt to make as large a down payment as she can to avoid or minimize PMI premiums. She should ask her parents and relatives for help if possible. She should also consider borrowing against her 401(k) plan or individual retirement account (IRA). While this is usually perilous, many retirement plans allow special consideration for loans when the purpose is to purchase a principal residence. Specifically, the loan may be paid back over a longer period of time than the usual five-year period without incurring tax penalties. If Sheila has a sizable balance in her plan and wishes to use a portion of that for a down payment, she should check with her plan administrator and tax adviser.

Traditionally, the industry's approach has been that women can take less risk than men and should stick to fixed-rate mortgages. I have done lots of loans for career women, and I've come to the opposite conclusion. I believe that many women are better able to accept risk than men. If Sheila's career is such that she has opportunities for upward mobility, she can be bolder in her approach to mortgage selection than if she is a teacher whose income is likely to remain relatively fixed. I would recommend that she consider taking advantage of the lower rates of two-step loans (5/25 and 7/23) and 5/1 and 7/1 ARMs.

Bachelor Who's Loaded

Tom French is a bachelor who made a lot of money early in his career and invested it wisely. But he was so busy in his career that he put buying a home on the back burner. In addition, falling real estate values deterred him; but now the market in his area is turning around, and he is thinking that investing in real estate would be a good idea.

He's right. Every study I have ever seen shows that the long-term cost of owning a home is less than the cost of renting. If housing values are increasing, it is good timing for Tom. A person with abundant assets can afford to be very opportunistic about carrying a mortgage. Specifically, Tom is definitely not a candidate for a 30-year fixed-rate mortgage. If rates are at low levels, which I will define as being able to get a 5/1 ARM for 7.5 percent or less, Tom should take a loan and buy down the rate, as long as he can get a ⅛ percent reduction in the rate for every additional ⅜ percent point.

If rates suddenly jump higher than they have been in the past year—say above 8 percent when they have been below 7.5 percent—the likelihood is that rates will eventually drop. In that case, Tom should choose a 3/1 ARM or a 5/1 ARM with zero points and refinance when rates drop.

If rates are 7 percent or less, Tom should give serious consideration to getting a 15-year loan and buying down the rate, as just described. If his income is commensurate with his accumulation of assets, the larger payment is incidental.

Minority Couple

Bill and Martha Williams live in the inner city of a large metropolitan area, where they grew up. Bill has a good job in the construction industry. They are doing well financially, and they have saved enough money for a down payment on a home. As their children approach school age, they are considering moving to the suburbs, where they believe the educational opportunities are better. But they are worried about the higher cost of housing in the suburbs and whether they will qualify for a loan. They are also concerned about whether they will be treated fairly by a lender.

Although I hear from supposedly reliable sources that *redlining*—withholding loans in certain areas considered to be poor risks—is still practiced, the federal Equal Credit Opportunity Act and similar state legislation have alleviated the bias in lending in recent years. Nonetheless, it is not unreasonable for Bill and Martha to be concerned about this issue. Most national lenders are under constant regulatory scrutiny to ensure they don't engage in discriminatory lending practices. Under the provisions of the Community Reinvestment Act (CRA), lenders are urged to increase their lending in certain areas deemed to have been adversely impacted in the past. Lenders also target people whose income is less than the average income for their community.

Such lenders often will bend over backward to lend to people meeting minority criteria if for no other reason than because it will help them meet their mandated targets for such loans. In particular, such borrowers may actually receive preferential treatment. When they choose to, lenders can be somewhat flexible about income, credit, and qualifying ratios. In Bill's case, however, his income as a construction worker will fluctuate more than that of someone on salary, and fluctuating income is always a cause for concern among lenders. Having said all of that, I'm sure there are still lenders who will not work as hard as they should for certain borrowers, so Bill and Martha must choose a lender carefully.

The topic of community homebuyer lending is very complicated. One lender I use showed me a 10-page matrix explaining all the rules and various alternatives. Picking the right option is not an easy task. Bill and Martha need to find an expert in this field. They should seek advice from their real estate agent and then call the larger lenders in their area. They should be very specific about their needs so they can be connected with the right people. (The average loan rep will not be knowledgeable in this field, so Bill and Martha should continue the search until they find an expert.) Finally, most CRA programs are available for only 15- and 30-year fixed-rate loans.

SUMMARY

The decision that will have the most significant impact on your long-term cost of home ownership is the type of loan you choose. Most people follow the crowd and get whatever loan is most popular at the time, a costly mistake for most of them. I hope that I have provided sufficient incentive for you to spend some time analyzing your needs and that the examples will help you make an intelligent choice.

12

QUALIFYING

They are unwilling to make up or change their minds until the strong impression of unavoidably visible evidence compels them to do so. That's their frame of mind when they say, "We'll cross that bridge when we come to it."
—JOHN LUKÁCS

KEY POINTS

- Qualifying is not a totally rational process.
- Qualifying is based not just on facts, but on documentation.
- There are a number of ways to package your income that will help you avoid problems if you know the difficulties ahead of time.

The purpose of this chapter is to give you some background on underwriting, the process through which a lender determines whether you are qualified for the loan you have requested. The advent of the Internet has actually meant that this process can be easier for some borrowers. I will give you some information that applies to all borrowers and then explain qualifying for borrowers with stable, straightforward incomes.

NOTE In my first book, *How to Save Thousands of Dollars on Your Home Mortgage,* I devoted two chapters to qualifying—one somewhat like this one and a second devoted to the topic of borrowers with complicated incomes. All indications are that borrowers who use Internet lenders tend to have straightforward income characteristics, so in this chapter I do not discuss borrowers with complicated incomes. Furthermore, at least for the short term, the typical Internet lender's staff will be doing well to keep up with simple loans. If your income picture is complicated by bonuses, stock options, capital gains, or partnership income, your tax returns are probably more than 20 pages long and most online lenders may not have the experience and training to handle this type of more complex borrower profile. I encourage you to get my first book and study Chapter 15, "Qualifying 201." If, subsequently, you believe you are well prepared, you might consider using an Internet lender. However, I wouldn't recommend one of the high-visibility, high-volume lenders geared toward doing quick, easy loans.

OVERVIEW

Underwriting and qualifying are mysteries to most people. A typical comment I hear from lenders is, "We do commonsense underwriting." A day later, the person who said that may tell a customer, "We can't approve your loan because your borrower's ratios are 40.1 percent and we can't go over 40 percent." That doesn't seem like common sense to me. Today, however, we have computerized automated underwriting, technology that uses artificial intelligence to evaluate borrowers. These systems promise to result in faster processing, lower costs, and better service for our customers, and I for one am committed to using them as much as possible. These programs judge applications as a whole rather than focusing on trivial details—a common failing of the traditional underwriting process.

Using traditional underwriting methods, the vast majority of applicants have to deal with time-consuming paperwork and demanding loan processing and underwriting systems that are highly bureaucratic and run by human underwriters who must interpret the rules and apply them to each application. Artificial intelligence is changing the rules somewhat, to the advantage of the borrowers.

In short, the purpose of underwriting is to ascertain whether you are a good risk. The loan application package is designed to answer the three questions an underwriter has about you:

- Do you have sufficient, stable income that will enable you to make the loan payments on time?
- Does your credit history reflect that you pay your other bills on time?
- Does your property provide adequate collateral (value) to protect the lender's interest?

The balance of this chapter addresses the first question; the latter two questions are dealt with in other chapters.

THE QUALIFYING MODEL

The qualifying process basically draws a line between loans that will be approved and those that will be denied. An underwriter compares borrowers' incomes against their proposed housing payments and other obligatory payments to determine their eligibility. Above the line, you're approved; below the line, your loan will be denied. Who decides where the line is? Industry gurus study a large number of households to try to get a handle on what people can really afford. Having said that, it is no secret that even on a given income, because of spending habits and approaches to personal responsibility, some households are always in financial trouble and others are always comfortable.

Still, with enough data, we can start separating the two groups. Calculations of this kind give lenders a high degree of confidence that when they approve a loan, the borrowers will be comfortable with the payments, and it will be a "good" loan. You may have heard of the numbers 28/36, the most commonly accepted ratios used by lenders selling loans to the Federal National Mortgage Association (FNMA) and the Federal Home Loan Mortgage Corporation (FHLMC). There are no hard-and-fast rules, and many lenders use ratios more liberal than this, but every lender has a certain ratio comfort zone. The ratios used by the strictest lenders—*A lenders,* as they are referred to in the trade—are lower than those of the B lenders, who will approve loans that the A lenders turn down. All lenders, whether class A, B, or C, calculate the ratios, so it's important to discuss them. They are at the heart of the process of having your loan approved.

Ratios

A study done many, many years ago by the Department of Housing and Urban Development (HUD) determined that when less than 28 percent of a family's gross income was devoted to housing expenses and less than 36 percent of gross income was devoted to housing expenses plus recurring obligations, most people didn't have trouble making their mortgage payments. Conversely, when people devoted more than those percentages of income to those categories, they were more likely to be late on their loan payments and more likely to be candidates for default at some time in the future. These ratios define the dividing line between those whose loans are approved and those whose loans are denied.

Consequently, the first thing an underwriter does is to calculate those ratios. The *top ratio* is the ratio of your housing expense to your gross income, which is income before withholding for taxes, Social Security, and Medicare. Your housing expense is the sum of the mortgage loan payment (principal and interest), property taxes, and insurance (hence the acronym PITI, for principal, interest, taxes, insurance). Next, the underwriter adds the payments on your recurring bills, such as car loans and credit card payments, to arrive at a total monthly expense obligation. That number is divided by the gross income to arrive at the *bottom ratio.* The underwriter then compares your numbers against the standards required by the lender, perhaps 28 over 36 or some other number.

In short, qualifying is the process of comparing your income ratios and other factors such as credit history and down payment against the target ratios your lender uses to determine whether you are likely to be a trouble-free customer.

Automated Underwriting

A significant change to this process has been the development of automated underwriting (AUs) by FNMA and FHLMC. The goal was to reduce the time and expense of underwriting as well as the amount of paperwork, and to improve the quality of loans these agencies purchase. While Internet lending could have succeeded without AU, and AU would have succeeded without the Internet, their almost concurrent development has to be viewed as a victory for consumers. FNMA's Desktop Originator/Desktop Underwriter and FHLMC's Loan Prospector are welcome changes in an industry that has cried out for modernization and simplification.

The good news is that, as just stated, the new automated underwriting systems are making the loan approval process speedier and much more efficient. In the AU process, your employment, income, assets, and credit history are entered into a program that is connected directly with the FNMA or FHLMC computer. The computer's program compares your characteristics against a model and then either approves your request, denies it, or refers it to a human underwriter for further investigation. These models tend to be quite liberal, approving loans that no human underwriter, who typically feels all ratios should be 28/36 or better, would approve. With a clean credit report, even if your ratios are 40/50, you stand a good chance of being approved. If your income is simple to understand, you should breeze through the process, unlike borrowers using traditional methods.

NOTE You've probably heard of the Housing Affordability Index, prepared by a local university or government agency, which is the estimate of the percentage of households that can afford to own a median-priced home in a particular area. These statistics are derived by comparing median income with the median price of a home. You usually hear about it when housing prices jump, meaning people at the margin who qualified for a median-priced home a month ago would not qualify today. These statistics almost invariably use 28 percent of gross income (as just discussed) as the maximum allowable housing expense for qualifying. Obviously, if the AU models will approve borrowers with ratios almost twice as high, the Housing Affordability Index is of dubious value. That is another reason to seek advice and assistance from an expert—a mortgage professional—rather than from the newspaper. Borrowers who are concerned about qualifying should be encouraged by this advancement.

Any borrower seeking a loan on the Internet has a right to expect that his or her efficient, forward-thinking lender will be using either of these systems. By doing so, a lender can approve your application within an hour. Why wait a week or two for some lender to fiddle around with your loan when you can have such instantaneous satisfaction? Of course, lenders still have to get an appraisal, check your income documentation, and review your contracts and title reports, but the AU models typically require substantially less documentation. Consequently, when you are in the process of selecting a lender, one of the first questions you should ask is whether he or she uses one of these AU systems. If not, move on to another lender.

EMPLOYMENT AND INCOME STABILITY

The first task in qualifying is to evaluate the stability of your income. As a general rule, employment at the same job for more than two years is considered satisfactory. Some occupations such as construction, which provide income that is inherently more volatile, or at least more variable, require you to show that you have been earning money consistently for a longer period of time and have demonstrated ability to manage your financial affairs. If you have held several jobs in the same field in the last couple of years, you may be asked to prove future stability in the form of documentation from your current employer. A borrower who has been changing jobs for advancement within the same line of work will usually be more favorably considered than someone who has a record of frequent job changes without obvious advancement—what I call "job-flopping," as opposed to job-hopping.

The key to qualifying is income stability; if a borrower has maintained stable income even in the face of an erratic employment history, he or she will likely be approved. In addition, a borrower's financial history is important. Likewise, a borrower who has demonstrated a pattern of regular saving will have a much better chance of having an application approved than someone who spends all of his or her income.

Exceptions and Additional Documentation

There are a couple of exceptions to the preceding rules. If you are a recent college graduate, obviously you aren't going to meet the two-year rule, so plan on giving your lender a copy of your degree or transcript to prove that you just graduated. Likewise, if you were away on a long trip (in particular, if you were out of the country), out of work due to prolonged illness, on maternity leave, or have some other reasonable explanation, be straightforward with your lender regarding the circumstances. Don't wait for your loan to be denied before explaining a gap in your employment record. In all of these cases, I suggest that you include a letter from your current employer to show that your future looks stable even if the recent past does not. This also applies to overtime. For example, if a nurse gets overtime on a regular basis—say he or she works four 12-hour shifts per week—the lender may not count that income if there isn't a two-year history of such earnings. Again, a letter from the employer will help.

A person who has recently retired will be relying on Social Security income, retirement benefits, and income from stocks and bonds, none of which will show up on the previous year's tax return. If this is your situation, be aware that you will have to document this income. First, ask the Social Security Administration for an *Award Letter,* which describes the level of benefits to which you are entitled. Your former employer's Human Resources Department or the pension administrator can provide documentation about the level of your retirement pay. Income from a portfolio is more complex, especially if you have money in an individual retirement account (IRA), 401(k), or other tax-deferred plan. Though your assets may be earning a good return, this income will not yet have shown up on your tax returns. Assuming that you are more than 59½ years old, you are probably entitled to take distributions. Many underwriters have a tough time figuring such income, so you must help them by getting your financial planner or CPA to write a letter explaining your future income. In addition, even though you may have consistently earned a 10 percent return, most underwriters will assume that you will make only what the banks pay on CDs, perhaps 4 or 5 percent. So, for example, if you have $100,000 in your plan, they will give you credit for only $5,000 per year.

These days, when people are more often taking responsibility for their own investment decisions, capital gains income on a portfolio may be an important component of income. But if you, as an investor, have been selling your losses and keeping your gains, your tax return will be showing losses when, in fact, you may be making handsome, sizable gains.

TIP For conventional [not Federal Housing Administration (FHA) or Department of Veterans Affairs (VA)] loans, lenders use gross income before deductions to calculate qualification ratios. If you earn $1000 per month, deductions for Social Security, Medicare, and federal and state taxes will leave you only $700 or $800. But the amount used to determine qualification is $1000. A borrower who has income that is not taxable—Social Security or pension income, child support, or income from tax-free investments such as municipal bonds—is at a disadvantage in the system. To compensate for this, lenders use a procedure referred to as *grossing up,* whereby the underwriter increases the tax-free income figure by 20 to 30 percent to make it equivalent to taxable income. Using this system, a person with $1000 in nontaxable income would be considered to have constructive income of $1200 to $1300. If this applies to you, and it is important in qualifying, be sure to go to a lender who will use this procedure. Have your loan rep or processor check with the underwriting department to determine the factor to be used before you apply.

Do You Have Enough Income?

In my experience, people start thinking about buying a home when their income has risen to the point where they feel comfortable with the proposed payment on the home of their choice. The overwhelming majority of such borrowers usually qualify themselves, meaning they have a good comprehension of their financial capabilities and know the level of housing payment they can afford. That is not to say that these people understand all the components of the qualifying process. Perhaps they don't know much about property taxes, insurance, or homeowners' association dues and how they figure in, but usually when I ask people how much they can afford, they quickly respond with something like, "$1400 per month." About 90 percent of the time, they are correct. Nonetheless, before parting with $50,000, $100,000, or $500,000, the lender wants to make sure that you have sufficient income according to *its* calculations. This is what qualifying is all about.

Documenting Income

If you are an employee of a large company, you are probably paid a fixed hourly wage or a fixed salary every month, in which case no one will have problems determining your income. If your salary is $36,000 per year, you know it, your company knows it, and, subsequently, the lender knows it. No problem. If your rate of pay is $10 per hour, that's clear, too, although a lender will want to confirm that you always work 40 hours every week and that any overtime being factored in is consistent and ongoing.

Income is one thing; documenting it is another. No question about it, the mortgage industry's driving need for documentation can drive you mad. Even for people with simple, salaried income, documentation can be horrendous. In a typical case, a lender will ask for some or all of the following:

- W-2s for the previous two years [should be consistent with the Verification of Employment form (VOE)].
- A current paycheck stub, or perhaps two, to document one full month's income.
- A telephone verification of employment (if the lender requires a full Residential Mortgage Credit Report).

- Another paycheck stub within 30 days of closing (some lenders).

- A prefunding telephone employment check to make sure that you weren't just fired (although not all lenders require it, some will do this).

- A VOE, sent to your employer. This will show your date of employment, your current rate of pay, your income for the current year and the previous two years, and the likelihood of continued employment. These are seldom required with AU but may be useful in explaining unusual variations in income, such as maternity leave.

If your income is easily determined, and if you are working with a lender that uses AU, you've cleared one big hurdle, because you probably are going to have to show only last year's W-2 and a current paycheck stub or two. However, if you are among the tens of millions of people whose lives and incomes are more complicated than that, this is only the beginning. You'd be well advised to buy a copy of my first book, *How to Save Thousands of Dollars on Your Home Mortgage*, in which I cover complicated income streams in more detail.

Qualifying Yourself

To demonstrate how the mortgage industry makes those calculations, I'm going to suggest that you to complete a worksheet that is very similar to the one a lender uses. (Figure 12.1 shows what the worksheet looks like.) If you have a computer (and I'm assuming you do, otherwise you wouldn't be reading a book about using the Internet), I encourage you to re-create this worksheet on a spreadsheet program such as Excel or Lotus 1-2-3. The easiest way is to download the Qualify program from my Web site at www.loan-wolf.com/download.htm. Not only can you calculate your ratios, the worksheet allows you to compare four different alternatives side by side. I think you'll like it. Refer to Appendix 1 for a list of other Web sites that have qualifying programs available to you.

The worksheet is set up to compare several alternatives, not just one example. That way you can compare various alternatives side by side. For example, you can compare how you qualify for houses of different value. You can also set up the worksheet with the same loan amount and then check how your ratios vary with different loan programs and different interest rates. We'll go over this worksheet line by line, so keep referring to Figure 12.1.

1. Enter the property value of the home you are considering buying.

2. Enter the loan amount, which is the property value minus your down payment.

	Alternative 1	Alternative 2	Alternative 3	Sample
1. Property Value				$125,000
2. Loan Amount				$100,000
3. LTV				80%
4. Interest Rate				7.875%
5. Loan Payment				$725.07
6. Property Taxes				$114.58
7. PMI for Loans over 90%				
8. Property Insurance				$33.33
9. Homeowners' Dues				$128.00
10. **Sum = PITI**				$1,000.99
11. Recurring Bills				$325.00
12. **Sum = PITI + Bills**				$1,325.99
13. Borrower #1 Monthly Income				$2,400
14. Borrower #2 Monthly Income				$1,200
15. Net Rental Income				
16. Interest and Dividends				$100
17. Other Income				
18. TOTAL INCOME				$3,700
RATIOS				
19. Top Ratio				27%
20. Bottom Ratio				36%

Figure 12.1   Loan qualification worksheet.

3. Calculate the loan-to-value (LTV) ratio (line 2 divided by line 1).

4. Enter the interest rates of the various alternatives you are considering.

5. Calculate the loan payment (using either the payment function on a computer with a spreadsheet program, a financial calculator with a payment function, or a calculation from Appendix 2).

6. Enter one-twelfth of the annual property taxes, which is frequently about 1 percent of the property's value.

7. Figure the private mortgage insurance (PMI) premium. Use Table 12.1 to approximate the amount. (Note that 0.75 percent is ¾ percent. Divide by 12 and enter.)

8. Enter the property (fire or casualty) insurance premium. Unless you have a quote from an agent, use $400 or $500 and divide by 12.

9. For condos and planned unit developments, enter the monthly homeowners' association dues.

10. Add lines 5 through 10.

11. Insert your car payment(s) plus 5 percent of outstanding credit card balances.

12. Add lines 11 and 12.

13. Enter the first borrower's monthly income.

14. Enter the second borrower's monthly income.

15. Enter the net income from rental properties.

16. Enter interest and dividend income.

17. Enter other income not included earlier.

18. Calculate your total income by adding lines 14 through 19.

19. Calculate top ratio (line 11 divided by line 20, expressed as a percentage).

20. Calculate bottom ratio (line 13 divided by line 20, expressed as a percentage).

The sample column at the far right of Figure 12.1 shows what a typical borrower's numbers might look like. Completing this worksheet should help you zero in on a range of homes that you can afford. More powerful analytical tools are available for those who prefer to work on a computer, and you might investigate them. Most important, when you complete this worksheet you can be confident that an underwriter will analyze your application the same way and be more likely to approve your application quickly.

Table 12.1   Calculating PMI Premiums on a $100,000 Loan

LTV	PMI	Premium
95%	0.75%	$62.50 per month
90%	0.5%	$41.67 per month
85%	0.3%	$25.00 per month

Ongoing Bills and Other Recurring Obligations

I want to expand on recurring obligations, shown on line 12 in the worksheet. If you have outstanding credit card bills, you receive monthly statements showing the minimum payment due, which sometimes will coincide with the amount listed on your credit report and sometimes not. Table 12.2 shows what a portion of a credit report might look like.

Using the information on the report, your lender would calculate the payment on the ThirdBank Visa at 5 percent of the balance of $1780, or $89 per month, even though the statement may require a minimum payment of only $35. That's another reason to get a credit report now! The 5 percent may sound harsh, but it is not unreasonable; if you foresee a problem, that is, if you are pushing the bottom ratio and your report shows "Flexible" on all of your bills, you may want to take additional steps. Make copies of your monthly statements showing the actual minimum payment due and submit them with your application. You should also do this if you have cards that you pay off in full every month. Creditors report to Experian (formerly TRW), Trans Union, and the other credit report agencies on a monthly basis. If the balance on a card is $1806 on the fifth of the month when they report, and you pay it in full on the sixth, $1806 will appear on the credit report and the lender will be unaware that you paid it off. Therefore, the lender will add 5 percent of $1806, or $90 per month, to your monthly obligations, which will push up your ratios. To avoid this, submit copies of four, five, or six months' worth of statements with your application to show that you pay off the card balance every month.

There is some good news here, too. Note that the last car payment in the sample credit report had a balance of only $756, reflecting that only three payments remain. The rule is that if you have fewer than 10 months left on an obligation, it will not be counted.

TIP   If your ratios are a little high, and you have, say, 15 months left on a high car payment, you can send in six extra payments right now so that the lender's next report to the credit bureaus will show fewer than

Table 12.2   A Portion of a Sample Credit Report

Creditor	Balance	Payment
FirstBank Visa	$ 2,602	Flexible $65
SecondBank M/C	$ 2,468	Flexible $52
ThirdBank Visa	$ 1,780	Flexible [see comments in text]
ABC Auto	$12,456	48 @ $461 [meaning it is a 4-year loan]
XYZ Auto	$ 756	36 @ $256 [see comments in text]

10 payments remaining. The lender will delete this from your bills so it won't negatively affect your ratios. This does not, however, apply to car leases, because at the end of the lease, you have to give the car back, and, presumably, get another car with another car payment.

The purpose of doing all of these calculations at home *before* looking at houses or talking with lenders is to give you a good idea of how mortgage lenders will view your application. For example, if you calculate your ratios to be 40/50, you know that you are reaching for too large a loan. Most people, however, will discover that they are in the ballpark. Remember, most people know what level of housing payment they can afford. That said, after reading this book and coming to a conclusion about the kind of loan that is best for you, have your lender preapprove you for a loan sufficient to purchase the home you want.

SETTING STANDARDS

An A loan from an A lender will have the lowest rates. If that's what you want to qualify for, shoot to keep your numbers under 28/36, and you should have no trouble getting approved. If, however, your ratios are higher than that, don't be discouraged. There are a number of exceptions to these limits, and many lenders will routinely approve higher-ratio loans, especially if they use an AU system.

Next, as a means of assessing the risk of your loan, lenders will look at loan-to-value (LTV) ratio. If you are putting only 5 percent down and want a 95 percent loan, you will have to have all your ducks in a row. There is simply not enough equity in the home to protect a lender in the event of default, so you will have to prove income that is more stable and stronger than average, and you will also have to have an excellent credit history. If you are putting 20 percent down, these criteria are relaxed. If you are putting more than 25 percent down, the lender will be even more tolerant. Table 12.3 gives you some examples from one lender's manual.

Table 12.3   Qualifying Ratio Varies with LTV

LTV	Acceptable qualifying ratio
If LTV is >80 percent	28/36
If LTV is <80 percent and income is:	
<$75,000	40/40
$75,000–$150,000	42/42
>$150,000	44/44

As you can see, these ratios are more lenient than those previously discussed. Even traditional lenders will approve high-ratio loans as a result of Community Reinvestment Act (CRA) programs. Most of the large banks have responsibility under CRA to fund a target number of loans every year. If you think you are a candidate for a CRA loan, check at bank Web sites. (I was able to find only one bank that devoted a page to this topic, so you may have to work a little harder to find an accommodating bank in your area. Just ask when you call, because virtually all lenders have CRA responsibilities and programs.)

My experience with automated underwriting is that it is far more lenient than a human underwriter would ever be. I had a loan with a 55 percent ratio approved recently—all the more reason to work with a lender that uses AU on all of its loans.

It should be clear by now that higher income and a higher down payment can work to your benefit. Here are a couple of other important points:

- If you've gone through the worksheet calculations, and your analysis shows that your ratios are high, your search for a lender should concentrate on those with more liberal underwriting policies. The policies dictate whether you will be approved, and therefore are more important than the rates. That is, you must go ratio shopping first, prior to rate shopping. As sure as God made little green apples, some lenders will turn down loans because the ratios are 1 percent higher than some standard they have been told to enforce.

- Any competent employee of a lender will know how flexible the underwriters are, but you need to get employees to be honest with you about this. This is another reason why preapproval is important. You can get preapproved either for free or for the cost of a credit report (about $20). If you run up against a problem, you have plenty of time to find another lender that is more flexible.

FHA AND VA LOANS

The preceding discussion centered on conventional financing. But many buyers are interested in *FHA loans*—those insured by the Federal Housing Administration—or (for those in the military and eligible veterans) *VA loans*—loans guaranteed by the Department of Veterans Affairs. In this section, I want to discuss qualifying for these programs. First, it's important to point out that most Internet lenders do *not* process FHA and VA loans on the Internet, so your search may be a little more involved than that of the average borrower who is looking online for a conventional loan. One that does deal with FHA and VA loans is Quicken Loans, which I discussed in Chapter 10, "Getting a Mortgage on the Internet: Part Two." By the time you read this, others may be following suit.

Second, keep in mind that anything connected with the government involves extra paperwork, and will therefore be more time consuming than if handled by private industry. FHA and VA loans used to take as long as 90 days to approve and fund! Even half that time is unacceptable from a service standpoint. The good news is that very recently, both the FHA and VA announced that they will accept the underwriting decisions of the AU systems in underwriting loans they will purchase. This will dramatically reduce processing time. Moreover, some lenders have *direct endorsement authority*, which means they can approve your loan without submitting it to the FHA or VA. If you are hoping to get an FHA or VA loan, I strongly suggest that you deal with such a lender, so make sure that the first question you ask when you are interviewing lenders is whether they have direct endorsement authority. If you do not get a straight answer immediately, move on.

Traditionally, FHA and VA loans (the industry calls them *govies*) have been the best option for those able to make only minimal down payments. Today, eligible buyers can still get a VA loan with no down payment at all, and the FHA offers programs to accommodate 3 and 5 percent down payments. In addition, FNMA and FHLMC have recently announced similar programs. Both the FHA and the VA have dozens of special programs to assist various special groups—from those with disabilities to Native Americans. For example, the FHA's 203(k) rehabilitation loan program will provide funds to purchase *and* rehabilitate a property, which is really good news for the borrower who wants to purchase a fixer-upper.

Another important factor to keep in mind is that historically the FHA and VA have been almost universally more lenient than other lenders both about qualifying ratios and credit—although with the advent of AU, the differences may have lessened or disappeared altogether. So, given the less strict down payment requirements and the more lenient underwriting, why doesn't everyone get one of these loans instead of conventional financing? There are four very specific reasons:

1. VA loans are available only to those who have qualified by virtue of their military service.

2. Maximum loan amounts, while close to FNMA/FHLMC limits, are typically lower. In the case of the FHA, the limits vary by county, depending on HUD's determination of housing costs in that area. FHA limits may be $100,000 less than FNMA/FHLMC limits. For up-to-date information, check out your local FHA office in the phone book, or go to www.hud

.gov/fha/sfh/sfhhicos.html, where you will find a list of the
loan limits for all areas.

3. Although this is a moving target, the mortgage insurance premium (MIP) on government loans is currently slightly higher
than the PMI premiums on conventional loans. This difference becomes more dramatic as the down payment amount
increases.

4. Pricing on government loans has recently been substantially
deregulated. Formerly, HUD established a fixed interest rate
that was below conventional rates, and the seller of the property had to make up the difference (sometimes many thousands of dollars). Builders didn't care because, frankly, they
factored in this probable expense when they determined the
cost of their homes. Sellers in the resale market frequently
would not accept offers from FHA or VA buyers because they
did not want to pay the points required to bring the rates up to
competitive levels. Today, the market rates on FHA and VA
loans are influenced largely by the same forces that determine
the pricing on conventional loans, except that FHA and VA
loans are more expensive. At the time of this writing, the difference is about ¼ percent in rate or 1 point in fee, a huge
amount.

Finally, let me add one more reason. Although no one wants to
talk about this, I believe that some borrowers choose conventional
financing first and then, if eligible, switch to a govie if they get turned
down. This means that FHA and VA borrowers, as a group, have
become somewhat stereotyped as less qualified in general. Sadly, this
has led to a situation whereby the lenders will take advantage of their
customers who aren't qualified for other, more competitive programs.
My funding sources confirm that the commission income to brokers
on government loans averages about 1 point higher than on conventional loans. Remember that government loans are also priced about 1
point higher, so the total difference is 2 points, or $2,000 on a
$100,000 loan. No doubt HUD and the VA assume that market forces
will act to keep things fair, but I do not see that happening. This is yet
another reason to heed my advice about searching for a trustworthy
lender. If you want an FHA or VA loan, you need to be especially
wary. It is too soon to tell whether this will be true of Internet lenders
doing these loans.

One final note on the plus side: Sometimes a condominium project will have been approved by HUD when it was built. It may be that
too many units in the project are occupied by renters, disqualifying the
project for lending by conventional lenders. The good news is that the

original HUD project approval will likely still be in effect, thus qualifying you for an FHA loan when all other sources won't approve it.

OTHER LOAN PRODUCTS

Subprime Loans

Only a couple of years ago, you would have been hard pressed to find anything but A lenders on the Internet. Today, many lenders routinely offer *subprime loans,* also know as *B/C loans,* to borrowers who do not meet the stricter standards of the secondary market. Be wary if you are told that you don't qualify for an A loan and your lender offers to switch you to a B/C program. A subprime lender told me recently that almost 50 percent of his clients could have qualified for A rates if someone who knew what he or she was doing had packaged the loans. Those clients either had chosen an incompetent lender or, worse, one more interested in increasing his or her compensation. The compensation on B/C loans is typically two or three times that on A loans. For example, on a $150,000 loan, an A lender may make $2,000, whereas a B/C lender funding the same size loan might charge $5,000. This is an important consideration if you are considering getting your loan on the Internet, because online you have fewer ways of determining the competence of the lender personnel you are dealing with.

No-Income-Documentation Loans

Because AU makes life simple, most Internet lenders concentrate on *conforming loans*—those bought by FNMA and FHLMC. As a result, the *EZ Qual* or *no-income-documentation* loans have been overlooked by most lenders. (Neither FNMA nor FHLMC makes these loans, because these organizations want to see income documentation.) However, EZ Qual loans are alive and well, especially for jumbo loans [those greater than the current (year 2000) limit of $252,700]. You will be expected to have good credit, and, for fixed-rate loans, to be able to make a larger down payment—say 25 or 30 percent—to qualify for these loan programs. There are exceptions to this. Many portfolio lenders that do adjustable-rate mortgages (ARMs), such as savings and loan associations (S&Ls), originate loans for their own portfolios (rather than selling them). These lenders routinely do EZ Qual loans with 20 percent down. I get faxes from lenders offering to make these loans for borrowers with only 5 percent down—but at a steep price. If you want an EZ Qual loan, you'll probably have to search beyond the well-known lenders.

Equityline loans are also available on the Internet, although my first choices for these are the credit unions and large banks that may make competitively priced loans with zero up-front fees. I'd check local sources first before going to the Internet.

SUMMARY

In some ways, the real estate industry mortgage has become more rigid, with the rule books getting thicker and thicker every year. Yet, from my point of view, the industry is more ready today than ever before to accommodate borrowers with almost any profile. Internet lenders offer more programs at competitive rates than ever before and compete well across the board with traditional lenders. But before you enter the fray, again I caution you to do your homework by qualifying yourself using the tools described in this chapter. Then use that knowledge to your best advantage, negotiating from a position of power. I want you to be among those consumers most empowered to carve out an attractive deal.

13

CHECKING CREDIT

It's not what we know that gets us in trouble. It's what we know that ain't so.

—WILL ROGERS

KEY POINTS

- Your credit rating is an important factor in determining whether you will be approved for a loan.
- The better your credit rating, the better the pricing you will get.
- Lenders may view the slightest amount of derogatory information as an excuse to downgrade you to a B/C loan, which is more profitable to them.
- There are a number of ways you can clean up your credit and improve your credit rating.

A cornerstone of the mortgage underwriting process is the assumption that people will act in the future as they have in the past. Past income is an indicator of future income, with allowances made for raises and promotions. If borrowers have paid their bills in a timely manner in the past, they will probably continue to do so. There is ample justification for this belief: My experience indicates that people with an excellent credit history will maintain it 99 percent of the time. The flip side of that coin—that those who were flakes in the past will be flakes in the future—is just not true. Many responsible people have professional, health, or financial problems that thrust them into a period of financial difficulties; after they solve those problems, they often return to financial stability and resume their responsibilities. Of course, there *are* flakes—people who seem not to understand the words, "I hereby promise to pay. . . ." It is difficult for lenders to differentiate between the two, because flakes often are very successful at masquerading as responsible citizens.

CREDIT REPORTS

The mortgage industry tries to determine creditworthiness by running credit checks. Two types of credit reports are acceptable: the Three-Bureau Merged Report and the full Residential Mortgage Credit Report. The Three-Bureau Merged Report is prepared after a local agency checks with three credit-reporting bureaus, such as Experian (formerly TRW), Trans Union, and Equifax. This report typically costs about $20. The Residential Mortgage Credit Report is more inclusive, because the agency also conducts a telephone verification of the applicant's employment and a check of public records for judgments or liens filed against the borrower. The additional work increases the cost to about $50.

   TIP Almost all lenders now accept the Three-Bureau Merged Report, so tell your lenders they can get any report they want but you will only pay only $20. You'll save only $30—but it's *your* $30.

   As a borrower, you want the opportunity to check the report before a lender sees it to confirm its accuracy. This is essential, because industry sources estimate that over 50 percent of the reports contain some inaccuracies, and that 90% of these inaccuracies are negative. So as soon as you even think about buying a home or applying for refinancing, get your credit report from one of the bureaus; better yet, spend $20 and get a merged report. It takes time to correct errors, and you'll need all the time you can get.

   Figure 13.1 shows a sample report prepared by the credit agency I use. Study the report carefully.

What's in the Reports?

The bureaus retain records on consumer accounts for 7 years and on bankruptcies and other legal claims for 10 years. That's a long time, considering most of us can't remember what we did last week. A common response of people when they see their report is, "I can't believe that they keep track of that stuff!" Well, they do, so you have to deal with any error that pops up years later.

   The reports I use have a useful format. The data are divided into the following categories: credit scores, open accounts, closed accounts, collection accounts, and derogatory accounts. The first category shows all accounts on which you currently maintain a balance. This is used to determine the amount you pay on your bills when the qualifying ratios are calculated. A lender will compare this list with your application to determine whether you have disclosed all open accounts—obviously, the lists should correlate. Lenders get upset if you neglect to mention important accounts. This section also shows any account that a creditor reports as open, even though you may not have used it for years. The

INDEPENDENCE MORTGAGE CO

Preview Credit Report 03/07/2000

INFORMATION
Network
4344 Latham St., Suite 110
Riverside, CA 92501
(909)788-8070

Bureau(s) Inquired: XP (800)831-5614:
Date(s) Ordered: XP: 03/07/00

Ordered By: InfoNet	Loan Officer:	Branch:

Consumer Information

Borrower: CONSUMER, JONATHAN QUINCY   **Co-Borrower:**
548-60-3388

Current Address: 10655 N BIRCH ST , BURBANK, CA 91502

Scores

Fair Isaac JONATHAN QUINCY CONSUMER *999-99-9909 (?1)
Score: +205 Factor 1: 06 Factor 2: 01 Factor 3: 02 Factor 4: 11
Factor 1: Number of finance company accounts
Factor 2: Current balances on accounts
Factor 3: Delinquency reported on accounts
Factor 4: Current balances on revolving accounts

Fair Isaac JONATHAN QUINCY CONSUMER *999-99-9909 (?1)
Score: +611 Factor 1: 02 Factor 2: 22 Factor 3: 21 Factor 4: 03
Factor 1: Delinquency reported on accounts
Factor 2: Account(s) not paid as agreed and/or legal item filed
Factor 3: Amount past due to accounts
Factor 4: Too few bank revolving accounts

Account Name Account Number Reported-Under	Date Open Reptd	Hi-Cred Loan Typ	Payment Terms	Bal	30	60	90	Mo Rev	Last Late	Account Status ECOA Payment Pattern

Open

CENTRAL BANK 23802654388 JONATHAN QUINCY CONSUMER 999-99-99 (?1) XP: 1132912	12/93 12/93	$22,350 AUTO	$465 048	$11,050	0	0	0	31		CURRENT ACCOUNT INDIVIDUAL CCCCCCCCCCCCCCCCCCCCCCCCCC

Special Comment: [Balance Date: 6/96]

| HEMLOCKS
8285130111261
JONATHAN QUINCY CONSUMER 999-99-99 (?1)
XP: 2313849 | 02/95 02/95 | $900
CHG ACCT | ---
REV | $0 | 0 | 0 | 0 | 17 | | CURRENT ACCOUNT
AUTH USER
BNCCCCCCCCC-CCNNC |

Special Comment: [Balance Date: 6/96]

Collection

| CREDIT AND COLLECTI
98E543182136
JONATHAN QUINCY CONSUMER 999-99-99 (?1)
XP: 3980999 | 09/94 09/94 | $500
UNKNOWN | ---
UNK | $250 | 0 | 0 | 0 | 20 | | COLLECTION ACCOUNT
JOINT
9999999999999999999 |

Special Comment: [Balance Date: 4/96]

Derogatory

| MOUNTAIN BK
3562A0197325346R1234535
JONATHAN QUINCY CONSUMER 999-99-99 (?1)
XP: 1119999 | 03/93 05/96 | $43,225
SECURED | $956
060 | $19,330 | 3 | 0 | 0 | 39 | 5/96 | DELINQUENT 30-3
JOINT
1CCCCCC1CCCCCCCCCCCCCCCCCC |

Late 30: 10/95
Subsequent lates occured before: 3/94
Special Comment: [Balance Date: 5/96]

| BAY COMPANY
525556601
JONATHAN QUINCY CONSUMER 999-99-99 (?1)
XP: 2390446 | 01/68 03/96 | $1,400
CHG ACCT | $10
REV | $55 | 1 | 1 | 1 | 99 | 2/96 | CURRENT WAS 90
AUTH USER
CCC321CCCCCCCCCCCCCCCCCCCC |

Late 60: 1/96 Late 30: 12/95
Special Comment: [Balance Date: 5/96] Account previously in dispute - now resolved - reported by subscriber

Inquiry Information

Figure 13.1   Full page 1 of a typical credit report.

Closed Account category is not important unless there are some derogatory items. If you have closed an account yourself, be sure the reference doesn't say, "Account closed by Grantor," the implication being that you didn't pay so they closed it!

The next section addresses credit scoring; most of the rest of this chapter is devoted to derogatory accounts, called *derogs* in the industry, and actions you can take to eliminate erroneous information and improve your rating.

CREDIT SCORING SYSTEMS

Credit scores will be of growing importance in the coming years. Many retail stores and other lenders have been using scoring systems for years, especially when they have to make an instant decision to extend credit. The Federal National Mortgage Association (FNMA) now requires that all loans sold to it include credit reports with credit scores. The scoring systems were developed by Fair, Isaac and Co., hence the acronym FICO. Experian's scoring system uses the FICO designation. Equifax's system is called Beacon, and Trans Union's is Empirica. The scores are never the same, partly because all the bureaus have different credit data reported to them. On a Three-Bureau Merged Report for two borrowers, six different scores will appear. Lenders typically use the middle value in their calculations, meaning that if the scores are 686, 672, and 661, the lender will use 672 in its determinations.

Here's the problem. These statistical models use an algorithm that takes the data, processes them, and comes up with a score. When you look at 100,000 people, there is a strong correlation between these scores and the rate of foreclosures. For example, if you were going to buy a $50 million loan portfolio from a bank, you could process the credit information and come up with the likelihood of default in that portfolio. That would affect your desire to buy it and the price you were willing to pay. In the world where loans are bought and sold in high volumes, this is important.

In spite of the protestations of Fair, Isaac and Co. that it never intended its credit scoring system to be used to predict the likelihood of a particular borrower's loan going into default, the mortgage industry chose to ignore this advice.

 TIP To find out more about the topic of credit scoring, go to the Federal Trade Commission's Web site at www.ftc.gov/bcp/conline/pubs/credit/scoring.htm. You may also go to the Web sites of each of the bureaus, as listed later, or to the horse's mouth at www.fairisaac.com. Another excellant discussion of scoring is at www.realestateabc.com/loanguide/fico.htm.

Because lenders like things easy, they have adopted underwriting rules that judge individuals on a case-by-case basis based on their credit scores. Even the people who designed the system say that lenders should not do this, but they do! For example, I know of one borrower who had a 659 score—not bad—but the lender would not make the loan because the program called for a minimum score of 660. I'm not kidding. I have heard lenders make comments such as, "I can't do that loan because the FICO score is less than 700," or "If the score is less than 660, we won't consider it." One major lender turned down a loan with an 80 percent loan-to-value (LTV) ratio for a borrower with $25,000 in the bank, $131,000 in his pension plan, a 15-year history of owning his own company, and ratios of 23/24. His sin? He prefers to pay cash for things and had just a few cards that showed a short history of usage. This borrower scored low due to his brief credit history, and no one—not even the chief underwriter—would override the computer, despite the fact that this customer's overall financial strength was greater than that of 90 percent of all borrowers.

Underwriters should be looking for a reason to *approve* loans, but that is just not the case in the real world, Internet or no. In my view, if the FICO score is high enough, lenders should ignore the minor derogs, because the scoring system says these are not important. If an applicant has a score that is lower than desirable, the underwriter should look at the specifics of the report to determine whether the borrower is being unreasonably penalized for some petty derog several years ago.

The good news is that the automated underwriting (AU) models used by FNMA and FHLMC have credit evaluation systems that are more user-friendly than the raw scoring system. The new systems focus on the credit history and are forgiving of derogs that are more than a couple of years old. In my experience with AU, if the credit history in recent years is reasonably good, the loan will be approved even if the underlying scores are lower than 620, the cutoff for many A lenders.

In contrast, for those lenders using traditional underwriting, credit scores provide a new excuse to deny a perfectly good loan. With that in mind, you need to learn which factors lead to lower scores and what actions you can take to improve your credit score.

Though the systems at each of the major bureaus will produce different scores, they have a number of common factors. Lenders develop criteria similar to the following based on those scores.

- If the score is above 720, borrowers may qualify for improved pricing.
- If the score is above 680, the loan will qualify for special, or streamlined, processing. Translated, this means the lender is happy with the borrower and won't ask as many questions, so approval will be faster.
- If the score is between 620 and 680, the lender will evaluate the borrower further.

- If the score is less than 620, an A lender may want to see off-setting positive factors that will justify approving the loan.

FICO scores may be a blessing to some borrowers, but they will be a curse to others. Streamlining the process for squeaky-clean borrowers is laudable, but the bureaucratic mind tends to focus on what is wrong rather than what is right. Therefore, I caution you: Do not underestimate the anguish this mentality can cause you.

A buzzword among lenders these days is *risk-based pricing*. This is especially true for the subprime lenders—those who lend to people with less than perfect credit. Theoretically, a large purchaser of loans could establish criteria as shown in the preceding text and adjust the pricing matrix accordingly. If you are a credit-impaired borrower, you should seriously investigate this avenue, because the pricing may be more attractive than the typical subprime pricing approach ("How much can we nick them for?").

Score Factors

The credit scoring process is purposely made mysterious because industry professionals believe that if it were known, someone would figure out a way to beat it, thus making it meaningless. I have seen a lot of credit reports since this system was introduced, and I have come to the following conclusion: At a basic level, the system works, but like all other rule-driven systems, it is sometimes unduly harsh on certain individuals.

We do know that the following factors will reduce your FICO score:

- A number of open accounts (the weight lenders give to unused accounts is not clear)
- A number of open accounts with balances
- A number of accounts with balances close to or at the limit
- A number of inquiries from other creditors
- A number of accounts with derogatory information
- A number of collection accounts, tax liens, or judgments

At first glance, most of these criteria make sense, but on closer inspection, they don't account for lifestyle differences due to income. Three credit cards may be too many for one person, but may not adversely affect the financial situation of another. Perhaps more important, the FICO system does not take into account those people who use credit cards for convenience and pay them off every month. More ridiculous is that an executive who travels extensively and routinely runs up as much as $10,000 on a credit card but pays it off when he or she receives the expense check is still penalized under this system.

Another problem with scoring is the time it takes to change a score. Under the old system, if you had an error on your report, you could ask the creditor to send you a letter to correct it, show the letter to your lender, and the lender would ignore the derog. Under the new system, even though you obtain error apology letters from a creditor, it will take some time—perhaps several months—before your FICO score changes. This is not desirable when you are under a deadline to buy a house.

The point is that if your FICO score is lower than the lender's limit, you may be in for a disappointment. That is why I recommend that you get your credit report early in the process so you have time to correct errors. If your FICO score seems lower than your credit warrants, don't deal with a lender that places emphasis on FICO scores. As I write this, about half of the lenders I know don't seem to use these scores—but the other half do, so your lender shopping should include this question: "How does your underwriting department use FICO scores to evaluate loans?"

A more recent development is the introduction of legislation in California that will require the credit bureaus to tell consumers what their credit score is. Perhaps as a result, Fair, Isaac and Co. has recently announced that it will allow the bureaus to disclose scores. For recent developments, go to the company's Web site at www.fairisaac.com.

Getting a Credit Report on the Internet

By law, consumers have always been able to get their reports from one of the major credit report agencies by calling or writing them. In a few states, the law says they must be provided free of charge, but most will require a small fee (currently $8 or less). Now, in addition, you can order the report online by going to these Web sites:

Equifax	www.econsumer.equifax.com/equifax.app/welcome/pgconsumerproducts
Experian	www.experian.com/product/consumer/online.html
Trans Union	www.transunion.com/creditreport/

Just be aware that there are serious issues of confidentiality here, so the agencies are very careful about releasing information. As of this writing, only Equifax will provide the actual report online, and then only after a verification process to assure that you are you. Thereafter you will be e-mailed a password that allows access to your report. The other two agencies will take your order online but will mail the report only to the home address that's in your file.

A number of other sites will allow you to order a Three-Bureau Merged Report online, but in all cases it will be mailed to you. Because the information in these reports is not shared among agencies, I recommend that you order a complete report, usually for about $30. Check these Web sites:

Qspace   www.qspace.com/qspace/
Credit411   www.credit411.com/

Finally, be wary about any Web site that offers a free credit report. Invariably, you get the free report only if you sign up for some kind of credit notification program, usually at a cost of over $50 per year. You may want this service, but you should know about it ahead of time.

CREDIT PROBLEMS

This section is intended to demonstrate how underwriters in general view credit reports. I'll pinpoint some problems you may encounter, then explain how to solve them.

I divide credit problems into three categories: insignificant, minor, and major. *Insignificant* refers to a small number (say three or four) sporadic 30-day late payments on revolving debts such as a Visa card. *Minor* problems include a regular pattern of late credit card payments or late car payments, especially within the last 12 months. *Major* problems reflect late payments on real estate loans, foreclosure notices on a mortgage, repossession of a car, or personal bankruptcy. Other serious problems are collection accounts, judgments, and tax liens.

Ironically, major problems can arise in the most innocent ways. Let me give you a few examples.

- You check into your local hospital and rack up a $5000 bill. At discharge, you pay $1000, or 20 percent of the bill. The hospital then sends a $4000 bill to your insurance company, which subsequently pays only $3935. The hospital does not call to alert you that you still owe $65. It sends the unpaid bill to a collection agency. That agency notifies Experian that you didn't pay a bill. Although required by law to do so, the hospital may even fail to write you a letter. For the cost of a postage stamp, the hospital may end up collecting only $20 of the $65 balance. But you now have a derog on your credit report, and your FICO score drops a notch.

- You hire a painter to paint your house for $3750. He destroys some plantings that cost you $250 to replace. You pay $3250 and tell him you'll pay the other $250 when he acknowledges that $3500 is all you owe. He takes you to small claims court for $500. You show up with pictures of the ruined plants and tell the judge you're willing to pay the $3750 less $250. The judge finds in your favor and you write out a check for $250—

which you were willing to pay in the first place. Unfortunately, this shows up on the public record as a judgment filed against you, though later satisfied—in other words, it appears exactly as though you'd lost and are the kind of person creditors must take to court. If you find yourself in this sort of situation, when you write the check, have the painter (or whoever) sign a Notice of Release of Lien and file it with the court. Otherwise, it will show up years later as an unsatisfied judgment.

- You co-own a boat with your neighbor, but eventually you tire of it, so when your partner calls one day and says, "I just sold the boat to Harry," you're elated. Your partner sends you a check for your half, $4400. However, if your county collects taxes on personal property like boats, failure to submit a bill of sale with the new owner's address will mean you find yourself presented with another tax bill next year. If you say to yourself, "This isn't my bill, we sold the boat," and don't pay it, the county will file a tax lien against you for the amount due, maybe $76.45. Voilà! Another derog on your credit report: an unsatisfied tax lien. Not only will you have to explain this, you may be required to pay it as well.

- No doubt you have credit cards with payments due on various days of the month. If you're like me, you probably pay them in batches. Sometimes this results in payments received by creditors after they send you the next bill. Well, technically, those payments are late. Whether creditors report such delinquent payments to the credit bureaus is up to them. My experience is that some do and some don't. It is not at all uncommon for credit reports to reveal some kind of derogatory information on people who are actually quite scrupulous with their finances. Frequently, this occurs on seldom-used accounts like credit cards of department stores—which, incidentally, seem to be the fastest on the trigger in reporting delinquent payments.

Most of the time, people are totally unaware that a late payment made years ago is still sullying their record. Believe it or not, even more innocuous behavior can result in a less-than-perfect credit report. Illegible handwriting on credit applications may result in information being misread or misreported. Keyboarding errors when data are entered into a computer may go undetected until someone requests your credit report years later.

Remember, get a credit report early.

Repairing Credit

I'll begin by using the example of a credit card to demonstrate how to undo a damaging entry on your report. First, and most important, remember that you have every right to get any inaccurate information corrected. Assume the company reports that you have a few 30-day late payments. The first step is to call the company and calmly say, "I just got my credit report and found that you reported that I made late payments. I believe that I have never been late with my account." In my experience, many creditors are happy to remove this blight from their reports as a matter of accommodation and convenience to the customer—even though you may actually have been late once or twice. Frequently, when you call, the agent's computer screen may not show any late payments, either because the derog really is an error or maybe because such information is maintained internally only for two years and the alleged incident happened three years ago. If whatever records the company does have don't say you were late, the derog has to be taken off. In other cases, if only sporadic, minor late payments show up, the first-line people you talk with may be authorized to delete them. You might, however, be asked to send them the portion of the report with the offending entry to show exactly how it is entered before the creditor can correct it.

If, however, the customer service rep tells you that he or she has to check with someone else, request a callback in 15 minutes to confirm the adjustment. If you get some waffling from the representative, it may mean that only a supervisor has the authority to make the change you are asking for. If that happens, don't waste time; ask nicely but firmly, "May I please speak with your supervisor?" Then explain your problem again to the supervisor.

| TIP | I recommend you go to the Federal Trade Commission's Web site, www.ftc.gov/bcp/menu-credit.htm, and read and/or download the excellent brochures there. Two I recommend are *How To Dispute Credit Report Errors* and *Fair Credit Reporting.* The site also has a great deal of other information relating to credit, but these publications are the most applicable to this situation.

In general, you'll find that credit card companies, especially the banks, are a little tougher to deal with than department stores. As with any business, however, some are better than others. If you get an unfriendly reception, consider canceling your card and finding a friendlier bank.

Usually, affiliation credit card issuers are the easiest to deal with. For example, many trade groups, professional associations, charitable organizations, and alumni groups offer credit cards where a portion of every dollar you charge is donated to the organization. At one such bank where I have a card, consumers talk with a "customer satisfaction representative," who is just that. A company that describes its employees that way is going to be a lot easier to deal with than the average bank.

Getting Action.   When the creditor agrees to correct your report, don't hang up the phone thinking that you're home free. It will probably take 45 to 60 days for the change to work through the system—too long if you're trying to get your mortgage approved. Ask the creditor to write you a letter clearing the report, then fax it to you immediately. Be sure to get the name of the person you are talking with. If the letter doesn't arrive within 24 hours, call that person; you don't want to start from scratch with someone new. Figure 13.2 shows a sample "clearing-your-report" apology letter.

The creditor may send a notice directly to the bureau and one to you, which is even better. When you have all the proof you can get your hands on, send it to the agency that generated your credit report so it can eliminate the derogatory items. Be sure your report is retyped; don't settle for a supplement to the original report. You want to ensure that the underwriter sees a squeaky-clean report.

| TIP | Creditors are notorious for "forgetting" to follow through on correction commitments, even though they are legally required to do so. To ensure that you get action, write letters to Experian, Trans Union, Equifax, and the other reporting bureaus disputing the derogatory reports. Then order another credit report 90 days later to verify that the changes you instituted have been carried out.

Paying Off Credit Cards with a Refinance.   Many lenders have a rule that states, "The payoff of revolving debt by a refinance will not improve your ratios." The obvious assumption is that you'll go out and run up your cards again. If you decide to pay off your bills with a refinance, believing that zero balances on your cards will improve your

---

Regarding account 372 555 1212

Dear Mrs. Wilson,

We have reviewed the history of this account and find that all payments were made on time. Our report of late payments is incorrect. We will forward our correction of our report to the bureaus.

We apologize for any inconvenience this may have caused you.

Sincerely,

Mary Bostwick
Credit Supervisor

Figure 13.2   Sample letter clearing an incorrect credit report.

ratios, you may be unpleasantly surprised. My advice is to add yet another question to your loan shopping list to be asked up front, even before you fill out the application: "How does your underwriting department treat the payoff of consumer debt with a refinance?"

| TIP | If you run into this problem and you find no other way around it, there is a solution, albeit a cumbersome one. Oddly, many banks with this onerous policy do not use it in their equity line department. That means you can apply for an equity line, pay off your bills, and then ask for a new underlying loan. The lender views such an action in a different light and may approve your loan.

A kinder, gentler lender's policy manual might say, "In order not to count the payment, you must also close the account." Others don't care at all.

Additional Pitfalls.   Credit reports also list any recent inquiries to the bureaus. Invariably, these result from new applications for credit that you have made or perhaps requests for increases in the limit of existing accounts. Nevertheless, you will be asked to explain these because the lender may assume you are running up credit balances that will mean additional payments beyond what is shown on your credit report and that will affect your qualifying ratios. And, unless you are highly qualified, do not buy a car while you are looking for a house or are in escrow. There is no surer way to ruin your deal. If you are highly qualified and want to buy a new car, first sit down with your lender and ask, "How would an additional $485 monthly payment affect my qualifying ratios?"

Letters of Explanation

Most lenders ask borrowers for letters explaining any derogatory items or recent inquiries on their credit reports, regardless of how insignificant. However, if you have a high credit score (for example, a FICO score over 680), some lenders will now waive this requirement, although there are exceptions to this. One lender adopted a policy of not requiring letters on minor consumer credit derogs more than two years old. Can you remember why you made a late payment five years ago on an infrequently used card? No one else can either, so why bother to ask? I applaud this practice and recommend it to other lenders.

More serious derogs still require an explanation letter, especially if they've occurred within the past 24 months. These include 60- or 90-day late payments on credit cards; late payments on installment debt such as car loans; collection accounts; repossessed cars; judgments; tax liens; and bankruptcy. These are important, and underwriters pay attention to them, so you should devote sufficient energy to crafting the letter to achieve the result you want: loan approval. Sample letters are shown in Figure 13.3 to give you an idea of what lenders like to see. Your loan officer should also be able to help you write these letters.

The most important point regarding credit problems is that you should realize that lenders *want* to help you clear your recent history. They are, therefore, likely to understand about problems that were confined to one particular period of time or that had a distinct, definable cause. Loss of a job or severe health problems can happen to anyone and can cause finances to become strained to the point at which payments are missed. If this has happened to you, tell your lender. That will help to classify you as a person who *had* a problem rather than as someone who *is* a flake.

Late Payments on Real Estate Loans

In the past, mortgage lenders didn't report mortgage credit histories to the credit bureaus. Now, however, almost all do, which could cause problems for you. Here's how. You are obligated to make your payment on the first of the month, but almost universally, lenders give you a 15-day grace period. (Sometimes it's 10 days! When you sign loan documents, check this out.) If you don't make your payment until the seventeenth of the month, you will owe the lender a penalty, typically

---

To whom it may concern:

I wish to respond to the items on my credit report.

My family and I spend a month vacationing in Japan every year. Because of the duration of our stay, it is possible a bill that arrives shortly after we leave won't be paid until the 32nd or 33rd day or 34th day. I'm sure that this is the source of the late payments shown on the report.

Also, I moved my office twice in 1991, once to temporary quarters and then to the office condominium I purchased. As a result of two consecutive moves, some of our mail was delayed and did not get to us promptly. I own my office now and do not plan to move.

As to the collection account, the landlord of the building where I maintained offices in 1990 and 1991 attempted to collect non-contractual charges from his tenants. We refused to pay, and he harassed all of the tenants, including referring the matter to a collection agency. The report says that the account was paid, but that is not true. Because the charges were not proper, the matter was ultimately dropped.

We have always paid our creditors, and I appreciate the privilege of having good credit. I hope that this response will reassure you as to my record and my determination to maintain my good credit standing. **(a)**

Figure 13.3 (a–d) Sample borrower letters of explanation.

To whom it may concern:

I wish to respond to the items on my credit report.

____ card—One company sold its accounts to another. It sent me a bill for the annual fee but I did not renew the card. Its charge-off is merely an internal reversal on the company's books of a charge for which I am not liable.

M___ Department Store—This bill came when we were on a trip to Europe. We have been current with the account for 14 years.

ABC Motors—I bought a new BMW. I paid cash for the car and did not finance it.

(Author Note: If you apply for a mortgage shortly after purchasing a car for cash, be prepared to provide a copy of the title to the lender to prove you don't have a car loan. When you finance a car, the lender keeps the title until you pay off the loan.)   **(b)**

To whom it may concern:

Regarding our credit report, we do not have an account at S__C__ and have never bought anything there. I called the company and it had us confused with someone in Lawndale. They said they will correct the error.

I have no recollection of the other items, all of which happened between two and seven years ago.   **(c)**

To whom it may concern:

We applied to both ABC Savings and XYZ Savings for this same loan. I canceled both applications, although it appears that XYZ ignored my request.

The B___ Bank inquiry was in response to our application for a check guarantee/debit card. This card was issued to us and is the first item listed on our credit report.   **(d)**

Figure 13.3   *(Continued)*

5 percent of the amount of the payment due. You probably already know this, but here's something you may not be aware of: Credit reports are set up to report 30-, 60-, and 90-day late payments. There isn't a column for payments received *after* the grace period but *before* 30 days. Therefore, the lender frequently reports these as a 30-day late payments. Ironically, when granting credit, lenders don't worry about 15-day late payments, but the underwriting manual tells them to be concerned about payments made more than 30 days late. You see the problem.

There's more. Some lenders keep detailed records for only 24 months. Say you were 18 days late (not 30 days late) on your March 1993 payment. After March 1995, the lender reports it as follows: "Number of times 30 days late: 1; date of late payment: N/S." (N/S stands for "not stated," which the lender uses because he or she didn't keep records and doesn't remember the date.) When you apply for a new loan, the new lender looks at your credit report and assumes that you were late last month. If you have such an entry on your credit report, have your loan rep immediately send a verification-of-mortgage form to that lender to get a more detailed loan history. Then go back through your records, dig out the most recent 12 months of canceled checks, and make copies—front and back—to show the lender that you haven't been late in the last 12 months, which is the only period lenders usually care about.

After you've purchased your home, I urge you to be scrupulous about making your mortgage payments on time. Mortgage lenders hate late payments on mortgages. If you get into a financial bind someday, let the Visa card slide, but do whatever you have to do to make your mortgage payment on time. Failure to do so can be very expensive, as it can instantly turn you into a B/C borrower and cost you thousands of dollars in the future if you buy another home or want to refinance.

Delinquent Property Taxes. If you are engaged in a refinance transaction, the preliminary title report ("prelim") shows the status of payment of property taxes. I once received a prelim showing that a borrower was delinquent not only on his current tax payment, but also on tax payments for the prior two years. The bottom line is that underwriters hate it when you don't pay your taxes. They consider it a grave offense. If you are about to refinance your home and haven't paid your taxes, pay them. Your lender will demand that you pay them before the transaction closes. When you pay, do so in person with a cashier's check. Get a receipt and give this to your loan rep to pass on to the title company. Make sure that the preliminary title report shows all taxes have been paid. If it does not, have it retyped. If an underwriter sees the delinquency, even with the subsequent payment, you'll have to write a convincing letter of explanation, but if you have the prelim retyped, the lender will never know it happened.

The same is true for other tax liens or judgments that may have been filed against your property. The lender will require that they be paid prior to closing anyway, so you might as well get it taken care of up front.

MAINTAINING GOOD CREDIT

This section is composed of a number of valuable tips you should implement as appropriate to ensure that your credit record is clean and stays that way.

- If you own a new or one-year-old car, even if you paid cash for it, the lender is going to assume that you have a car loan, even if you are a person of substantial wealth. The lender's way of confirming ownership is to require you to show the pink slip, title, or whatever your state uses to prove ownership. If there is a loan on the vehicle, the lien holder will keep this until the loan is paid. It is annoying at the very least, and perhaps even insulting, to have to show that you have clear title to a car. To avoid the issue, when you fill out the application, omit the year your car was manufactured and state its value conservatively. I will quickly add that you should not lie, about this or anything else, especially if you actually have a loan on the car that doesn't show up on the credit report. Sometimes these car loans show up on the backup credit reports that lenders get.

- I don't know why more family lawyers don't suggest this, but if you are going through a divorce or have gone through one, make sure you and your ex-spouse split up the credit cards. Take the cards you want and have your ex-spouse expunged from them. Cancel all joint accounts, but note that you are both liable for cards with existing balances because the credit was granted on the assumption that you would both be responsible for debts. You can, however, close the account to new purchases so that when the balance is paid, the account will be closed. If necessary, apply for a new account with a new card. As part of the divorce proceedings, demand that your ex-spouse do the same. I have seen too many cases where, three or four years later, the ex-spouse creates problems. If your ex-spouse uses these cards, the balances show up on *your* credit report. If your ex-spouse forgets to make some payments, this shows up on your credit report as well. It is very hard to prove that these aren't really your debts.

- Instead of being a cosigner with your child on a car loan, ask the bank if you can *guarantee* the loan. If you are a cosigner, the bank will report the loan to the credit bureaus as yours, under your Social Security number as well as your child's. You're just as liable as a guarantor, but the loan is reported only on your child's Social Security number, not yours. Banks are not used to implementing this guarantee alternative, so you will almost certainly have to talk with a manager before you can find someone who even remembers what a guarantee is!

- In a *rolling late,* you miss a payment, make the next five on time, and then make up the missed payment. The creditor may report this as five 30-day late payments, four 60-day late payments, or three 90-day late payments even though only one payment was actually late. The lender has the contractual and probably the legal right to apply any payment received to the oldest outstanding payment, so the report is not technically incorrect. However, your lender will be a lot more understanding if you have canceled checks and monthly statements from the creditor to show what went wrong.

- I have seen innumerable situations where people pay off a car loan early only to have late payment reports show up later. It is as if banks have two computers, one to keep track of balances and the other to keep track of payments due. When you pay off the loan, computer 1 doesn't tell computer 2, so computer 2 still expects a payment from you. When it doesn't get one, it calls the credit bureau and reports you as late. When you pay off the loan, do so in person if you can, and get a dated receipt.

- This may sound silly, but it happens all too frequently. Let's say you are selling or refinancing your home. The settlement agent gets the legal Demand for Payoff document from the lender being paid off. It's the legally binding document that says something like, "They owe us $135,357.54 plus interest at the rate of $28.50 per day from 03/01/97." Your escrow is supposed to close on April 10. The settlement agent will collect from you the balance plus 40 days' interest, 30 days in March that would have been paid with the April 1 payment and 10 days in April, plus maybe an additional day to make sure the lender gets it. You don't make the payment on April 1, assuming that the escrow company or settlement agent will just make the payment when the old loan is paid off. However, if escrow is delayed until April 15 and the lender doesn't get the payment until the next day, the loan payment becomes delinquent. In addition to the extra five days' interest, you'll also incur a late fee, and probably a derog on your credit report as well. To satisfy the lender you aren't a flake, you'll have to show the closing statement on that transaction, and it'll be trouble enough just finding it two years later. To avoid this, when you are refinancing, make your regular monthly payment to the lender on the first of the month or earlier (yes, you can pay early, too!). That way the lender will have time to update its Demand for Payoff, so interest will be collected only from April 1 and you won't be late.

- If you hold too many credit cards and have a shopping problem (i.e., addiction), I recommend the following solution. It's called the *310 trick*. Take all your credit cards, put a rubber band around them, set your oven for 300 degrees, and put the cards in there for 10 minutes. Bingo. No more temptation!

- Check your credit every year or so at least, just to see what's on there and to make sure that if some erroneous information has crept in, you can correct it at that time.

- If you do not have many accounts, or if your accounts have been newly established (for example, you recently graduated from school and are just entering the labor market), lenders will want you to show some history of handling credit responsibly. It may even be that your FICO score is low because of this. To fix this, go to your parents and ask, "Please add me as a cardholder on a couple of your clean credit accounts, preferably ones with zero balances." The bank or department store will send you an application and add you to those accounts. Then, when the next reports are sent to Experian and the other bureaus, these accounts will also be reported as your accounts. Instant credit history. If your parents are reluctant to keep you on the account, have them close it and open up another one. Then it shows up as a closed account with satisfactory payment history. I hear some of you saying this is cheating. My response is that a lot of this credit stuff is game-playing, and it's okay to play back!

CREDIT REPAIR AGENCIES

Expunging derogatory data from credit reports is a complex, time-consuming task, and many people find it difficult to go through these steps on their own. Hence the rise of credit repair agencies, which offer to do this for you and promise glowing results. Unfortunately many (even most) have bad reputations—so bad that the Federal Trade Commission has determined that many of them are scams, as reported at www.ftc.gov/bcp/conline/pubs/alerts/repralrt.htm. Therefore, if you feel you can't clean up your credit report on your own, I recommend that you carefully investigate any credit repair agency, including calling customer references before you sign on with one. But I want to stress that you can do this work yourself if you will just devote the time to it. Believe me, it is worth it.

One place it is safe to go for help is the Consumer Credit Counseling Service, a nonprofit agency that offers assistance through its more than 1,450 offices nationwide. This agency has helped millions of people, and if you have a severe problem, I can think of no place I can recommend more highly. There is now a Web site at www.nfcc.org that has lots of useful material as well as help with locating an office near you. Online counseling is also offered at the Web site. You can also reach the agency by phone at 1-800-388-2227 to find a local office, or write to:

National Foundation for Consumer Credit
8611 Second Avenue, Suite 100
Silver Spring, MD 20910

SUMMARY

The mortgage industry's decisions about potential customers are built on the bedrock of credit history. If you have a good credit history, you'll get along just fine, but it is all too easy for errors to creep into the system. These errors will cost you a lot of grief and a lot of money. Correcting past errors and keeping errors out in the future requires some vigilance and effort, but is well worth it. I assume that you will take my suggestions in getting the loan to finance this home, but make it a point to get a credit report every year or so to make sure it is correct.

UNDERSTANDING APR, BUY-DOWNS, AND DISCOUNT POINTS

Streams are for wise men to ponder and for fools to pass by.
—Izaak Walton

KEY POINTS

- The government-mandated approach to interest rate comparison, the annual percentage rate (APR), is not useful for consumers.

- Every lender has a target net yield for every loan program. A large number of different rate versus fee options have the same net yield, so the lender doesn't care which one you choose. However, from your perspective as a borrower, some of these choices are better than others.

- Choosing the best rate versus fee alternative is going to save you a bundle over time, and there is a simple method of organizing the information to make this choice easier.

- Most people choose the wrong rate versus fee option, usually a zero-point loan.

I'm a fisherman, and as I grow older, I see more and more parallels between fishing and life. Many of the opinions borrowers have about lenders and mortgages are based on platitudes. The lenders hope you will be foolish enough to believe these clichés because it will be more profitable for them if you do. I take a different approach: I want you to ponder the process, just as the wise angler ponders the stream. The good news is that analysis is not that difficult once you learn the process. The techniques you will learn in this chapter will save you tens of thousands of dollars.

TRUTH OR CONSEQUENCES

Historically, purveyors of credit have confused people about interest rates. Someone would buy a $300 TV and the salesperson would say, "Do you want to finance it? We only charge 10 percent interest." That rate sounded reasonable, so the consumer would say yes and the salesperson would do the following calculation.

$$\$300 \times 10\% = \$30$$

$$\$30 \times 3 \text{ years} = \$90 \text{ total interest}$$

$$\$300 \text{ for the TV} + \$90 \text{ interest} = \$390 \text{ divided by 36 months}$$

$$= \$10.83/\text{month}$$

This may look reasonable, but it isn't. The annual percentage rate on this transaction is actually almost 18 percent, not 10 percent. The interest rate calculation, $30 × 3, assumes that the entire principal is repaid at the end of the third year. Because the consumer is making payments and reducing the principal every month, the average loan balance in this transaction is only $150, not $300. If the real rate were only 10 percent, the total interest due would be only $48, not $90. The actual payment at 10 percent is only $9.68, a difference of only $1.15 per month. That may not sound like much, but if the store earned an extra $1.15 on every TV, every month, the money made from misleading the customers would really add up. Think about this as it applies to mortgages. Clearly, getting a mortgage is a much more complex process than financing a TV set, and there is a huge difference between a 3-year consumer finance loan and a 30-year mortgage.

To correct such abuses, Congress passed laws that were intended to ensure truth in lending. These laws required, among other things, that lenders had to give consumers information disclosing the annual percentage rate on any proposed loan. Although these laws have done much to improve consumers' understanding of the cost of financing TV sets, they have done almost nothing to correct similar problems in the mortgage industry. Simply put, mortgage financing is different from and more complex than common consumer finance. In general, if someone offered you an APR of 18 percent, and someone else offered 10 percent, it would be an easy choice: 10 percent is a lot less than 18 percent. But with mortgages, it's never that simple.

In calculating the APR on mortgages, the lender must factor in certain costs affiliated with the loan, called *prepaid finance charges.* First, the lender keeps the interest accrued between the date of funding and the end of the month, so that the first payment isn't due for at least 30 days. That means if you borrow $100,000 at 10 percent and zero points on the first day of the month, the lender keeps 30 days' interest, or $833.33. Throw in processing fees, underwriting fees, document fees, and so on, and the lender will fund only $98,500, not $100,000.

The APR is then calculated based on your paying interest on the amount financed, which is only $98,500 (the loan amount less those prepaid finance charges). Obviously, the APR is always going to be higher than the note rate. The APR in our 10 percent, no-point loan turns out to be 10.185 percent.

If you don't see much difference between 10 percent and 10.185 percent, let me share a secret with you. Almost no one in the mortgage industry understands APR very well, either. Lenders hire computer programmers, give them the regulations from the Federal Reserve Bank, and tell them to program the computers to calculate APR on the forms the lenders give to customers. Ninety-nine percent of the lenders don't even know how to calculate it themselves.

The greater flaw in the APR calculation is not mathematical, but behavioral, because it assumes that the borrower will keep the loan for the entire period of the loan. In reality, however, 95 percent of loans are paid back far sooner, and that means the APR calculation is wrong 95 percent of the time.

Here's another way of expressing the problem that gets to the heart of the way many people shop for loans. Let's assume that Bob and Becky Phillips are buying a new home and are making the rounds of local lenders. They come into my office and ask, "What is your APR?" Being a little coy, I ask what they have already been quoted. They say, "10.185 percent." Then I quickly calculate that I can get an APR of 10.185 percent if I have a 10 percent loan with zero points (from the preceding example). I also know that my lenders offer this same loan in as many as a dozen other rate versus fee combinations, one of which is 9.75 percent and 1 point. Let's look at these two choices this way:

	Rate	Points	APR
Alternative 1	10%	0	10.185%
Alternative 2	9.75%	1	10.051%

So I say to the Phillipses, "I've got that beat; my APR is only 10.051 percent." The Phillipses are happy because I quoted an APR of 10.051 percent, which is lower than 10.185 percent, the previous best rate they had found. The government agrees with them; my loan is better. So the Phillipses and I agree to do business. But did they get a better loan? The entire mortgage industry says, "No, these two pricing alternatives loans are just two different ways of looking at the same loan." When lenders do their calculations, both loans have the same net yield. I used the APR calculation to sell the Phillipses on my loan. As we'll see later, if they stay in their home longer than four years, my loan *is* better for them, but not for the reason they thought.

The heart of the issue is that you need a more realistic calculation to help you analyze alternatives. What you want is not some esoteric calculation, not even your neighbor's APR. What you want to know is, "What is *my* APR?" To determine that, you should amortize the points and other costs over the period you'll actually own the home. Let me demonstrate this simply. Assume you choose a 10 percent loan with exactly 1 percent in prepaid finance charges. Table 14.1 shows the calculated effective interest rates, amortizing the costs over the time you have the loan.

As you can see, the actual APR becomes a valid number only if you keep the loan for 30 years. But as I said earlier, you are probably not going to keep either your home or your loan for 30 years.

In the upcoming section on buy-downs and discount points, you'll learn that the mortgage industry offers many rate versus fee alternatives that are based on a formula that hits a target yield figure. To understand the difference between the reality of the market on the one hand and APR on the other, refer to Figure 14.1, where I have charted the rates offered by one lender and then calculated the APR on each alternative. You can see that there is very little in common between the two lines.

Let me put it another way. Consider what your reaction would be if the government instructed car dealers to give buyers a disclosure statement showing the price per pound of the cars they offered, and advised consumers to compare the value of cars by comparing the price per pound. Of course, there is some relationship between a car's weight and its value; common sense tells you that a small car like a Volkswagen Beetle isn't going to cost as much per pound as a Ford Expedi-

Table 14.1   Effective Interest Rates Vary with Period of Ownership

Period of ownership	Effective interest rate
1	11%
2	10.5%
3	10.33%
4	10.25%
5	10.2%
30	10.123% (? APR)

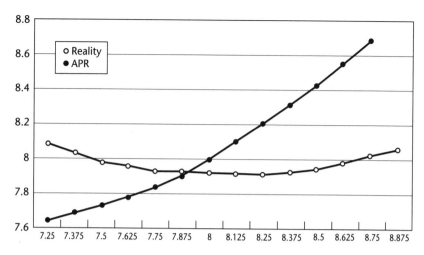

Figure 14.1   APR versus the reality of the market.

tion—but obviously this method of comparing car prices is silly. Similarly, the graph in Figure 14.1 demonstrates the fallacy of using APR as a means of comparing loans.

Let's go back to the Phillipses. They were analyzing my answer using the APR line on the graph, while I was using the market line. In using the government's method, they failed to analyze the situation in the most meaningful way. Most important, they may have failed to get the best loan. In summary, I think the financial markets know more about yields than Congress does, which is why no one I know of looks at APR to make decisions. I don't think consumers should, either.

APR AND ADJUSTABLE-RATE MORTGAGES

When it comes to adjustable rate mortgages (ARMs), things are even more complicated. In calculating the APR on an ARM, the government-mandated method throws consideration of the loan's index—by far the most important issue—out the window. It does the calculations for the teaser rate period and assumes that once the rate adjusts to the value of the index plus margin—say in year 2—it stays there for the life of the loan. Ladies and gentlemen, I am here to tell you that this is a patently absurd assumption. The actual rate in years 2 through 30 is going to vary widely (maybe even wildly), but it is not going to stay at today's rate. Whatever the difference between one index and another—sometimes one is better, sometimes the other—the government's approach makes it appear that whichever loan has the lower index plus margin today is the better loan. Again, that's just plain wrong. I repeat, comparing APR is not the best way to shop for an ARM either.

No doubt the folks at the Department of Housing and Urban Development would ask, "What other number do you want us to use?" The answer is that there is no way of knowing today how the interest rates are going to vary over the next 30 years, so there isn't an appropriate number. It's not the number; it's the method itself that is flawed. Consumers need an ARM disclosure that graphically compares the performance of a given index against the performance of other available loan indexes. With that in mind, we'll move on to take a more in-depth look at rate versus fee alternatives.

| NOTE | Currently, ARM loans are not being offered by many lenders on the Internet, probably due to the fact that they are too complex for inexperienced customer service people to understand and thus be able to explain to customers.

Understanding Rate versus Fee Alternatives

Before I begin this section, I want to tell you how essential this information is for Internet borrowers. The two most important sections of this book in terms of saving you the most money are this one and the one on determining loan type. Getting a loan costs money, and what I tell you here will enable you to get some of it back. Another way of saying this is to state that *paying points is the only good thing about getting a loan.* Once you understand this, you'll wonder why anyone does those zero-point or zero-cost loans.

| NOTE | Alarmingly, most borrowers—as many as 80 percent at some lenders—are choosing the zero-point option. Why? Because they do not understand what you are about to learn. When I get "blind" rate requests—phone calls from people I have never met before—almost invariably they are asking for zero-point, 30-year fixed rate loans. Unfortunately, this is a combination of features that have opposite and mutually exclusive objectives.

In a typical scenario, if a borrower couple is going to be in their home for seven years, then if they pay $2000 up front, they will get back that $2000 plus another $2000, thus "paying" for all of the other ancillary costs of the loan. They don't get back their money right away, but they sure do over time. In effect, that makes their loan free.

We're going to go back to the two loan alternatives we discussed in the APR section. We compared a loan at 10 percent for zero points and one at 9.75 percent and 1 point. This trade-off confuses most people, so I'm going to demystify it right now. Let's go through this example using my method, and assuming we are borrowing $200,000. Table 14.2 shows the results.

Table 14.2   Rate versus Fee Alternatives

	Loan 1	Loan 2	Difference
1. Establish the loan balance	$200,000	$200,000	
2. Determine the rates	10%	9.75%	
3. Determine the points	0	1	
4. Calculate the annual interest	$20,000	$19,500	$500 savings per year
5. Express the points as dollars	$0	$2,000	$2,000 up front
6. Divide cost by savings		$2,000/$500 = 4 years	

This process proves that if you pay an extra $2000 now, you'll save $500 every year in interest. After the fourth year, you'll get back your $2000 and still save $500 every year thereafter. What do we learn from this? If we are going to be in the house for more than four years, we should pay the point and collect the savings. Most people find this method much more meaningful than trying to decipher the difference between 10.185 percent APR and 10.051 percent APR. I hope you agree. Actually, almost all lenders offer many more than just two alternatives. This method works well in analyzing them all, as we'll see later in the chapter.

   NOTE   I can just hear someone running these numbers on a spreadsheet and saying, "The difference between the payments is $36.83 . . . and that gives a different answer." This is not right because using the payment reduction introduces the amount of principal reduction that is included in the payment into the equation, skewing the answer. Thus you should only use the interest amount, not the payment amount, in making these calculations.

   How far should we carry this? What if we had a 10-year break-even point? You might ask, "If I'm going to be in this property for 10 years, why isn't it a good deal?" The answer is that rates might come down even more, so it might be advantageous to refinance in year 5. If you did, you'd have recouped only half of your up-front costs. That's a mistake because you would have wasted money.

   TIP   I recommend one-, two-, and three-year break-even deals. Four-year break-even deals can work out if you are sure that you are going to benefit from them.

   My method forces you to ask questions about how long you are going to be in the home, what interest rates might do, and so forth. As difficult as this might be, it's a lot wiser than assuming you will be there for 30 years. You should not assume rates are as low as they're going to get, because you don't know that, and neither do I. Rather than worry about the hazards of predicting the long-term future, make decisions that you are going to be happy with for the next few years. When you get a loan, you aren't going to consider refinancing unless there's a major rate change. Beyond that, it's anyone's guess.

The Importance of Alternatives.   Let's delve into this a little deeper, keeping in mind that while the lender may be indifferent to pricing alternatives, for you there are some that are better than others. The numbers in Table 14.3 are eight actual rates and fee alternatives from a lender's rate sheet. Some lenders have even more than this. Check out the wholesale rate sheets I have included in Appendix 2.

On the first day you discuss pricing with your lender and the day you lock in your loan, be sure to get all the applicable numbers from your lender and analyze them according to the method shown here. Note that many Internet lenders do not include more than one or two alternatives. To do these calculations, you want all the numbers, not just the ones posted on a Web page.

The first thing I want you to notice is that the rate versus fee trade-offs are not orderly; if they were, there wouldn't be much point to going through the process. Because lenders round off rates and points to the nearest one-eighth percent, the results aren't rational. Some will be slightly in your favor and others will be in the lender's favor. You want to choose one that is in your favor. That's why it is so valuable for you to go through this exercise.

Note that in column 1 of Table 14.3 there is a ⅛th percent difference among the rates. Column 2 shows the points associated with each rate. Column 3 shows the difference between the points at this rate and

Table 14.3   Pricing Options for 30-Year Loans

Rate	Points	Difference	Break-even point
7.875%	0		
7.75%	0.125	0.125%	1 year
7.625%	0.375	0.25%	2 years
7.5%	0.75	0.375%	3 years
7.375%	1.125	0.375%	3 years
7.25%	1.75	0.625%	5 years
7.125%	2.25	0.5%	4 years
7%	2.75	0.5%	4 years

the points associated with the rate on the previous line. Next, we are going to divide the difference between points in column 3 by ⅛th to determine how quickly you get your money back. Look at Column 4. It shows the break-even time in years.

Let's say that initially you were considering a zero-point loan at a rate of 7.875 percent. Now it's time to lock in. You have all these numbers from the lender and you want to figure out whether there are better alternatives. You can get 7.75 percent by paying 0.125 point (or ⅛ point, expressed as a fraction). You'd pay ⅛ point to get down to 7.75 percent; you'd get back that ⅛ percent in the first year and every additional year you have the loan. You can see that that works out to a one-year break-even point. If you have the loan 10 years, you'd get ¹⁰⁄₈ back for ⅛ cost. That's terrific. Look at the next loan. It costs 0.375 (⅜) point to get a rate of 7.625 percent. That's 0.25 (¼) point more than the 0.125 point associated with 7.75 percent. That's good, too—a two-year break-even point. Does that make sense? It does to lenders, because they all say, "You can have a lower rate if you just pay a little more up front. Pay me now or pay me later."

The next two loans offer a three-year break-even point, also attractive for most people. But when you get to 7.25 percent, it takes five years to break even, and that's not a good deal in my opinion. So the ideal rate would be either 7.625 or 7.375 percent. Again, I can make no rational case for the 7.25 percent option, and thus none for either 7.125 or 7 percent.

In order to get the 7.375 percent rate, you as the borrower would probably be perfectly willing to pay the 1.125 points, because it's such a good deal. Many experts say that zero-point loans are the best, and sometimes they are. But for the overwhelming majority of borrowers— those who really are going to be in their homes for 5 or 7 or 10 years— it makes more sense to pay some points and get a better rate.

I know this methodology is tough to grasp, until you work a few examples for yourself. Recently, I processed a loan for a professor of physics who can probably solve differential equations in his head, and even he struggled with this concept at first. However, it is important, and I recommend that you play with some examples from the wholesale rate sheets in Appendix 2. It will become clear after a few tries. Remember, if you don't choose the alternative that's best for you, the lender will choose what's best for the lender, and it will cost you.

TIP If you bought this book, I will assume you are sufficiently computer proficient to set up a spreadsheet to do these calculations and graphically display the results. To download the spreadsheet from my Web site, www.loan-wolf.com/readers.htm, type in your e-mail address and the password, which is *goal*. After a few examples, it will become easy; soon you will be able to look at a schedule and quickly calculate the break-even points.

To illustrate this further, I've tried to simplify this concept by portraying the data graphically, as shown in Figure 14.2. In the figure, you can see that there are two common characteristics. First, it is obvious that as the rate gets lower, the buy-downs become more expensive. The implications are clear: As the cost goes up, the loan will reach a point where it's too expensive. Second, the numbers usually bounce all around.

Look at the same lender's pricing options for 15-year loans in Table 14.4, and then view its graphical representation in Figure 14.3.

Note that two of the break-even points are zero. Who in the world would take 7 percent if he or she could get 6.875 percent for the same points? Well, more than a few people do exactly that, either because they don't know how to get this information or because their lenders won't give it to them. You, on the other hand, will be well armed and very knowledgeable and will get the most advantageous deal.

Rates versus Fees on ARMS

If you decide that an ARM is best for you, remember that it may start at a teaser rate of 4 or 5 or 6 percent, but after its first adjustment in a year or sooner, the real interest rate is going to be at index plus margin—perhaps 7.5 percent or 8 percent. Thus it is more important to know the index and margin and add them together to figure out what the real rate of the loan is going to be.

There isn't much difference between pricing alternatives with ARMs because the period of variability of rate versus fee options is so short that the lender has only a very limited period in which to recoup its costs. Therefore the differences between alternatives are typically less than those for fixed-rate loans. To compare ARMs, I know of no other way than to just sit down and do a period-by-period analysis. Using a computer spreadsheet, it's more tedious than difficult.

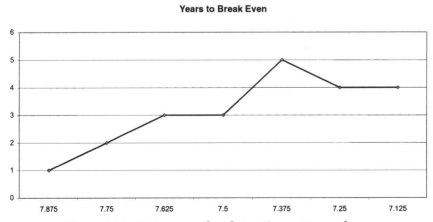

Years to Break Even

Figure 14.2 Rate versus fee alternatives—30-year loan.

Table 14.4   Pricing Options for 15-Year Loans

Rate	Points	Difference	Break-even point
7.5%	−1		
7.375%	−0.875	0.125%	1 year
7.25%	−0.5	0.375%	3 years
7.125%	−0.125	0.375%	3 years
7%	0.25	0.375%	3 years
6.875%	0.25	0	0
6.75%	0.75	0.5%	4 years
6.625%	1.125	0.375%	3 years
6.5%	1.625	0.5%	4 years
6.375%	1.625	0	0
6.25%	2.125	0.5%	4 years
6.125%	2.625	0.5%	4 years
6%	3.125	0.5%	4 years

Finally, be very careful about prepayment penalties on ARM loans, especially if you are paying zero points. Also find out whether the loan has the potential for negative amortization. This is almost surely the case if the start rate on the loan is below 6 percent. For more details, check out the more complete discussion of ARM loans in my first book, *How to Save Thousands of Dollars on Your Home Mortgage.*

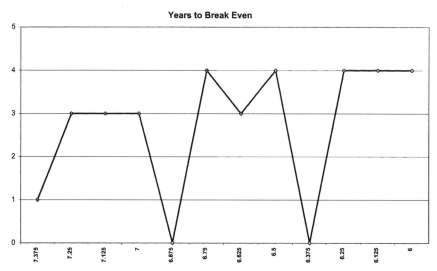

Figure 14.3   Rate versus fee alternatives—15-year loan.

SUMMARY

I hope you feel incredibly smart right now. You should! Set up the spreadsheet and ask your loan rep for the rate versus fee alternatives. You may be the first person who ever asked, and when you show the rep the results (why you went through the process), he or she will be impressed, never having seen this type of analysis before. Whether you choose a fixed-rate loan or an ARM, you're going to have to do some work to find the loan pricing alternative that is best for you. I promise that if you go through this process, the result will be well worth the effort.

15

ENSURING LENDERS TREAT YOU FAIRLY

Avarice, envy, pride,
Three fatal sparks, have set the hearts of all
on fire.
—DANTE ALIGHIERI, *THE DIVINE COMEDY*

KEY POINTS

- Many borrowers and lenders view their relationship as adversarial, and sometimes they are right.

- In spite of numerous disclosure laws, borrowers never have as much price information as lenders.

- Breaking through the professionals' secrecy barrier—getting lenders to share information with you—is the key to getting the best pricing.

- If you can't find a lender who will share information willingly, there are other steps you can take to gain the knowledge you need.

The mortgage business is different from other types of businesses. Consider this typical commercial transaction: You see an ad for a shirt in the newspaper and you go to the store and buy the shirt for the price at which it was advertised. Americans expect commerce to be conducted in this manner. But in the mortgage business, the consumer makes the decision to buy shortly after the home goes into escrow. However, the price isn't established until the buyer is ready to close, perhaps 30 or 60 days later. In the case of new construction, six months may elapse. During that period, the borrower is at the mercy of the lender. That's not bad as long as the lender is trustworthy! The question is: Are lenders trustworthy?

Various laws, written to give the borrower information about the costs associated with loans, require lenders to disclose rates, fees, and costs to consumers. These include the Truth in Lending, Itemization of Amount Financed, and Good Faith Estimate of Closing Costs forms mandated by the Real Estate Settlement Procedures Act (RESPA). The assumption is that once customers have the information, it'll be difficult for the lender to change terms later, to the borrower's detriment. This is totally incorrect. In the non-Internet market, lenders routinely change rates to their advantage if they think they can get away with it. This is less of a problem on the Internet because so many lenders are posting rates daily on their Web sites. If you are within the time frame you wish to lock, you can see exactly what the lender is quoting that day. If there is a difference, ask why, and don't let them blow you off.

WHOM DO YOU TRUST?

Lenders are in business to make money. Though they like to project the image that their industry is highly regulated, in practice the bank examiners and regulators from the Office of Thrift Supervision concentrate on the financial viability of institutions. Occasionally, they may check to see whether the Equal Credit Opportunity Act forms are signed, but they do not look into pricing to determine whether a bank is bamboozling its customers. Enforcement of disclosure laws mandated by RESPA is not the job of the people who visit lenders regularly. It is up to the Department of Housing and Urban Development (HUD), which has only several dozen investigators nationwide—far too few to do an adequate job of investigating the millions of transactions that occur annually. The regulators assume that the market will take care of pricing and that customers wouldn't agree to pricing unless it were reasonable. I see no evidence to support that assumption either. If you want to be treated fairly, don't count on some regulator; it's up to you.

The mortgage market is volatile, changing from day to day. Unless you lock in immediately, you are at the mercy of the market. That's the way most of the American economy works. But a lender can use this volatility to disguise methods of improving its profits on your transaction. Most of the time this goes on at a level that is invisible to consumers, which gives lenders, with their greater knowledge of the market, the opportunity to take advantage of their customers' ignorance. Let's see how this can happen.

Remember that there is no correlation between the rates quoted on the initial disclosure forms (those given to you at the time of application) and the rate you eventually get. The actual rate isn't determined until you lock in. This loophole in the law creates an opening that allows lenders to abuse customers if they think they can get away with it. To demonstrate the amount of volatility, Figure 15.1 charts one lender's points at the same interest rate for a two-month period. As you can see, for A loans, pricing changes daily, and this is typical of all lenders. This period, by the way, is not appreciably different from any other period I might have chosen.

Let me elaborate on this pricing situation. To begin, it's naive to think, "If I am doing business with a trustworthy lender, I don't have to worry about this." Indeed, a theme you have heard me repeat throughout this book is that you should search for your own advocate, a lender you can trust. Fortunately, many lenders do not let their employees change pricing from one customer to another, and the larger the institution, the less likely the employees are to fool around with pricing—the bureaucracies are just too cumbersome and inflexible. Other companies would consider it a violation of ethics to allow their employees to control pricing. Still other lenders dictate only a minimum level at which their reps may quote rates on any given day. The employees in those companies in fact are not only encouraged to charge the customer higher rates, some lenders teach classes that explain how to do it better.

In a multibranch operation, a branch's profit is directly dependent on pricing, and the branch manager's bonus is almost surely based on the profit. That's okay, but when the lenders split excess commissions with their loan reps to encourage them to engage in such practices, it is unethical. The industry even has a term for this type of incentive compensation—*overage.* The overage is additional profit created by charging higher-than-market prices. Some lenders even attract high-performance sales reps by offering a better split of the overages. What we have here is a conspiracy between management and employees to squeeze more money from you.

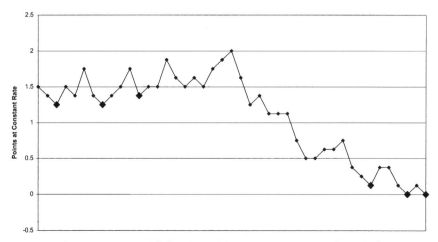

Figure 15.1   Variability in pricing over a two-month period.

Of course, profit-making organizations have the right to generate extra profit, but they should do so by creating extra value, not by taking advantage of customers' ignorance. The more unethical lenders regard market volatility as an ally because it creates a situation in which the true price becomes elusive to customers, and thus the lenders have a better chance of charging more and increasing profits at the expense of their unknowing customers. Let me make the point this way: Suppose that the market weren't volatile, that during the 60-day period between application and locking in, the rates were absolutely flat and unchanging at 8 percent. Obviously, your rate would be 8 percent. If there is volatility, however, the situation changes. Let's say that, during the same time span, rates move from 8 percent to 7.75 percent, back up to 8 percent, then to 8.25 percent, and back down to 7.875 percent. Which rate are you going to get now? Lenders know the rates on a minute-by-minute basis because that's their business. If your lender is being fair with you, any change, up or down, will be passed on to you. However, you may not have known about this volatility, and even though you do now, you want to make sure that your lender is being honest with you by looking at the quoted rates at the precise moment you are locking in.

LENDERS PROFIT AT YOUR EXPENSE

For this discussion, we're going to return to the topic of rate versus fee alternatives, which we discussed in the chapter. We'll examine how they work at the wholesale level—the lender's cost of funds. Keep in mind that most borrowers are not aware of the choices available to them. To begin, let's assume you and I own a mortgage company, and that the company to which we sell loans sends us a rate sheet every day. It works the same way in a bank. Recall from Chapter 14, "Understanding APRs, Buy-Downs, and Discount Points," our matrix of rate versus fee alternatives. The same type of matrix is shown in Table 15.1.

How did we get this chart? Let's say, for this example, that as lenders we propose to charge 1.5 points over the cost as our markup. Every morning we'll take the price list from our money sources and add 1.5 points to the wholesale price to determine the retail pricing on the retail daily rate sheet we give to the loan reps. Table 15.2 shows how we do this. Note that the customers only see the pricing shown in boldface type, the same as the price list above.

Our analysis in the previous chapter proved that a borrower could pay extra points and get a lower rate. But yield works the other way, too, meaning a loan with a higher yield—a higher rate—is worth more. It provides greater income to the lender, so it's worth more. That value is reflected as a negative number in the matrix. It's negative because, as we will see, it represents what our source for funds will pay us, not what the customer pays.

Table 15.1   Rate versus Fee Alternatives

Rate	Retail points
7.875%	0
7.75%	0.125
7.625%	0.375
7.5%	0.75
7.375%	1.125
7.25%	1.75
7.125%	2.25

Let's work through an example. If the customer chooses 7.25 percent, we can see from the rate sheet that he or she will pay us 1.75 points. When we sell the loan, we will have to pay 0.25 point to our source, keeping the 1.5-point difference, our planned profit. If the customer chooses 7.625 percent, he or she will pay us only 0.375 point. When we sell the loan, the source will pay us 1.125 points, called a *rebate*. That 1.125, plus the 0.375 we received from the customer, yields our planned profit of 1.5 points. Our money source will pay us, as the broker, the rebate of 1.125 points because we have delivered a loan that yields more—7.625 percent instead of 7.25 percent. You can see why it's worth more.

Look at Table 15.2 again, especially the top rates with the negative numbers in the third column. Remember, the ultimate source of money

Table 15.2   Customer versus Lender Pricing Information

Rate	Retail points	Wholesale points
8.25%	N/S	−2.25
8.125%	N/S	−2
8%	N/S	−1.75
7.875%	**0**	−1.5
7.75%	**0.125**	−1.375
7.625%	**0.375**	−1.125
7.5%	**0.75**	−0.75
7.375%	**1.125**	−0.375
7.25%	**1.75**	+0.25
7.125%	**2.25**	+0.75

pays us those points. What are we going to do with the money? The customer could benefit if we, as lender, were willing to pass it on. Or we could keep the money as an incentive to sell the customer a higher-rate mortgage.

Let's see how this can affect the borrower. Let's say that we've approved a borrower when the market is as shown in Table 15.2. We know that whichever rate versus fee alternative the customer chooses, we will make 1.5 points, the spread we created between wholesale and retail rate sheets. Our customer has been thinking about 7.875 percent and zero points, shown in boldface as #1 in Table 15.3. (Remember, it doesn't make any difference which rate he or she chooses because this situation works for all of them.) Then, a month or two later when we're ready to close, the market has improved, and rates are 0.375 percent lower. Our source sends us a new rate sheet in which the entire matrix shifts downward by 0.375 percent, but the relationship between rates and fees stays the same. Here's a portion of that rate sheet, along with the previous rate sheet numbers.

Note that the rates are 0.375 percent lower. At a specific rate, the points are 0.75 point higher than before. Remember that we quoted 7.875 percent at zero points (#1). At today's lower rates, we could lock in at the new zero-point rate, 7.5 percent, shown in boldface as #2.

The question confronting us, the lender, is, "What do we tell the borrower?" If we run an honest company, we call the borrower and say, "Good news; rates have improved and your loan will cost you only 7.5 percent, an even better rate than the 7.875 percent you were expecting." As I said, many lenders instruct their employees to follow the rate sheet. But others look on situations like this as unique profit opportunities. Here's what they do.

The branch manager calls the loan rep into the office and says, "We're going to lock in the Smith loan today. What do you plan to charge?" The loan rep knows that the borrower was quoted 7.875 per-

Table 15.3 Rate Sheet Adjusted Due to a Drop in Rates

	Rate	Old retail points	New retail points	Old wholesale points	New wholesale points
#1	**7.875**%	<u>0</u>	−0.75	−1.5	−2.25
#3	**7.75**%	0.125	−0.625	−1.375	<u>−2.125</u>
	7.625%	0.375	−0.375	−1.125	−1.875
#2	**7.5**%	0.75	<u>**0**</u>	−0.75	−1.5
	7.375%	1.125	0.375	−0.375	−1.125
	7.25%	1.75	1	0.25	−0.5
	7.125%	2.25	1.5	0.75	0

cent and may still be expecting 7.875 percent. He also knows that we, as lender, will make an extra 0.75 point if the customer still thinks that 7.875 percent is a fair rate. We're not talking chicken feed here. On a $200,000 loan, 0.75 point amounts to $1,500. So the rep calls the borrower with the "good news" that his or her mortgage was approved as originally quoted. If the borrower agrees, we fund the loan, pocket an extra $1500, and nobody's the wiser.

If the borrower objects because he or she has heard that rates have dropped, the loan rep says, "I'll have to see what I can work out for you," and hangs up. The rep may still try to finagle extra profit by calling back a little bit later and saying, "I managed to get you 7.75 percent." If the customer approves that pricing, the lender still makes a bonus. If we look at Table 15.3, #3 shows that when we sell this 7.75 percent loan, we get paid 2.125 points (also shown in boldface.) We've made our planned profit of 1.5 points, plus an extra 0.625 point or $1250. I can hear someone asking, "Is this legal?" Yes, it is perfectly legal as long as the compensation is disclosed in the RESPA forms that accompany the loan documents. If you, the borrower, don't read or don't understand all those forms you sign at settlement, it's your problem, not the lender's.

CHEATING ON THE INTERNET

While the examples I just described reflect patterns of behavior of a number of offline lenders, you can be assured that these tactics occur in online lending, too. However, because of the competitiveness of the A paper market, it is less likely to happen to A applicants. In contrast, those with spotty credit and low credit scores who are looking for B/C loans need to proceed cautiously. At one company, primarily an A lender, I was told that one rep made over $10,000 in overages just one month—and that's $10,000 over and above his base income!

Still other lenders, I am led to believe, are masters at getting a commitment to sell a certain but small percentage of their loan volume into the secondary market. Let's say that the market is at 7.75 percent but we want to advertise a lower rate 7.5 percent—0.25 percent under the market—to attract price-conscious borrowers. We have to pay money up front to get the secondary market source to accept a below-market loan, but it is only a small commitment. Sure enough, the phones ring, the reps take lots of applications, and a few people actually do get the advertised rate. After the commitment is filled, however, the reps tell the borrowers, for example, "Your loan was approved, but we couldn't get it on the 7.5 percent program. We could only get you approved on a program that is at 7.75 percent." The borrower may grouse a bit, but if it's five days before the scheduled closing date, what he or she do about it? Not much. Do not underestimate the ability of lenders to try to get away with this kind of bait-and-switch tactic. Unscrupulous loan reps will not work for a lender unless the company affords them the opportunity to engage in this kind of nefarious activity.

Regardless of your credit situation, be just as cautious in Internet borrowing as you would at your hometown bank. Remember my warning that those who shop focused on price rather than on a finding a trustworthy expert risk discovering later that the "hot quote" was given to them by a bandit. If you are an A borrower, so much pricing information is available that there is simply no excuse for letting yourself be taken advantage of.

Do not believe that the marketplace will keep this from happening. As the time draws near to close the sale, the seller of the property becomes the lender's unwilling coconspirator, because he or she won't give you enough time to get a loan from another lender.

OTHER SHADY TACTICS

You know that I am a fan of automated underwriting (AU) systems, but there is dark side to them, too. In the first place, it takes very little skill for the processing department to get a loan approval using an AU system. If the borrower's characteristics fit, the AU system will approve it. That can lead some lenders to "cherry-pick" loans, working with those who are approved and blowing off those who are denied. Perhaps it was a simple input error that caused the denial, but if the employees don't understand how to fix it, the customer loses. Perhaps you're thinking, "But if I'm approved, what difference does it make?" Well, do you honestly believe that all your interests are going to be well served by dealing with a company that treats its customers like that? You may not be cheated in terms of the immediate pricing, but if you are deprived of service that has some other, perhaps greater, long-term cost implication, that's short-changing you.

Some lenders make it a practice to lock in and close their customers' loans as soon as they can. Without question, if you take 45 days to approve and fund loans, the percentage of loan applications drops because some people will change their minds or find out about some competitor and get their loans there. If you shorten the period to 30 days, the fallout will be less. If it is shortened to 15 days, the fallout ratio will drop even further. If a notary shows up at the borrower's doorstep with loan documents three days after making application, my guess is that fallout is very, very low. Many people will sign the loan documents and proceed with the transaction, just because they are a little overwhelmed, don't have time to check alternatives, and don't know how to back out. They just think it is too much trouble to switch lenders once the documents have been signed. Speedy service can be in the customer's interest, but if such speed causes him or her to override caution, then the door is open for abuse. Some large companies do engage in this practice.

Prepayment Penalties

You need to be aware of another shabby practice. Some lenders have two price lists: one for loans with a prepayment penalty and another one without the penalty. The penalty is hefty, mind you: If you pay off the loan within the first three years, you have to pay a penalty of 2 or 3 percent of the loan balance. On a $200,000 loan, that's $4,000 to $6,000, a huge charge to incur if you decide to sell or refinance your house.

Here's the insidious part: If the loan rep delivers a loan with a prepayment penalty, he or she may get an extra commission, perhaps $300 or $500! Obviously, an honest agent would give you the choice, saying, "You can save an extra half-point if you're willing to accept the prepayment penalty period." That way, you can make an informed choice. But it is totally inappropriate for the broker or loan officer to make the decision for you when he or she stands to gain an extra income. Customers typically don't see this happening until they are signing loan documents—and sometimes they don't even catch it then. If the customer does notice, the loan rep might suggest that all lenders have prepayment penalties today. Not true. Alternatively, the rep might say, "You're not going to be refinancing anytime soon, so it won't hurt you." Maybe, maybe not. The point is, it ought to be *your* decision, not theirs.

Servicing Released Fees and Yield Spread Premiums

A number of class action lawsuits have been filed against some large lenders alleging abuse of customers. Specifically, the borrowers allege that the practice of money sources paying rebates to brokers is illegal. Such terms as *servicing released fees* and *yield spread premiums* are used to describe compensation paid by a lender to a broker. The way I see it, the lender has to pay its employees in its retail division, so paying a broker to do the same thing—originate loans—shouldn't be any different. If the broker and the lender have agreed to a commission of 1.5 points, the customer pays something less than 1.5 points, and the balance of the broker's commission will be paid by the lender to the broker as a rebate.

As strongly as I feel that zero-point loans make no sense for 90 percent of those who choose them, they have value for some people, and elimination of servicing released fees and yield spread premiums would eliminate the ability of the broker's customers to take advantage of low-point pricing. That's clearly unrealistic. As discussed in Chapter 14, making these choices is a very important part of your rights as a borrower. HUD has ruled that such rebates and premiums are not, per se, illegal, but I think that the courts, HUD, the Fed, and Congress will have more to say on this. I am always concerned when the government attempts to regulate economics, its track record in the last 100 years being spotty, to say the least. Nonetheless, ever since lenders have had the ability to get rebate pricing, many have used it to their advantage, not their customers' advantage. For that reason, I favor brokers retaining the ability to earn part of their compensation this way, but I also believe that the disclosure requirements should be significantly strengthened to curb unethical practices.

If you are working with a broker, you want to be aware of and negotiate total compensation paid to the broker, not just the rate and points you pay. Refer to Table 15.3 and note that there are a number of alternatives in which the broker's compensation is made up partly from fees paid by the borrower and partly from those paid by the source of funds. If you have agreed that your broker will earn a fee of 1.5 points, then it doesn't make any difference which alternative you choose. Let's say you are getting a $200,000 loan. When you get your closing statement with the loan documents, it will show the fees like this:

Loan origination	$1,500 (equals ¾ point)
Yield spread premium (POC)	$1,500 (the other ¾ point)

The acronym POC stands for *paid outside of closing,* and it means that the lender has paid a rebate to the broker. In this example, that's all right, because that was our agreement. But you should always check this and add up the numbers to make sure the compensation conforms to your agreement. If not, don't sign until the documents have been brought into accordance with your agreement.

SUMMARY

I hope you don't finish this chapter with a jaundiced view of the mortgage industry. Most of the professionals I know are honest, hardworking people who always try to get the best results for their customers. But you need to be aware of the "bad guys," because, as in all business arenas, they're out there. In the mortgage industry, they're often manning the phones at some Internet lender's call center. Making more money by taking advantage of customers using the practices I described here is sometimes the very reason they are in the mortgage business.

We're talking about the single most expensive purchase most people will make in their lives, so it is important to know what to look for and what to look out for when evaluating the people you choose to work on your team.

16

CALCULATING CLOSING COSTS, LENDER FEES, AND OTHER FEES

I cannot find anything better in a man than that he know, and nothing worse than that he be ignorant.

—KING ALFRED THE GREAT

KEY POINT

- In addition to points, the appraisal fee, and the credit report fee, lenders charge a number of other closing costs. These items appear on the Good Faith Estimate of Closing Costs and the closing statement (HUD-1 form) that you'll get from the escrow company or other settlement agent. You have a right to know, question, and understand these charges early in the process and again at closing.

A typical closing statement today lists an appalling number of fees and charges. To the uninformed customer, it seems as though everyone in the extended industry wants—and is getting—a piece of the action, which you pay for. Many of these fees will be charged by firms you will never have heard of, and you won't know what they did for you, so it will be unclear why you have to pay them.

The U.S. Department of Housing and Urban Development (HUD) requires lenders to give borrowers a little guide entitled, optimistically, *Buying Your Home: Settlement Costs and Helpful Information.* Unfortunately, it's printed in small type and doesn't exactly read like a novel, so few people get around to reading it. This document is also available at the HUD Web site at www.hud.gov/fha/sfh/res/sfhrestc.html. Not only is it a little more readable in the downloaded version, while online you can search it for the topic that interests you. The purpose of this chapter is to supplement this information so as to make it more accessible and comprehensible.

Whether you like it or not, these fees are here to stay, so you might as well try to understand them. Don't try to find a lender that doesn't charge them; lenders will just cover them some other way. These fees and costs are divided into three separate categories: legitimate, garbage, and other.

LEGITIMATE FEES

I'll address the legitimate lender fees first. There are a number of them, so fasten your seat belt.

Loan Origination Fee

The loan origination fee encompasses that portion of the points paid to the lender (or broker) for marketing, counseling customers, taking applications, processing, underwriting, coordinating, and funding loans. Traditional lenders, whether brokers or direct lenders, have fee schedules that typically earn them income of about 1 to 2 points; however, competition brought about by Internet lending has caused a revision of that pricing structure. Because online lenders have cut their incomes to be competitive, do not expect this fee to be further negotiable with them. And, as I discussed at length earlier in the book, more important in your decision should be whether a lower fee may come at the expense of lower levels of service—which may ultimately cost you more.

Loan Discount

This portion of the points is the trade-off of rate versus fee, as discussed in Chapter 14, "Understanding APRs, Buy-Downs, and Discount Points." You lower the rate on your loan by increasing the loan discount or buy-down. On a closing statement, if you are dealing with a broker, these fees will be shown like this:

Loan origination fee	$1500
Loan discount	$1000

While the discount is supposed to be the voluntary amount you pay to buy the rate down, a bank or other direct lender may not separate these fees but may lump them together. Just because the disclosure doesn't show a loan origination fee, don't assume that you are getting something for free.

Appraisal Fee

This is the money you pay to an appraiser for evaluating the property and preparing a formal report of its value for the lender. In many areas, this fee will range from $250 for a tract home to over $500 for a luxury home. If you qualify for Fannie Mae's or Freddie Mac's automated underwriting (AU), you may be approved for a "drive-by" appraisal, which will cost about $50 or $75 less than a normal appraisal. And note that Internet lenders, too, require an appraisal, because 99 percent of lenders are prohibited, either by state law or their regulators, from funding real estate loans without an appraisal. In short, lenders have no choice. Moreover, an honest appraisal is one of the most important protections against fraud. In Chapter 6, "Estimating What It's Worth," I mentioned the potential for computerized appraisals, but I don't think they will have an impact anytime soon. If you pay for the appraisal, by law you are entitled to a copy; ask for it as soon as it is completed, not after the transaction closes. Discuss this with your lender when you pay for the appraisal; if a written request is required, write one and give it to your lender with your check.

Credit Report

This is the fee (usually varying from $20 to $60) paid to a credit reporting agency to develop your report. Currently, the secondary market accepts a Three-Bureau Merged Report, which costs about $20. However, a few lenders still require a Standard Factual Data Report, a more complete $50 report that includes the merged report; a public records check for bankruptcy filings, liens, judgments, and so forth; and a phone verification of the borrower's employment. Self-employed borrowers should be aware that some lenders will also require a business credit report to verify that your business, as the source of ongoing income, is financially stable.

Flood Certification

Federal law requires that borrowers in "federally related transactions" (which means darn near everybody) buy national flood insurance if they are in a designated flood zone. The flood certification fee is paid to a company to determine whether your property is in such a flood zone. The charge is in the $20 to $30 range. Even if your property is on the top of a hill or in the desert, lenders still require this certification. Legislation was recently proposed to add a $12 federal fee to help pay for the cost of updating the flood maps. Obviously, even if you're not in a flood zone, you'll still pay it.

Flood Insurance

If it is determined that your property is in a flood zone, the lender is legally mandated to require you to purchase flood insurance. It carries an annual premium and is sold by regular insurance companies but underwritten by the federal government. Like all insurance, it seems expensive until you need it, and then it looks like a bargain.

Tax Service

Because a local taxing authority, usually the county, can take your house away from you if you don't pay your property taxes, your lender wants to make sure you pay them promptly. This one-time fee, usually $60 or $70, is paid to a tax service company, which will get the report of tax payments every year from the county tax collector's office after taxes are due; it names all those who haven't paid their taxes and reports this information to their lenders, who in turn will send out reminder notices to delinquent customers.

Settlement Fee

This is known as the *escrow fee* in some states. (In many parts of the country, the term *escrow account* is used interchangeably with *impound account,* described later in this chapter.) In California, transactions are handled through escrow companies, some of which are departments within title companies. Other states may use title companies or attorneys. Settlement agents handle the details of the property transfer; they prepare deeds, order title insurance, hold the buyer's deposit and down payment, assure that other requirements of the transaction are completed in a timely fashion, handle the funding of the new loan and payoff of the old loan, allocate taxes and insurance, record legal documents with the county, and, finally, pay the seller the proceeds of sale. Who pays the settlement fee is a matter of custom depending on the area you are in. If it is customary for the buyer and seller to split this 50-50, that's what the instructions will indicate. Custom notwithstanding, there is no reason you cannot include the following statement in your offer to purchase: "Seller to pay settlement fee." As for refinancing transactions, a special deal can usually be negotiated with a settlement agent, because refinances are easier than purchase transactions. Ask your lender to negotiate such a rate for you, perhaps in the $400 range. Sometimes the title company's settlement department will charge less, although you should ask your lender about the level of service to expect.

Notary Fee

This fee is usually included in the settlement fee as just one facet of the service the settlement agent provides. In states that allow it, it makes sense to hire a mobile notary who will come to your home in the evening or on the weekend so you can sign loan documents, usually for a fee in the $75 range. Many people who have difficulty taking off work find this more convenient, and, for people who don't get paid when they're not at work, cheaper than taking several hours off from work to go to the settlement agent's office to sign.

Title Insurance

When you buy a home, the seller pays for a title insurance policy that protects your interest as the new owner. I recommend that every purchaser demand such a policy and not close the transaction without one. Mortgage loans are *secured transactions,* meaning the lender has a secured interest in the property in addition to your promise to pay. Title insurance assures the lender that the collateral for its loan (that is, your home) is free of defects of title, such as encumbrances, liens, or claims by others. You pay for a policy that is issued concurrently with the one the seller paid for. If the lender has to foreclose, it is protected by the equity in the property without consideration of other claims. When you refinance, however, you have to pay for the whole policy, usually between $500 and $1000. This is one of the largest expenses in a refinance.

Sub-Escrow Fee

Settlement agents used to handle receipt of the proceeds of your loan and making the payoff to the old lender. But many lenders today do not want to send a $200,000 cashier's check to an escrow company or settlement agent they have never heard of. They prefer the safety of funding through a title company, and you will pay for this. This $75 or $100 compensates for the additional risk involved in handling large sums of money. Sometimes, if the law in your state allows, and if the premium you pay on your title policy is high enough, your title company may be willing to waive this fee, but you have to ask.

POC

Paid outside of closing (POC) means funds that didn't pass through the settlement agent's hands. It can signify nothing more than the money you already paid for the appraisal. That is legitimate. POC can also mean a rebate, yield spread premium, servicing release fee, or extra income paid by the lender to the broker over and above the loan origination fee. Let's say you agreed that your loan broker was to make $1600 on the transaction. The closing statement might show the following:

Loan origination fee	$800
POC—Lender rebate	$800
POC—Appraisal fee	$275
POC—Credit report	$20

Because the loan origination fee and lender rebate add up to the agreed compensation, this is legitimate. However, POC may disguise secret compensation, as we discussed in the previous chapter. It may mean that the lender has paid the broker extra money for delivering a loan at over market yield, meaning you are going to pay an over-market payment each month. When you ask about it, it is not uncommon for a settlement agent to say, "Don't worry; that's not something you pay." Well, you should worry, because it is something you pay, but not through escrow.

GARBAGE FEES

A number of miscellaneous fees are charged by lenders to cover the escalating costs of doing business. Mortgage lending is a profitable business if managed properly, but it is highly competitive, and margins are thin, which is why there are a lot of casualties among banks, savings and loan associations (S&Ls), and other lenders. Getting a loan approved and funded may seem like a simple deal, but the average loan transaction can involve as many as 50 phone calls (seriously!) and a lot of other work to assemble a file that contains a hundred pages or more of documents. A major problem with Internet lending is that there is a much higher fallout ratio than the 30 percent in traditional lending. Someone must pay for the cost of attracting and then handling those who inquire about or apply for loans. No one is charging up-front fees, but the costs are still there. Who pays for the cost of processing the fallout? You do. When your loan is funded, part of the revenue you generate goes to pay those costs. And this isn't going to change because the industry is not likely to start charging applicants an up-front deposit that would be refundable when the loan funded but otherwise would be forfeited. So we are stuck with a system whereby lenders do a lot of work for free and then charge various fees to offset the ever increasing costs of servicing customers and meeting all the regulatory requirements. In the lenders' defense, the costs of doing business have escalated dramatically. Because of this, every lender charges these fees, and there is a reason behind every one. One columnist was critical of this practice, saying that these fees were "pure profit"; but they really are pure revenues, and they offset a lot of things lenders do that are pure cost.

So-called garbage fees are a double-edged sword. The "good" side is that, among large, ethical lenders, the fees do not vary significantly, so it is a waste of your time to shop for costs. I have a spreadsheet on which I keep these fee amounts, and they do not vary much; most are between $650 and $750. The cheapest, at $550, is just for AU loans. An attractive feature of the Internet is that most lenders give fairly detailed listings of costs, although you may have to poke around a little to find them. Others do not list closing fees at all, even though they are the ones who set them. A few high-volume lenders, particularly those who advertise the best rates, have higher costs than average to make up for the low rates. They do not post their closing costs on their Web sites and won't give you the closing costs until after you fill out a lengthy application. Note that subprime lenders who lend to those with impaired credit may load up on extra fees because they feel that the borrowers may not have many choices.

The bad side of garbage fees is that they get more complicated than most laypeople can, or want to, handle. There is a tendency to overanalyze the situation and assume that it is important to get every lender's costs. Among ethical lenders, there is very little difference, but if you are going to compare costs, it is imperative that you create a spreadsheet and enter every number for each lender. Once you've done that, don't include title, settlement, or escrow fees, recording costs, and the cost of fire insurance—not because they aren't costs you will pay, but because they are not costs charged by lenders and are thus irrelevant to the cost comparison between lenders. Worse, because third-party costs are not "their" costs, some lenders lowball these costs to make the total look good. You'll pay the real costs, not the lenders' estimates, because lenders normally have no control over these costs. Note that some lenders just use national averages for some charges, while others use specific information down to the county level.

Finally, an increasing number of lenders are quoting guaranteed closing costs, and probably more will do so in the future. Frankly, even if lenders don't control some of the costs, they sure know what they are likely to be. Though I've never been asked to make such a guarantee, I would if that's what it took to make a customer happy. Just be sure that you as a customer are not mesmerized by the word *guarantee.* I ran the numbers at one site and found that its guaranteed cost, which included ½ point, was the same as my total costs, charging 1 point. Some people might see ½ *point* and the word *guarantee* and think that they were getting a better bargain than they really were.

Here's a listing of the garbage fees:

Processing Fee

As the paperwork has multiplied in this business, most lenders and brokers have started collecting $200 to $400 to pay for handling costs, courier fees, and long-distance calls because they're dealing with lenders who are thousands of miles away. You might think that this is just part of overhead, but long-distance phone calls and FedEx shipping of documents have become part of every lender's cost structure and their price structure.

Underwriting Fee

Like the processing fee, this is another contribution to overhead. In some cases, when lenders contract with outsiders like private mortgage insurance (PMI) companies to underwrite loans, it is for a fixed fee of perhaps $75 or $100. Yet the typical charge is from $300 to $450, the excess paying for overhead and the cost of the 30 percent of people whose loans were denied or canceled. This fee may be lower for AU loans.

Document Fee

There are 40 to 50 different documents in a typical loan package today. These used to be typed by hand onto preprinted forms. Today, they are generated by laser printers. The national document services that lenders use charge about $50 for the entire package. But someone has to prepare the order—what goes in all those blank spaces—which raises the cost to $150 or $200. Here's another reason for the difference. The secondary market and quality control people are absolute tyrants about correctness; they are totally unforgiving about mistakes, so the penalty for error is high. In fairness, someone has to make sure that every single one of those papers is signed properly and that the file is complete. You have to pay for someone to check them all to ensure accuracy.

Wire Transfer Fee

Lenders charge this fee, typically about $50, because their banks charge them $10 to wire money to the escrow or title company. (Charging you $50 for a service that costs $10 is an illustration of why these are called garbage fees.) But look at it this way: The wire is instantaneous, so the lender can fund your loan quickly. If they had to prepare a cashier's check and physically send it, they'd have to cut the check a day earlier and FedEx it to the settlement agent. The extra day's interest you'd pay would be more than the wire fee.

OTHER SETTLEMENT ITEMS

The following costs are not true lender costs, but you have to pay them anyway as a part of closing.

Interest

This topic really confuses most people, so here's the explanation. Interest on mortgage loans accrues on a daily basis and is paid in arrears, after the fact. On the first of every month, you pay the interest that accrued the previous month. In every month but the first one, your payment pays one full month's interest. If you purchase your home on the twentieth day of the month, you don't owe the lenders a whole month's interest, just 10 days' worth—from the day your loan funds until the first of the next month. You will not have to make a payment until the first of the following month for the interest that accrues in the month after you close. In this case, that payment is due 40 days after the loan is funded. If you are short on cash, schedule closing until the end of the month. Note that in preparing a Good Faith Estimate, some lenders calculate charges based on the worst-case scenario that you will have to pay 30 days' interest. Others try to snooker borrowers by assuming that each customer will only have to pay 15 days' interest. This makes their costs appear lower, when they really aren't.

Private Mortgage Insurance Premium

If you put less than 20 percent down, you pay PMI. These days, most people choose to pay the premium on a monthly, as-you-go basis.

Hazard or Casualty Insurance Premium

Both you and your lender want assurance that your financial interests are protected in case your house should be damaged or destroyed by fire or another catastrophe. Your lender is named as an additionally insured party on your policy. If you haven't already paid your agent for a policy, you are required to pay the first year's coverage at closing. Most lenders will accept a full cost replacement policy that insures that the home will be rebuilt in the same condition. Be sure to cover this with your insurance agent.

Escrow or Impound Accounts

A lender doesn't want to foreclose and find that you are also $2000 behind on your property tax and insurance payments—$2000 the lender will have to come up with. To protect its interest, the lender may require you to pay one-twelfth of the annual tax and insurance every month into a special account called an *escrow* or *impound account*. The lender then makes the required payments when they come due. Depending on when your transaction closes and when tax payments are due, you may have to make a sizable deposit to start the account. Be sure to ask your lender about the amount it will require.

Unless Congress passes new legislation superseding state law, check with your lender to see whether impounds are required in your case. In some states, like California, if your loan-to-value (LTV) ratio is less than 90 percent, the lender is not allowed to require such an account. In other states the lender may require an impound account for any loans. Here's another sneaky trick. Where state law forbids impound accounts, lenders who are used to getting them may charge an extra ¼ point—$500 on a $200,000 loan—to waive the establishment of an escrow account. In my opinion, it's not worth $500 to do it yourself. Grit your teeth and go on with life. The initial amount of your deposit will depend on in which month you close escrow and in which month your taxes will be due. Check on this early in the process so you are prepared.

SUMMARY

As a customer, you have a right to know the meaning and purpose of every charge you incur. The Real Estate Settlement Procedures Act (RESPA) gives you the right to a Good Faith Estimate of Settlement Charges within three days of application and again at closing. Unfortunately, there are few remedies in the event a lender's estimates deviate significantly from reality. If you get bamboozled, complain first to the lender's president; if that isn't effective, complain to HUD; but don't hold your breath waiting for a refund. Better to be wary and ask questions. Ask them at the beginning, ask them in the middle, and ask them at the end. Although garbage fees may be incredibly annoying, your efforts will be better spent concentrating on saving ⅛ percent on the note rate or ¼ point in fees than wasting time checking fees.

17

UNDERSTANDING 15-YEAR LOANS AND ACCELERATED PAYOFFS

The real measure of your wealth is how much you'd be worth if you lost all your money.

—ANONYMOUS

KEY POINTS

- The majority of the public thinks a 30-year loan is the standard loan. This chapter makes a case for the 15-year loan.
- You can save a huge amount on interest if you make higher payments.
- When you refinance, keep your payment the same, lowering the term of the loan, not the payment.
- Biweekly payment plans are beneficial for some people, and you don't need to pay someone else to do it for you. It's not complicated; you can handle it yourself.

Compared with other amortization alternatives, the 30-year loan has two features that make it a compelling loan for many people: It has a lower payment, and it is the easiest to qualify for. The payment is low because the 30-year loan is essentially an interest-only loan in the early years; that is, only a very small percentage of the payment is going toward principal reduction. At an interest rate of 10 percent, for example, 95 percent of the payment is going to interest and only 5 percent to principal. Keeping the payment low is important to first-time homebuyers who are stretching themselves to buy the largest home they can. Thus, the 30-year is their loan of choice. But for a significant number of other homebuyers, qualifying is not a major issue. For many of these people, the 30-year loan is not the best choice.

In fact, 99 percent of all lenders offer loans that are fully amortized in 15 years. Let's examine the benefits of those loans. At any given time, perhaps 30 percent of borrowers should have 15-year loans—yet these loans enjoy a smaller share of the market. Those who pass are missing an opportunity for significant savings.

MORTGAGE AS TOOL

A loan is a tool; it enables you to buy a home when you have accumulated only a small percentage of the purchase price. On the day escrow closes, the mortgage is your friend. Thereafter, you should treat it as your enemy and try to eliminate it as soon as you can. You accomplish this by reducing the principal quickly, which does not happen with a 30-year loan.

From the lender's perspective, most of the risk of approving a loan occurs during the first year. If, for one reason or another, borrowers are unable to make their payments, their problems usually become apparent during this time period. After that risky first year, however, lenders have a vested interest in keeping *your* interest coming in for as long a time as possible. Remember, most loans are sold in the secondary market, so your "lender" is merely collecting the payments—and is being paid handsomely for doing so. The fee is based on the loan amount, and the lender/servicer is happy if the loan balance stays high. If a lender has a servicing portfolio of $1 billion in January, and if the principal reduction is 5 percent during the year, the portfolio has been reduced to $950 million by December, and the lender's servicing income has declined by 5 percent. Obviously, lenders are not as keen on 15-year loans, which pay off even faster, thus reducing their income still more quickly.

BENEFITS OF A FIFTEEN-YEAR LOAN

Thanks to computers, analysis of loans is easy today. I am especially fond of the Mortgage Wizard program, which I used to create the next two figures so you can see graphically what happens with different amortization periods. Figure 17.1 shows the relative distribution of interest and principal on a $100,000 30-year loan. Note that more than one-half of the payments go to interest—almost twice the amount of the initial principal balance.

Now let's look at the same loan on a 15-year amortization schedule. In Figure 17.2, note that the interest paid drops from $215,928 to $93,427 and is less than 50 percent of the total payments. Also keep in mind that the interest rate on 15-year loans is about ½ percent less than

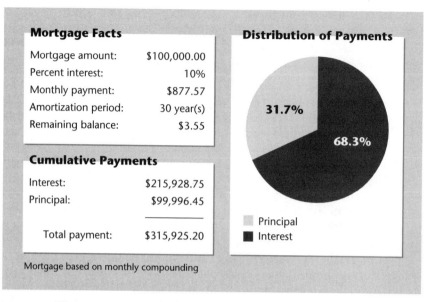

Figure 17.1   Distribution of payments on a 30-year loan.

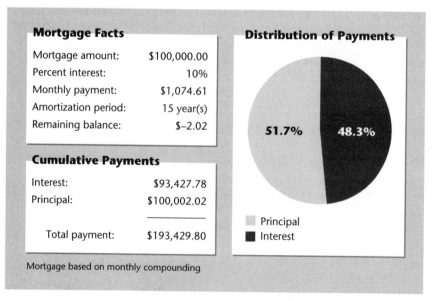

Figure 17.2   Distribution of payments on a 15-year loan.

that on 30-year loans. If you redo the calculations at 9.5 percent instead of 10 percent, you will find that the total interest paid drops even further—to $87,961, compared with $215,928. Now you can understand why I think 15-year loans are so terrific.

One of the arguments in favor of 30-year loans is that the homeowner can deduct mortgage interest from taxable income, a significant benefit. Fifteen-year loans are criticized because of the loss of tax deductions after 15 years. That misses the point. Unless the marginal tax rate is 100 percent, when you write a check, it still costs you money, just not as much. If we look at the taxes saved with a 30-year $100,000 mortgage compared with a 15-year loan, the difference over 15 years is only a little over $20,000. Even if you consistently invest the taxes saved (a big if), the benefit is only marginally better—not enough to compensate for the fact that after 15 years, the person with the 30-year loan still owes $75,000 on the original $100,000 he or she borrowed. The 30-year borrower paid $37,000 less in the first 15 years, but in the second 15 years, he or she still has to pay another $125,000, while the 15-year borrower pays zero!

It is true that if you were to take the money you save as a result of making lower payments on the 30-year loan—about $200 per month in our example—and invest it, you could come out ahead. But that's true only if what you earn on those funds is at least as high as the note rate. If you have an investment account that gives you a return of exactly 7.5 percent, those funds will grow and be equal to the remaining loan balance after 15 years. You then could just write a check out of that to pay off your mortgage. But if your average yield is lower than the note rate, you lose. How many people get those kinds of returns? Of course, in the last few years with the huge surge in stock values, it has been easy to beat 7.5 percent, but over a 30-year period, it's much harder. The active investor can adopt such a strategy, but the average consumer doesn't make use of the vehicles that allow him or her to earn that kind of return consistently year after year. And you must make the investments consistently or you lose.

Earning a Return on Investment of Twenty Percent

Most arguments against 15-year loans are theoretical and ignore one very practical fact—15-year loans are priced from about ⅜ to ½ percent cheaper than 30-year loans, as can be seen at the Freddie Mac Web site, www.freddiemac.com. For jumbo loans (those greater than the conforming limit, currently $252,700), the differential is even greater. Thus, with a 15-year loan, not only do you benefit from the accelerated payoff, but you save on the interest rate as well—a key point.

No doubt some of you are thinking, "This analysis is good *if* I keep the loan until maturity. But I'm going to sell my house in a few years and buy another. Can I still benefit from a 15-year loan?" That's a good question. The trick is knowing how to measure this advantage over a shorter term. Remember that even if there were no difference in rate, whenever you send in extra money on your mortgage payment, you get a return on investment (ROI) equal to the note rate; that is, if you had an extra $1000, there would be no difference between making a new investment with a 7 percent return and making a principal reduction on your 7 percent mortgage—except that when you pay down your loan, your yield is locked in, and very few investments offer that kind of guarantee.

My approach uses marginal analysis, which treats the lower interest rate as a bonus for being willing to commit to a 15-year loan's higher monthly payment. Then I assign this "bonus interest" as the marginal return on investment of the additional payment. Table 17.1 shows you what I mean on a $100,000 loan, assuming a ⅜ percent difference this time.

Your reward for committing to the $237.87 extra payment is a $31.25 bonus. Divide that $31.25 by $237.75 and you're up 13 percent on top of the 7 percent return you were getting anyway—a total ROI of 20 percent. Obviously, this kind of return is tough to beat in any market, but it's especially good today, when money market funds are yielding only 4 or 5 percent and certificates of deposit even less. If you put $237.87 in the bank every month, you'll only earn $52.92 in interest for the whole year, or $4.41 in interest per month, not $31.25.

SAVING VERSUS INVESTING

Let me get a little philosophical here. When most people talk about saving $200 per month, they make it sound as if they were investing that money. The fact is, the majority of people do not *save* these funds. When they don't spend as much money on one thing, they spend that money on something else. Spending money on something else is different from saving it. Thus, an additional advantage of the 15-year loan is that it encourages discipline, forcing borrowers to build equity in their homes.

Table 17.1   Bonus Interest on a Fifteen-Year Loan

	Rate	Interest	Principal
30-year loan	7.5%	$625.00	$ 74.21
15-year loan	7.125%	$593.75	$312.08
Difference	0.375%	$ 31.25	$237.87

Financial discipline is in short supply these days. The very fabric of our economy is powered in great part by the engine of consumption. Most people's wish lists include items such as a new house, a new car, a new refrigerator, or a new TV, rather than alternatives such as making additional deposits to the 401(k) plan at work, adopting a systematic investment plan, or saving for the kids' college education. In the last 20 years in which I have been a mortgage broker, many clients have told me, "I want the 30-year loan, but I intend to make extra principal payments to pay it off faster." But when they come into my office again five years later, perhaps to refinance or to buy a new home, 80 percent of them haven't paid an extra nickel. The truth is, a lot of people simply do not have the self-discipline to make this commitment on their own, or other things pop up every month that take priority over paying something extra on their mortgage. I encourage you to examine your motivation and discipline when making this decision. Your choice will have a long-term financial impact: Own your home free and clear 15 years from now or still owe 75 percent of what you do today. The 15-year loan is one of the most powerful investment tools available for homeowners.

If you go through this kind of analysis on your loan and it seems as if the 15-year loan is just too much for you, consider a 20-year loan. Most lenders offer 20-year loans at the same price as the 30-year loans, but several national lenders price the 20-year loan about halfway between 30- and 15-year pricing. That should be an incentive for you to ask those specific questions as you interview lenders. Another alternative is the 10-year fully amortized loan. This is not for everyone; but for someone who is already a few years into a 15-year loan, the pricing is the best in the market, about ¼ percent under jumbo 15-year pricing, making it the lowest fixed-rate loan in the market!

| WARNING | Beware of what I consider the worst alternative, the 40-year loan. True, the payment is lower on a 40-year loan than on a 30-year loan, which might make a difference in qualifying, but on a $100,000 loan, lowering the payment from $665 to $621 is inconsequential compared with not building any equity.

THE REFINANCE TRAP

When rates are low, many people refinance into a new loan that lowers their interest rate. But there is a hidden trap here. Most people refinance into another 30-year amortized loan because it lowers the payment, and, as we have discussed, most people like the immediate gratification of a lower payment. Here's the trap. If they have been making payments on the old loan for, say, five years, when they refinance

Table 17.2   Elevated Interest on a Refinanced 30-Year Loan

	Balance	Payment	Rate	Years	Life-of-loan interest
Old loan	$189,000	$1,385	7.75%	25	$230,000
New loan	$189,000	$1,210	6.625%	30	$246,600 ($16,600 *more*)

into another 30-year loan, even though the payment drops, the actual total amount of interest due under the new loan will be more than under the old loan. Refinancing is a great opportunity to begin an accelerated payoff of your loan. Let me give you an example.

A teacher who consulted me was 5 years into a $200,000 30-year loan that had an interest rate of 7.5 percent and a payment of $1,398. Her remaining balance was $189,000. I could have refinanced her into a new 30-year loan at 6.625 percent, which would have lowered her payment to $1201, a savings of almost $200 per month. That is the way refinances are sold by the mortgage industry, and 80 or 90 percent of homeowners would jump on that! But I showed her the numbers in Table 17.2.

Sure, she could save almost $200 per month immediately, but she would have to make 60 more payments. Remember what I just said about the total interest going up. In this case, refinancing into another 30-year loan would raise the total amount of interest my client would have to pay by over $16,000—from $230,000 to $246,000. A better alternative would be to refinance and to keep making the same $1398 payment. The effect of making the higher-than-obligatory payment was to shorten the remaining life of the loan from 25 years down to 20 years, 7 months. Table 17.3 shows the results of that scenario.

Not bad. Most people would jump on the first alternative and ended up paying $16,000. This alternative would save my client $70,000. Actually, when we discussed it further, she said she was open to making an even larger payment. So we ended up getting her a 15-year loan at 6.125 percent. Table 17.4 shows what the final scenario looked like.

Table 17.3   Shortening Loan Term by Maintaining Payment Levels after Refinancing

	Balance	Payment	Rate	Years	Life-of-loan interest
Modified	$189,000	$1,398	6.625%	20.7	$159,358 ($70,000 savings)

**Table 17.4   Interest Saved in Refinancing from
a Thirty-Year Loan to a Fifteen-Year Loan**

	Balance	Payment	Rate	Years	Life-of-loan interest
15-year loan	$189,000	$1,609	6.125%	15	$100,000 ($130,000 savings)

My client's payment went up by about $200, but it all went to principal reduction—not exactly what you would call a cost. And you can see that by just being shrewd, she cut her total interest bill by $130,000. That's why you should adopt a similar strategy every time you refinance.

Here's a good rule of thumb: Set an objective of having your loan paid off on your last house 30 years after buying your first house. That means always seeking opportunities to make additional payments, and, whenever you refinance, to shorten the maturity of the loan. You'll find a further discussion of this topic in Chapter 18, "Managing Your Mortgage."

ALTERNATIVE RAPID AMORTIZATION PROGRAMS

For a number of reasons, a 15-year loan is unattainable for some people, especially if they can't qualify for it because the underwriter won't count a portion of a borrower's real income. For people who wish to adopt an accelerated payment schedule anyway, I work out special amortization tables to help them make additional payments that will help meet their objectives.

TIP   Amortization tables are included in all computer spreadsheet programs these days, and you can run sample amortization schedules yourself. You can also download an amortization worksheet by going to my Web site at www.loan-wolf.com/readers.htm. Type in your e-mail address and the word *goal* to enter the download area. Also available for download is the excellent Mortgage Wizard program I used earlier in this chapter. Check Appendix 1 for other mortgage programs available on the Internet.

Whatever your methodology, I encourage you to be aggressive in adopting a savings plan. After paying off high-interest-rate credit cards, foremost among your goals should be making the maximum possible contribution to tax-advantaged retirement programs, such as a 401(k) at your place of employment. After that is taken care of, adopt a rapid amortization schedule for your loan.

BIWEEKLY PAYMENT PLANS

There are 26 biweekly periods in a year, and if someone were to make one-half of his or her mortgage payment every two weeks, it would amount to the equivalent of making 13 monthly payments every year, thus amortizing the loan more quickly. The problem is that most lenders and loan servicers do not yet have a mechanism for collecting payments and crediting them to your loan on a biweekly basis. They are set up to accept 12 monthly payments per year and an extra payment amount if it is received with the regular payment. They do not have processing methods to accommodate 26 payments per year.

Some entrepreneur figured out that it is possible to accommodate both borrower and lender by establishing a special escrow account to accept the 26 payments from the borrower, and then, once a month, disburse loan payments to the lender, including the extra amount. Using this method will pay off a 30-year loan in about 23 years—a definite benefit. What's the catch? Well, there are two. First, most if not all services require that the payment be deducted every other Friday from your bank account. This is fine for many people, like those who are paid every other Friday, but for those who like to make payments when it is convenient for them, this feature is problematic. The second and more significant catch is that this process is expensive. Most services, even those offered by the banks themselves, charge a setup fee of $300 or $400, and then tack on a monthly processing fee. I do not question that providing this service should come at a price, but I think that borrowers can do this themselves at little or no cost. Let me show you how.

Remember that making a biweekly payment means there are 26 biweekly periods in a year. If you make 26 half-payments, it's the same as making 13 payments. There are three ways to accomplish this:

- Make a thirteenth payment once a year, at bonus time or some other convenient period.

- Spread out the thirteenth payment by adding 8.33 percent to every payment.

- If you get paid every two weeks, set up a savings or money market account and transfer one-half of your payment into it every two weeks; then make the payments to the lender as appropriate. (Be sure to maintain whatever minimum balance is required to earn interest on the balance in the account.)

Look at Figure 17.3, which shows the principal reduction for each method just described compared with a biweekly payment. You can see that each of these methods produces an almost identical result, and mine won't cost you anything if you do them systematically.

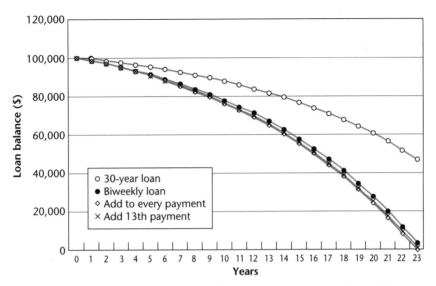

Figure 17.3   Results of various methods of accelerated payoff.

Before wrapping up this section, let's talk about human nature again. The plain fact is that if people had to write a check toward their 401(k) plan every month instead of having it automatically deducted from their paychecks, the number of participants in retirement programs would drop significantly. Don't you agree? That same phenomenon will be at work in making additional mortgage payments on a voluntary basis. The pressures on people's budgets these days are such that they would just defer making that extra payment until the next month, and then defer it again the month after that. For such people, a third-party managed biweekly payment plan can be well worth the money. But shop around for the services. Use the Internet, doing a search using the keywords *biweekly mortgage payments*. If such a program appeals to you, remember that you are going to be authorizing the transfer of thousands of dollars every year, so be sure to get all the information and review the contract carefully before signing up.

SUMMARY

Accelerated payment plans that pay off loans quickly are a highly underrated savings and investment plan for many people. If the additional payment is not a financial strain, you should consider a 15-year loan when you purchase a home. Those whose loans are good candidates for refinancing and who are convinced by the merits of my arguments should consider refinancing into a 15-year loan. The interest rate differential—an extra ⅜ or ½ percent—will provide more incentive to help finance the cost of the transaction. For others whose loans are already at or below the current market rate, adopting an accelerated plan of any type will yield significant long-term benefits.

18

MANAGING YOUR MORTGAGE

The individual who can modify or correct beliefs molded by personal interest or the influences of his rearing is rare. It is easy to be wise in retrospect, uncommonly difficult in the event.
—WALLACE STEGNER, *BEYOND THE 100TH MERIDIAN*

KEY POINTS

- Most people take their mortgage as a given in their lives, and do not understand the number of choices they have.
- Most people follow conventional wisdom about which mortgage to get; therefore, they get conventional results.
- Most people do not realize that their mortgage is just another financial instrument and that financial planning includes proper mortgage management, which can have awesome consequences.

I'm always amazed when I go into my local bookstore and see 5000 self-help books; there must be 1000 on investments such as stocks and mutual funds and 300 on dieting. They are testimony to the triumph of hope over experience. My guess is that 95 percent of people who buy self-help books are not helped, that 95 percent of the people who buy investment books do not benefit from the advice they read, and that 95 percent of people who buy diet books do not achieve permanent weight loss (which may explain why the next largest book category seems to be cookbooks). These books have one thing in common: They appeal to the human desire to get something for nothing or for very little effort, whether it's self-help without introspection and commitment, better investment returns with get-rich-quick gimmicks, or weight loss through schemes that do not involve discipline.

In contrast, you will find only a relative handful of books on mortgages in your local bookstore. Perhaps this is because most people do not think that there is anything glitzy about mortgages. In fact, proper mortgage management holds significant financial promise for most people—sometimes more than they can achieve with other types of investment management.

For most people, their largest asset is their home and their largest liability is their mortgage. People in general think seriously and regularly about the value of their home and how quickly that value is (or is not) increasing. Unfortunately, they seldom consider that a $10,000 reduction in their mortgage would have the same effect as a $10,000 increase in the home's value.

In short, there are terrific benefits to be had for the prudent homeowner who takes active management of his or her mortgage. If this seems obvious to you, I can assure you it is not to most people. Homeowners tend to get the same kind of mortgage that their neighbors got; they fit their mortgage payment into their budget, and go on with life, making payments seemingly forever. Specifically, most people get a payment coupon that says, "Pay $863.25," and that's what they send in, month after month, for as many years as it takes.

THE REWARDS OF PAYING OFF YOUR MORTGAGE LOAN

If you are wise, during your working life, you begin to prepare financially for your old age, so that you can spend your retirement years comfortably. Most reasonable adults these days acknowledge that Social Security payments are not going to be enough to provide for anything but the bare necessities of life. Consequently, let us define successful retirement as the ability to maintain a postretirement lifestyle that is comparable to your lifestyle prior to retirement. If you ask 100 people how to accomplish this goal, though, nearly all would say that you have to accumulate sufficient assets to provide the necessary income. Most would not mention the elimination of liabilities as another means to the same end. Here is my surefire retirement preparation technique:

> *Plan your affairs so as to have your mortgage paid off the month you retire.*

When you eliminate the largest single item in your expense budget, it will be a lot easier to live comfortably on a reduced level of income. If the expense level drops by the amount of the mortgage payment, most people will be sitting pretty. In order to pay off your mortgage at age 65 or some other defined retirement age, however, it is important to start the planning process some number of years before that, not at age 64. For example, whenever I am securing a loan for someone past age 45, I always ask questions that are designed to deal with the retirement question.

But the planning should start sooner. I propose what I call *life-cycle planning.* The earlier you start planning, the easier it will be to accomplish your goal. And most people simply do not comprehend the role of a mortgage in their financial life, other than as a means of purchasing a home and then as 30 years of making payments. They look upon it as a necessary evil and nothing more. The fact is that a mortgage can be managed just like any other financial instrument.

A Tale of Two Families

Far more often than you might imagine, different families may have identical circumstances but manage them differently for totally different outcomes. I want to give you a little insight into the power of making good decisions as compared with following conventional wisdom. We will consider two families over a 30-year period, from the time they buy their first homes until they are almost ready for retirement. We will assume that they purchase identical homes and have with identical initial mortgage amounts.

Joe and Jane always do what all their neighbors do. They get the most popular mortgage; they save money up front; and they reduce the monthly payment when they refinance. In fact, Joe and Jane are representative of most Americans—probably you, too, until you picked up this book.

Bill and Barbara, on the other hand, are the kind of folks who always do their homework. They select a loan that meets their needs (they will pay points if they can save more money in the long term); and when they refinance, they convert the savings to pay down their loan more quickly rather than reducing their monthly payment. They also enlist the aid of experts in helping them make their mortgage decisions.

Let's see how both families do.

Step 1: 1983.   In year 1, the families purchase $100,000 homes next door to each other. (We're going to assume that the homes appreciate about ½ percent per month, between 5 and 6 percent per year.) Both families put 10 percent down. (In our calculations, we're going to ignore private mortgage insurance, as both families have it and it doesn't influence the calculations.) Rates are just dropping from record levels, and both families get adjustable-rate mortgages (ARMs) with a 10 percent start rate.

- Joe and Jane choose the most popular loan for the period, the recently introduced ARM tied to the 11th District Cost of Funds Index. This is a negative-amortization loan, and Joe and

> Jane make the minimum payment and add the deferred inter-
> est to their loan balance.
>
> • Bill and Barbara choose a loan tied to the potentially more
> volatile T-bill index, and they make the obligatory payment.

Step 2: 1993.   Rates have dropped, and both borrowers decide to get
out of their ARMs and into fixed-rate loans.

> • Joe and Jane choose a 30-year fixed-rate mortgage and take
> advantage of another new industry feature, the zero-point
> loan. They get a competitive 7.5 percent rate and pay the nor-
> mal payment.
> • Bill and Barbara figure that they aren't going to be in the home
> too many more years, so they get a 5/1 ARM, also a new prod-
> uct. They also pay 1 point to buy down the rate to 6.75 per-
> cent. They figure that they have already been in the home for
> 10 years, so they calculate the payment required to amortize
> the loan over 20 years—only about $92 per month higher than
> that for a 30-year amortization schedule.

Step 3: 1998.   Because their houses have doubled in value, appreciat-
ing to $244,000, and they are making much more than they were 15
years ago, both couples decide to buy new $400,000 homes, trading
their equity in their old homes into their new homes and borrowing the
balance.

> • Joe gets a 30-year fixed-rate mortgage and again pays no
> points. His rate is 7.75 percent.
> • Bill gets a 15-year loan because he wants to have this home
> paid for more quickly. His rate is 6.75 percent because 15-year
> loans are cheaper and because he paid 1 point to buy the rate
> down.

Step 4: 2003.   Rates have dropped again, and both borrowers refinance.

> • Joe gets another 30-year loan, this one 1 percent lower at 6.75
> percent, dropping his payment by $222 per month.
> • Bill gets another 15-year loan and pays 1 point, dropping the
> rate to 6 percent. Because he is already 5 years into the last
> loan, he is actually on a 10-year amortization schedule. Thus
> he adopts a 10-year payment schedule on the new loan, one
> that will pay his mortgage off in just 10 more years. His pay-
> ment actually drops $21 per month from what it was on the
> old 15-year loan.

Step 5: 2013. Both homes have appreciated to $976,000! (If this sounds like a lot, remember that this appreciation rate is less than 6 percent per year, and that 15 years have gone by. Many homes are worth two-and-one-half times what they were worth 15 years ago.)

- Joe owes $189,875 on his mortgage.
- Bill owns his home free and clear.

Table 18.1 gives is a summary of where the borrowers stand.

During the first 15 years, Joe and Bill had substantially the same payments; but with the purchase of their new homes, Bill ratcheted up his payments by $371 per month over Joe and $555 per month during the last 10 years. In total, he paid out $86,243 more over 30 years. However, he reduced the interest cost by $108,607 and paid off the mortgage in its entirety.

Joe saved that $86,243, but he still has $345,818 in payments left ahead of him. What else does he have to show for that $86,243? Is it worth $345,818? Probably not.

Look at it another way: Bill lives in a house worth $976,000. He has no mortgage payment. Can he have a comfortable retirement? Joe's house is worth the same, but he has $189,875 less equity and he has still has to make payments of $1,440 per month for another 20 years.

This example should clarify to you the power of making good decisions, getting the right loan, paying points if you're going to be around for a few years, and adopting a more aggressive payment schedule.

FOR THOSE WELL INTO THEIR MORTGAGES

Of course, most people aren't just starting off, but are well into their mortgage life cycle. In Chapter 17, "Understanding Fifteen-Year Loans and Accelerated Payoffs," we discussed the teacher who came into my office to refinance her home. She and I agreed that refinancing into another 30-year loan would have been silly because almost no one

Table 18.1 Conventional Wisdom versus Astute Mortgage Management

	Joe	Bill	Difference
Remaining mortgage balance	$189,875.63	0	
Total payments made	$405,217.61	$491,540.71	$ 86,323.10
Total interest paid	$348,819.42	$240,212.35	$−108,607.07

wants to be making mortgage payments between ages 65 and 80. This is a powerful message: The goal of refinancing should be to lower the remaining term of the loan, not to reduce the payments.

For most people, however, the analysis is more complicated than the teacher's situation. They may still have children in college or may be obligated to a higher expense level of one kind or another, making a higher mortgage payment impractical. That does not mean it is not important to plan to get rid of the mortgage; it may just mean that it will be several years before the mortgage liquidation plan can be put completely into effect.

Let me share with you an example that illustrates this. Let's assume that Jack and Gwen are 5 years into a 30-year loan when interest rates drop, making refinancing practical. They are unwilling to consider a 15-year loan because they are still obligated to 5 more years of college expenses. They are in a position, however, to keep their monthly payment the same as it was prior to the refinancing. Typically, this will cause their new loan to be amortized over a 20-year period, saving 5 years of the remaining term of their current loan. Specifically, Jack and Gwen do not want to get another 30-year loan. Five years later, when the college expenses are eliminated, they will already have what amounts to a 15-year loan because they have been making payments for 5 years on a 20-year amortization schedule. At that time, they can consider increasing the payments even further and reducing the remaining term of the loan from 15 years to 10 years.

Table 18.2 takes you through the example to show you how this works.

There is no magic here. Just two people who stopped paying attention to conventional wisdom, which says you should always find ways to lower the payment. And do what with the money? Well, be creative!

Table 18.2   Reducing the Loan Term as Time Goes By

Age	Mortgage balance	Interest rate	Payment	Amortization
40	$100,000	8.5%	$768.91	Original loan
45	$ 95,490	7.5%	$769.91*	20 years
50	$ 83,008	7.5%	$985.32	10 years
60	0			

*This is higher than the obligatory payment, $667.68, but this way the loan gets paid off faster. Compared with where Jack and Gwen were headed with their original loan and its payment, they made 120 payments that were $216 higher than their old payment, totaling about $26,000. What they saved was five years of payments—60 payments of $691, totaling $46,134.

TIP A number of other calculators that can assist you with mortgage planning are listed in Appendix 2. The one I value most is the Mortgage Wizard program, an excellent planning tool that enables you to consider the effects of a number of different payment options on the payoff of your loan. You can download it from my Web Site at www.loan-wolf.com/download.htm.

SUMMARY

Most people have a passive relationship with their mortgages. When I meet with clients and ask questions about their mortgages, many do not know even the interest rate they are paying. A surprising number cannot even remember the name of their current mortgage lender. I advise you to have an active relationship with your mortgage. No doubt you were surprised by the analysis we went through in this chapter; almost everyone is. Now that you know, you can act accordingly.

19

SOME THOUGHTS ON FINANCIAL PLANNING AND BALANCING YOUR LIFE

If people bought what they needed instead of what they wanted, then some of those crooked concerns would go out of business.
                    —CLYDE EDGERTON IN *KILLER DILLER*

Once you get rich, you'd have to spend all your time staying rich, and that's hard, thankless work.
          —LARRY McMURTRY, *THE LAST PICTURE SHOW*

Those who think that money can't buy happiness don't know where to shop.
                    —LARRY McMURTRY, *TEXASVILLE*

KEY POINTS

- People have a strange relationship with their money, sometimes not a healthy one.
- I see so many facets of people's lives, I see things that others don't, and I hope that my observations are useful to you.
- Retirement planning is easier these days because the tax treatment encourages investing for retirement more than at any other time in history.
- Most people still miss some obvious opportunities to save, the biggest being the automobile trap.

Because I see so much of people's financial lives, I have learned a lot about financial success and failure. The purpose of this chapter is to share some of what I've learned with you so that it might help you to achieve greater success in your personal and your economic life.

| TIP | Explore some of the books about lifestyle and financial planning listed in Appendix 1.

My clients tell me things they won't tell their CPAs, stockbrokers, or financial planners. I have examined a lot of tax returns in my career, and tax returns tell the truth—or at least what the taxpayers think the IRS will believe is the truth. I see where people derive their income and where they spend much of their money. I see which investments make money and which ones lose money. I see which people have prudent ideas and which ones make foolish mistakes.

FINANCIAL PLANNING

To begin, I think it's possible to reduce financial planning to these three essential elements.

- Either you're going to die young or you're going to die old.
- If you die young, hopefully you've protected your loved ones by financially securing them with insurance.
- If you live to a ripe old age, if you've prepared financially, you can spend your later years in comfort rather than poverty.

The Power of Compounding

Americans tend to focus on the present, believing the future is so far away that they can put off making decisions about saving for another month, another year. Not so. Let me illustrate, again using Bill and Barbara and Joe and Jane, the two couples introduced in the previous chapter. In this scenario, at 25 Bill and Barbara start to save for retirement by putting $1000 into a retirement account. But they do so only for 10 years, stopping when they are 35. Joe and Jane don't start saving until they are 35, when they, too, begin to put $1000 per year into a similar account. But they continue to invest in the account for 30 years, until they are 65. Both accounts earn 10 percent per year. How do their accounts compare when they all reach 65? Bill and Barbara, who started earlier and only put $10,000 away, have an account worth over $336,000, while Joe and Jane, who put away three times as much, have an account valued at only $200,000. How? The power of compounding money over time.

Small investments made early have very powerful consequences. Remember this example. Saving has never been more rewarding than it is today because of tax-advantaged plans and the returns that you can get these days, unlike 20 or 30 years ago. Saving is a different ball game today, and you can be one of the winners. My advice to you is to make a commitment to saving, and to do it *today*.

Money Management

I read that the author of a magazine article had gone to a bookstore and measured how many linear feet of shelf space were devoted to books on investing. It came to 86 feet. My point? There are enough books about money management. No, I'm not going to add to that footage, but I am going to give you the benefit of what I have learned from my years in the real estate business, some of the insight I've gained looking at more than 2000 tax returns.

First, you do not need to be wealthy to have a comfortable retirement. The good news is that 7.9 percent of American families are millionaires today, up from the 3.5 percent number of a few years ago, no doubt due to the strong stock market and the increase in value of residential real estate. But you do not need a million dollars to retire in comfort. More is certainly better than less, so you should accumulate as much as you can. Now it is easier than ever, because not since Congress started taxing personal income have the tax laws been as generous to citizens as they are today.

The best great wealth-building mechanism for the average American today is the opportunity to contribute to a tax-deferred retirement plan such as an individual retirement account (IRA), 401(k) plan, or other retirement plan. Whatever contributions you make will grow without being penalized by current income taxes. Although you will have to pay taxes when you begin taking distributions from your plan, presumably you will be in a lower income status and a lower tax bracket. If your current combined federal and state tax rate is 40 percent, you save that amount in taxes when you make your contribution. But when you take the money out after you have retired, your tax rate is going to be much less, perhaps 20 percent. In the meantime, your money is growing faster than it would in a comparable investment or if you had to pay taxes on current income.

A recent study showed that most people do not ask for, nor are they given, much information about their retirement accounts either by their employer or the plan's administrator. I urge you to make a special point of keeping track of your investments, even if only through quarterly reports. Worse yet, a recent study showed that half of the people who changed jobs cashed in their 401(k) plans. Not only did these people have to pay taxes and penalties, they had to start saving all over again. Not a wise choice! If you have the opportunity to direct some of those investments, I recommend that you buy several of those 86 feet of books and educate yourself. In Appendix 1, I list several you can start with. I also list a number of Web sites that help you learn about investing, retirement planning, and organizing your investments.

A second wealth-builder is the ability to own your own home in an inflationary market and to use leverage by borrowing most of the purchasing price and paying back the loan with dollars that shrink in value as inflation wears on them. I have included in this book a number of ideas that have been helpful, but there are numerous others that are beyond the scope of this book. Again, refer to Appendix 1, where I suggest some excellent books on owning real estate. And don't forget the importance of what I discussed in the previous chapter: the power of paying off your mortgage, thus eliminating the largest budget expense, as a means of ensuring a comfortable retirement.

Investment Management

The most important investment advice I can give you is not financial. Rather, it is ancient wisdom. More than 2000 years ago, Socrates said, "Know thyself." If you are going to be a successful investor, you need to understand your own strengths and weaknesses. Each and every one of us, from novice investor to floor trader, sometimes make decisions to buy or sell investments either out of bravado or panic. You buy the wrong stock on a tip and lose most of your money, or you sell a winner too early. It is easy to panic when the market goes into the tank. It is also easy to fall in love with an idea and not be willing to admit, "Boy, was I wrong about that one!" The most common investment fault is refusing to sell a loser, instead waiting until it gets back up to what you bought it for before unloading it. Psychologically, taking a loss is, for some, an admission of a mistake, while waiting a year until the stock comes back—if it ever does—justifies itself. This is silly decision making. Sell the stock and buy something else. There are thousands of other stocks that will perform better than that loser.

We all have heard the expression *smart money*. Well, if there is such a thing, and I believe there is, there is also such a thing as *stupid money*. You want to do things that are smart. Buying and selling stocks based on tips and emotion is not smart. You can save yourself a lot of grief and money when you resist acting impulsively. You will never be able to become a totally rational person (no one can), but if you take the time to engage in introspection, you will be able to discern your various personal traits, both constructive and destructive. Once you understand yourself better, you will be able to recognize when you are being one or the other. You can learn to take an hour or a day to think before making decisions. You're investing for a lifetime; things really can wait until tomorrow.

And don't become discouraged because your portfolio doesn't match the return of the Dow Jones Industrial Average or some other index each year. No matter what investment strategy you adopt, if you have an intelligently balanced portfolio of large-cap stocks, stocks in smaller companies, some foreign investments, and bonds, you will find that the return on your entire portfolio is never going to be equal to the return of the best sector in the most recent period. That's okay, because a good portfolio should be a balance between risk and safety. Some investment advisors advocate buying nothing but no-load mutual funds, while others suggest buying individual stocks. Many advise buying quality investment-grade stocks and bonds, putting them away and not wasting time and energy trading them. Others advocate a more active management of the portfolio. In fact, any of these plans can work well, but you have to decide, based on your temperament, which is best for you.

Many people simply do not have the time or energy for investment management—or choose not to devote the time and energy to it. Their investment style is passive. Obviously, the buy-and-hold investor's results will not show up on his or her tax returns, because there is no tax event until a position is closed. The trader, on the other hand, may have a two-page Schedule D listing all his or her trades. For what it's worth, studies show and my experience corroborates that most frequent traders lose money, because they trade without putting in the time to invest intelligently. Recently there have been some exceptions to that, due not to the lower costs of Internet trading but to the greater access to information that has empowered traders to trade more intelligently. If you are willing to spend at least one hour per day studying investments, then you can probably find success as a more active trader.

Neither does it make sense to make investments and put them away for 30 or 40 years. Remember the tales of the trusts established in 1900 whose investments were limited to manufacturers of buggy whips and moustache wax? It is no different today; only the names have changed. Investments in the blue-chip companies of 20 years ago may have done well for an extended period, but you need to reexamine them from time to time. A portfolio established in 1990 should certainly be reevaluated in 1995, again in 2000, and again at regular intervals. You can't time the market, but you certainly can try to respond to fundamental changes in the marketplace. Today, as we enter the twenty-first century, the so-called old economy stocks are taking a drubbing and the successful ideas are almost all technology related: computers, communication, biotechnology, and, of course, the Internet. These sectors are forcing fundamental, broad-based changes in the economy, and not acknowledging their strength is not prudent investing.

EMPOWERMENT AND EDUCATION

Empowerment and education must go hand in hand. Empowerment without education is meaningless. Deciding how to invest your money wisely is no different from deciding how to make wise choices about getting a mortgage; you must figure out how much help you need. Talk with successful investors and see where they get their information. Some successful investors go it alone; if you are going to follow in their footsteps, ask how much time they spend studying and ask yourself if you are willing to make that same commitment. If you are willing to educate yourself about investments, then perhaps you can go it alone too. By educating yourself, I mean enrolling in a course about investments, getting some good basic texts about investments and reading them, and spending at least an hour a day doing research on stocks and mutual funds. I don't mean reading the magazine articles that shout: "Ten Stocks You Need to Own Now!" I don't mean hanging around chat rooms on the Internet or making your decisions based on e-mail tips you receive. If you are not willing to make the commitment to educating yourself, you are better off working with a professional.

As you accumulate more money, you can hire a planner or counselor on your own. And believe me, I practice what I preach: Even though I have an MBA, have spent about 30 of my 35 years in business as an investor, have a comfortable portfolio, and spend an hour a day studying and strategizing about investments, I still use a professional.

Spending versus Saving

Consumers drive the American economy, no question about it. But if you look at those who have accumulated a nice nest egg for retirement, by and large you'll find they have let other consumers drive the economy by spending. They have saved and invested their money. Perhaps it's time for you to take a penny-by-penny look at how you spend your money.

All of us spend money that, a week later, we wish we hadn't. We all buy clothes that we never wear. We all buy things that end up in a garage sale a couple of years later. If we were able to avoid these purchases, we'd all have quite a bundle at age 65. My point is, keep track of your expenditures and see where the money goes. When you are considering a major purchase, never buy it when you first have the impulse. Wait for 48 hours; perhaps you *can* get a long without it. If you can't, check out *Consumer Reports* before you buy and make your buying decision based on knowledge, not whim.

Buying on Credit

Assuming now that you have waited 48 hours and have decided you still want whatever it is, my next advice is to buy it, not borrow to buy it. This means you should pay cash for the purchase or charge it to a credit card that you will pay in full at the end of the month. If you want to accumulate a down payment for a house, you're not going to be successful if you are carrying credit card balances costing you 10 to 18 percent. For example, a $300 suit put on a credit card and paid off over time actually costs anywhere from $350 to $450 depending on how long it takes you to pay it in full. You can't afford to do that.

This leads to a discussion of what is for many people the second biggest purchase (after a home) that they make: a car.

The Automobile Trap

If you thought a car was for transportation, consider these statements.

> ."... *recognize automobiles for what they have indisputably become: mobile extensions of our living environment. Our cars reveal our individual triumphs, as well as our yearnings; in them we find a concentrated form of design that's capable of transporting us emotionally even as it transports us literally."*
> —PAIGE RENSE, EDITOR-IN-CHIEF,
> *ARCHITECTURAL DIGEST MOTORING*

> "... *automobiles are heavily laden with social meanings and are highly esteemed because they 'provide avenues of expression ... of the character, temperament and self concept of the owner and driver' ..."*
> —VANCE PACKARD, *THE HIDDEN PERSUADERS*

The automobile industry marketers really have the American consumer in their crosshairs. They are experts at creating a sense of need in the minds of millions of people, and then convincing them that this need can be satisfied only by spending $20,000 or $30,000 or $40,000 for a new car.

Ironically, I have noticed that an extraordinary number of the people who have developed their wealth themselves don't spend a lot of money on cars. They look on cars as a means of transportation, not as extensions of their egos, and that saves them a bundle. They usually drive cars that are 5 or 10 years old. By comparison, the people who always have two new cars in the driveway are usually in hock to their ears, because they don't just have two cars, they have two car loans, too. They also seem to have higher credit card balances, buy larger homes, and make payments on larger mortgages. This leads one to believe that cars are just one trap our consumer-oriented economy lays for consumers.

Let me share an example of how much cars can cost your family. Dick and Ben, who live next door to each other, buy identical cars for

$15,000 in year 1. Each finances his car and pays it off in four years. Then Dick buys a new car—a slightly more expensive car with a slightly larger payment—and finances it, too. Ben keeps driving his old car for another four years. He doesn't have a car payment, so he puts the same amount Joe is paying on his loan for his new car into a mutual fund account that grows. So while Dick keeps making a $400 car payment, Ben socks away $400 into an investment that grows in value.

At the end of that next four-year period, again Dick and Ben each buy identical, slightly more expensive, cars. Joe finances his, but Ben has saved enough with his $400 per month savings to pay cash for his and have a little bit left over. For the next 32 years, Joe keeps buying and financing cars every 4 years until a total of 40 years have gone by. Ben keeps socking away in savings every month whatever Dick is paying every month on car loan payments. Every eight years he buys a new car by tapping his savings account for the cash. Sure, from a lifestyle perspective, half of that time—20 years—Dick and Ben have been driving identical cars, but in the other half, Dick is driving a new car while Ben drives an older one. How much of a sacrifice is that? Let's see how it worked out financially.

At the end of 40 years, when Dick and Ben are both due to buy a new car, they look back over the last 40 years. Dick has bought and financed $263,000 in cars and has accumulated over $45,000 in interest payments during 40 years. On the other hand, in those 36 years of saving, Ben has accumulated over $800,000. That's a swing of over $850,000. That $850,000 alone is enough to ensure a quality retirement for most people. I showed this analysis to a car dealer friend, who said, "I hope my customers don't read your book."

I'm making two points here. First, obviously, is that you have to get over trying to impress people. Let go of the "keep up with the Jones" philosophy of life. Second, when you start saving, *really* save, by which I mean invest your money rather than spend it on something else.

Real Estate Investments

All homeowners have a real estate investment: their home. But many people have the desire to invest in other types of real estate, such as a rental or commercial property. If this is of interest to you, I strongly suggest that you first consider your own temperament. Some people are just not suited to be landlords—to deal with finding and qualifying tenants, to solve the myriad problems that go along with owning any property, and finally, to know when to sell the property. To highlight just how difficult an investment real estate can be, I share with you a maxim told to me by a friend who is a successful landlord.

"Any act of kindness will be viewed as a sign of weakness."

Sound harsh? I assure you, my friend is a nice guy, but the difficulty he has experienced with some of his tenants over the years has hardened his heart somewhat. If you want to make money in real estate, you have to be able to raise rents when it is called for and not think, "She's been such a good tenant, we don't want to lose her." If she's such a good tenant, she won't mind paying you market rent rather than having to move and pay market rent to someone else. You have to be able to handle lease and tenant and maintenance problems week after week, month after month, year after year. Finally, you have to be tenacious, to be able to weather the up-and-down economic cycles. The most important thing to realize about investing is real estate is that it is extraordinarily difficult to make money in a short period of time; you must be aware that this is a long-term investment. If you are considering investing in real estate, believing you do have the temperament, here are some guidelines:

- Buy carefully, because you are going to own for a long time.
- Buy single-family residences rather than condominiums.
- Buy vanilla properties that will rent and sell easily.
- Find good tenants, and maintain market rents.
- Keep your properties well maintained.
- Try to get your properties to break even initially, and to generate a positive cash flow as soon as possible.
- Apply all rent increases to reducing the mortgage. Ultimately, your tenants will have paid off the mortgage on the property free and clear.

If you are lucky, if property values surge, or if you are able to devote more money to investing in real estate, there may be a point in time when you can make a tax-free exchange, trading up to a small apartment building or complex. Such properties are usually more efficient to own and manage than one or two or three houses.

If you succeed in building up substantial equity in one or more properties, it probably will be possible to refinance them and then to take cash out on a tax-free basis. If you decide to do this, be sure to discuss it beforehand with competent accounting and income tax professionals. Finally, in Appendix 1, I commend David Schumacher's book *Buy and Hold: Seven Steps to a Real Estate Fortune* to you.

Investing in Small Businesses

You don't have to have much money to attract businesspeople who want you to invest some of it in their ideas. Whether the money is to be used to start a dot-com company (the most prevalent type of new venture today), manufacture a new carburetor that allows a car to get 100 miles per gallon, buy a motel, or open a trendy new restaurant, I offer one simple piece of advice that will save you a bundle of money: Don't do it!

There is a cadre of professional promoters out there whose job it is to find investment money for various ventures. They will show you a spreadsheet of pro forma operating results, which always look good. What they won't show you is what the *first* spreadsheet looked like, before they tweaked it to look good enough to show you. In the 1970s, it was real estate investment trusts (REITs). In the 1980s, it was limited partnerships. As the tax laws change, there is always a new gimmick touted by some huckster showing you how the investment will save taxes.

Instead, I advise you to invest in publicly traded companies to which Securities and Exchange Commission (SEC) disclosure rules apply and where you have *liquidity,* the ability to sell your investment when you want to.

The Lottery

The lottery is a tax on the mathematically challenged. Don't buy lottery tickets.

MAINTAINING PERSPECTIVE

When it comes to money and home ownership, it's important to keep things in perspective. Many people, particularly first-time homebuyers, become emotionally distraught when buying a home. Some even come to believe that their lives will be meaningless unless they can buy the home immediately. This is simply not the case. Consider this list of things much more important:

- A sense of spiritual well-being
- Good health
- Strong, healthy relationships with your family and friends
- Provisions for a comfortable retirement
- A rewarding and fulfilling career

All of these have nothing to do with owning a home. If you can't buy a particular home you want, when you want it, remember that there are many, many other homes out there. Denial of a loan may actually be a blessing at that moment in time. If you didn't qualify for the loan you wanted, it's probably a good indication that you should consider a smaller loan or a smaller home. Or that you need to do additional planning, save more money, clean up your credit—whatever it takes to meet your goals next year or the year after that.

Interest Rates

We've all read newspaper headlines such as "Fed Increases Interest Rates" or "Mortgage Rates Rise." To anyone in the market for a new home, this news is greeted with foreboding. Certainly, interest rates do have an effect on the affordability of housing for marginal homebuyers, but those of you who feel particularly sensitive to interest rates should look at Figure 19.1, which shows the rates on 30-year fixed-rate mortgages for the last 28 years.

This illustration should make you feel better. People continued to buy and sell homes even when the market was going through some tough times. We will have more tough times, and everyone will survive those, too. So when you hear that rates are going up, don't be discouraged, because it isn't the end of the world. Take a deep breath, and keep right on going.

REFLECTIONS ON LIFE

Over the years, I have collected a number of aphorisms that are the result of my reflections on the human experience, in particular the experience of watching my clients cope with the problems of buying and selling their homes. To some extent, these reflections transcend the

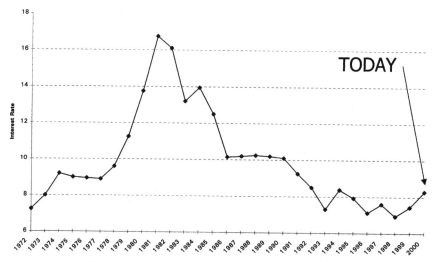

Figure 19.1   Rates for 30-year fixed mortgages.

merely commercial and offer answers to the questions that life poses to all of us sooner or later:

- People will do what they need to do, and you have to let them do it.
- Your worth as a human being is measured not by what you accumulate or what you achieve, but by what you give away.
- When people meet someone who knows someone they know, they often say, "Isn't it a small world?" No, it isn't—it's a very big world, 24,000 miles around with 6 billion people on it. However, it is a connected world.
- Success in life comes from finding something you can do well and that makes you happy, and then doing it to the very best of your ability.
- The task you are most reluctant to tackle is almost certainly the one you most need to do.
- Pay attention. Each life event should be a learning experience; and if you do learn from your experiences, you will only experience the negative ones once.
- You are measured not by what you believe in but by what you do.
- Keep an open mind; reexamine your beliefs, even your most strongly held beliefs, from time to time. And have the courage to say, "I was wrong."
- Life is not a training exercise—it is the real thing. Deal with what is on your plate now, not what might be there tomorrow.
- Be happy with what you have, where you are, now.
- Don't quit.

SUMMARY

Buying a home is a marvelously satisfying experience. I still remember the joy of spending the first night in my first home. Indeed, one of the greatest pleasures of my job is helping people realize their dreams of owning their own home. With the advent of the Internet, homeowners can become more involved in the decision-making process than ever before. Those who use these tools effectively can have a strong competitive advantage over those who use only traditional resources and who rely on others to make decisions for them. Home ownership is more satisfying and less costly when you prepare and inform yourself so that you make the right decisions along the way. I hope this book proves to be a meaningful part of your preparations and becomes a helper for you in buying and financing your home. More important, I hope it encourages you to make a financial plan, to treat your mortgage as part of that plan, and to remember to reexamine your mortgage on a regular basis so that you can make other wise choices when opportunity knocks. Good luck!

APPENDIX 1

GLOSSARY

As all of my readers are "connected," go to the glossary at my Web site (www.loan-wolf.com/glossary.htm). I urge you to check it out if you want an explanation of industry terminology.

INDEX OF WEB SITES

One of the shortcomings of a book is that you can't put in working hyperlinks. Some of the URLs are long and complicated, and I know it will not be much fun to type them into your computer. Hence I have created an index of URLs at my Web site. When you want to go to a site—you'll be at your computer anyway—go to http://www.loan-wolf .com/urlindex.htm. (Be sure to bookmark the page for easy return to it in the future.) You will see every URL in the book with hyperlinks to the sites. No typing! I hope you like this feature.

OTHER WEB SITES WITH GOOD ADVICE

I have a high regard for attorney Robert Bruss, who is a syndicated columnist and the author of a monthly newsletter. You can view the catalog of prior newsletters and articles at his site at https://secure .inman.com/bruss/catalog.cfm. These reports are available at nominal cost, and are well worth the very modest price. You can also check out the other Bruss articles that appear on a regular basis at the Inman News Web site at www.inman.com.

A good source for mortgage information is at www .mortgageprofessor.com. Jack Gutenberg's background is academic, so, as the name of his site suggests, he has a more professorial demeanor than my "from the trenches" perspective. His research is thorough and his advice helpful.

Another useful site with tons of information on all aspects of family life, including home ownership, is Our Family Place at www .ourfamilyplace.com. This site has earned my admiration because of its focus on making family life more of a joy. There are sections on finding time, gaining control, and personal finances. I think that the information on homeselling and homebuying is valuable. For example, in helping you develop priorities, the site makes an important distinction between *need* and *want*. You should too.

These experts and Web sites are not affiliated with any real estate company or lender. They do their own research and have excellent credentials. For these reasons, I value their advice. You should too, more so than the many self-serving articles that appear at so many real estate and mortgage Web sites.

Spreadsheets

Those who are looking for more fully featured programs should first go to my Web site at www.loan-wolf.com/readers.htm. Type in your e-mail address and the word *goal* to get to the download page. The following programs and worksheets are available there.

Mortgage Wizard.   This program is a very useful tool, especially in figuring out odd amortization periods.

Qualify.xls.   The General Purpose Worksheet. This is so much more useful than the available stand-alone programs that give you an answer to just one question. Most people want to compare various alternatives, and this worksheet allows you to do just that. For example, you can:

- Check out qualifying as you increase home value
- Check out the impact of varying the loan amount
- Compare different loan programs with different interest rates
- Do accurate refinance calculations

Discount.xls.   This is the worksheet you use to compare different rate versus fee alternatives. Fill in the rate sheet information from your lender, and the program calculates the break-even periods, just like in the book. It even graphs the results for you.

Amort.xls.   A simple amortization table. Mortgage Wizard produces one too, but this one is useful if you want to see the effect of increasing your payments a step at a time in future years.

Arm-comp.xls.   This is a useful table for collecting rate information from lenders on the various adjustable-rate mortgage (ARM) programs.

15year.xls.   This worksheet shows how to calculate the rewards of a 15-year loan. They are far greater than you think! Typically you will get more than a 15 percent return on investment. Be sure to use the same points for each alternative.

Termwrks.xls.   Calculates the marginal benefit of one loan term versus another, such as a 5/1 ARM versus a 7/1 ARM.

Mortgage Calculators

Here are some other sites that feature useful calculators, starting first with my favorites.

www.hsh.com/hbcalc.html .com/	Downloadable Homebuyer's Calculator
www.mortgage-minder.com/	Downloadable Mortgage Minder
www.interest.com/hugh/calc/	A terrific collection for every purpose
www.moneyweb.com.au/ tools/calculators.shtml	Another exhaustive collection
www.jeacle.ie/mortgage/	A slick interactive calculator
www.fool.com/calcs/ calculators.htm	Lots of calculators, but sometimes the answers can be confusing
www.nolo.com/calculator/ re_ency.html	A good array of calculators, except for "How much house can I qualify for?" which is too simplistic and, therefore, wrong.
www.dataquick.com/title/ default.asp	A graphically pleasing amortization program.

Home Improvement

Once you've bought your home, you may want to do some fixing up. The most complete source of information is at www.hometime.com. The site has an unbelievable amount of information about do-it-yourself projects, including many how-to ideas. There are also a bookstore, a list of videos, and plans for projects. Another resource is www.improvenet.com. You can get design ideas, use a kitchen budget estimator, look at plans, find a contractor in your area, and review thousands of home improvement products.

Michael Holigan's popular TV program on the Discovery Channel has spawned a terrific Web site at www.michaelholigan.com/home.asp. Among its features is a library of hundreds of articles and transcripts of portions of the show in the Library section. Tim Carter's Ask the

Builder site at www.askbuild.com/ can be a great way to get your questions answered. After seeing him for 10 years on TV, everyone knows about Bob Vila. He has a Web site too, at www.bobvila.com. There you can access a large number of home plans.

Here are some other good home improvement sites:

www.bhglive.com/

www.housenet.com/

www.pbs.org/wgbh/thisoldhouse/home.html

www.homewarehouse.com

www.hardware.com

If you want more education, buy a book at www.buildersbooksite .com, which has books on all aspects of design, architecture, and construction.

Other Useful Sites.   State Farm Insurance Company has software for saving data about your property and possessions. This is especially useful if you ever have to file an insurance claim in the event of loss. You can download the software at www.statefarm.com/insuranc/ homeown/propmttr.htm. When you enter all the data, remember to take the program and an extra disk to work! It's not going to do much good if your home computer burns up with your data on it.

Smartstart has a free service at www.startsmart.com/startsmart.dll that will handle the transfer of utilities, newspaper subscriptions, and so forth from your old hometown to your new home. Although it is not available in all areas yet, this is a pretty slick service.

The 'Lectric Law Library has a section for lay persons at www.lectlaw.com/lay.html. You can find discussions on almost any topic you can imagine. While this is obviously not a substitute for a lawyer, it is a useful place to start to understand how your transactions intersect with the law. A similar site with lots of free advice is Lawstar, at www.lawstar.net/fds/gens/lay.html.

HomeFair, at www.homefair.com/index.html, is owned by Homestore.com. It is an excellent source of information about relocation, insurance, and related homeowner issues. A useful tool is the Salary Analyzer, which compares the salaries required to maintain comparable living standards in different communities.

BOOKS

Obviously, I'm a believer in books—and, if you've gotten this far, so are you. I simply do not believe that people can become experts about anything by reading one-page blurbs at a Web site. Therefore, I commend the following books to you. You can order them through my Web site by going to www.loan-wolf.com/bookstore.htm. They are also available at bookstores everywhere or on line at www.amazon.com and www .bn.com.

Real Estate

Buyer Beware: Insider Secrets You Need to Know Before Buying Your Home—From Choosing an Agent to Closing the Deal. Carla Cross. Chicago: Dearborn Financial Publishing, 1998.

Not One Dollar More!: How to Save $3,000 to $30,000 Buying Your Next Home: A Plain English Guide. Joseph Eamon Cummins. Kells Media Group, 1995.

100 Questions Every First-Time Home Buyer Should Ask: With Answers from Top Brokers from Around the Country. Ilyce R. Glink. New York: Times Books, 1994.

The 106 Common Mistakes Homebuyers Make (& How to Avoid Them). Gary W. Eldred. New York: John Wiley & Sons, 1998.

Reverse Mortgages for Beginners: A Consumer Guide to Every Homeowner's Retirement Nest Egg. Ken Scholen. Apple Valley, MN: National Center for Home Equity Conversion, 1998.

10 Steps to Home Ownership: A Workbook for First-Time Buyers. Ilyce R. Glink. New York: Times Books, 1996.

Buy and Hold: Seven Steps to a Real Estate Fortune. David T. Schumacher. New York: Floating Gallery, 2000.

Financial Planning and Money Management

The Savage Truth on Money. Terry Savage. New York: John Wiley & Sons, 1999.

Invest in Yourself: Six Secrets to a Rich Life. Marc Eisenson, Gerri Detweiler, and Nancy Castleman. New York: John Wiley & Sons, 1998.

Last Chance Financial Planning Guide: It's Not Too Late to Plan for Your Retirement If You Start Now. Anthony Spare and Paul Ciotti. Rocklin, CA: Prima, 1997.

The Millionaire Next Door: The Surprising Secrets of America's Wealthy. Thomas J. Stanley and William D. Danko. New York: Pocket Books, 1998.

The 9 Steps to Financial Freedom. Suze Orman. New York: Crown, 1997.

Smart Money Decisions: Why You Do What You Do With Money (And How to Change for the Better). Max H. Bazerman. New York: John Wiley & Sons, 1999.

Charles Schwab's Guide to Financial Independence: Simple Solutions for Busy People. Charles R. Schwab. New York: Three Rivers, 1999.

APPENDIX 2

MONTHLY PAYMENT CALCULATOR

Mortgage calculators are certainly ubiquitous at Internet Web sites. It's hard to find a mortgage or real estate site that doesn't have calculators on it. Unfortunately, most of the functions of these calculators are trivial, like calculating monthly payments. That is important information, but you should do your homework using one of the spreadsheets or calculator tools mentioned in Appendix 1. When you are actually out looking at homes, you don't want carry your computer around with you, so here is a simple tool. Make a copy of the payment chart in Figure A2.1 and stick it in your pocket or purse. Using it, you can quickly interpolate between the numbers to find almost any payment to within $10 or $20, close enough for most purposes.

One of the databases I subscribe to has almost 100,000 lender versus program versus rate versus fee combinations, and they change every day. As a broker, every rate sheet I get looks like those shown in Figure A2.2, except some are a lot longer. Also, I receive about 60 pages of rate sheets every day by fax or e-mail and have another dozen lenders that post rates at their Web sites. In total, that's about 100 pages of data.

When I look at this staggering aggregation of data, it makes the rate-shopper's question, "What are your rates?" seem a little silly. I am showing these rate sheets here because I want to show you the complexity of the lender's world and to give you some insight into what to expect from your lender when it comes time to decide on a particular rate versus fee option. So take a minute to look at these rate sheets. It won't be long before things start falling into place. Note that these are wholesale rate sheets, to which I would add my fees when quoting a customer. This same bank also has a similar retail price sheet it gives to its own retail loan reps, but that sheet would include the bank's markup, so those rates would be slightly higher than the wholesale ones.

15-YEAR LOANS

30-YEAR LOANS

Loan amount	Monthly Payment at various interest rates						Loan amount	Monthly Payment at various interest rates					
	5%	6%	7%	8%	9%	10%		5%	6%	7%	8%	9%	10%
$50,000	$395	$422	$449	$478	$507	$537	$50,000	$268	$300	$333	$367	$402	$439
$60,000	$474	$506	$539	$573	$609	$645	$60,000	$322	$360	$399	$440	$483	$527
$70,000	$554	$591	$629	$669	$710	$752	$70,000	$376	$420	$466	$514	$563	$614
$80,000	$633	$675	$719	$765	$811	$860	$80,000	$429	$480	$532	$587	$644	$702
$90,000	$712	$759	$809	$860	$913	$967	$90,000	$483	$540	$599	$660	$724	$790
$100,000	$791	$844	$899	$956	$1,014	$1,075	$100,000	$537	$600	$665	$734	$805	$878
$110,000	$870	$928	$989	$1,051	$1,116	$1,182	$110,000	$591	$660	$732	$807	$885	$965
$120,000	$949	$1,013	$1,079	$1,147	$1,217	$1,290	$120,000	$644	$719	$798	$881	$966	$1,053
$130,000	$1,028	$1,097	$1,168	$1,242	$1,319	$1,397	$130,000	$698	$779	$865	$954	$1,046	$1,141
$140,000	$1,107	$1,181	$1,258	$1,338	$1,420	$1,504	$140,000	$752	$839	$931	$1,027	$1,126	$1,229
$150,000	$1,186	$1,266	$1,348	$1,433	$1,521	$1,612	$150,000	$805	$899	$998	$1,101	$1,207	$1,316
$160,000	$1,265	$1,350	$1,438	$1,529	$1,623	$1,719	$160,000	$859	$959	$1,064	$1,174	$1,287	$1,404
$170,000	$1,344	$1,435	$1,528	$1,625	$1,724	$1,827	$170,000	$913	$1,019	$1,131	$1,247	$1,366	$1,492
$180,000	$1,423	$1,519	$1,618	$1,720	$1,826	$1,934	$180,000	$966	$1,079	$1,198	$1,321	$1,448	$1,580
$190,000	$1,503	$1,603	$1,708	$1,816	$1,927	$2,042	$190,000	$1,020	$1,139	$1,264	$1,394	$1,529	$1,667
$200,000	$1,582	$1,688	$1,798	$1,911	$2,029	$2,149	$200,000	$1,074	$1,199	$1,331	$1,468	$1,609	$1,755
$210,000	$1,661	$1,772	$1,888	$2,007	$2,130	$2,257	$210,000	$1,127	$1,259	$1,397	$1,541	$1,690	$1,843
$220,000	$1,740	$1,856	$1,977	$2,102	$2,231	$2,364	$220,000	$1,181	$1,319	$1,464	$1,614	$1,770	$1,931
$230,000	$1,819	$1,941	$2,067	$2,198	$2,333	$2,472	$230,000	$1,235	$1,379	$1,530	$1,688	$1,851	$2,018
$240,000	$1,898	$2,025	$2,157	$2,294	$2,434	$2,579	$240,000	$1,288	$1,439	$1,597	$1,761	$1,931	$2,106
$250,000	$1,977	$2,110	$2,247	$2,389	$2,536	$2,687	$250,000	$1,342	$1,499	$1,663	$1,834	$2,012	$2,194
$260,000	$2,056	$2,194	$2,337	$2,485	$2,637	$2,794	$260,000	$1,396	$1,559	$1,730	$1,908	$2,092	$2,282
$270,000	$2,135	$2,278	$2,427	$2,580	$2,739	$2,901	$270,000	$1,449	$1,619	$1,796	$1,981	$2,172	$2,369
$280,000	$2,214	$2,363	$2,517	$2,676	$2,840	$3,009	$280,000	$1,503	$1,679	$1,863	$2,055	$2,253	$2,457
$290,000	$2,293	$2,447	$2,607	$2,771	$2,941	$3,116	$290,000	$1,557	$1,739	$1,929	$2,128	$2,333	$2,545
$300,000	$2,372	$2,532	$2,696	$2,867	$3,043	$3,224	$300,000	$1,610	$1,799	$1,996	$2,201	$2,414	$2,633
$310,000	$2,451	$2,616	$2,786	$2,963	$3,144	$3,331	$310,000	$1,664	$1,859	$2,062	$2,275	$2,494	$2,720
$320,000	$2,531	$2,700	$2,876	$3,058	$3,246	$3,439	$320,000	$1,718	$1,919	$2,129	$2,348	$2,575	$2,808
$330,000	$2,610	$2,785	$2,966	$3,154	$3,347	$3,546	$330,000	$1,772	$1,979	$2,195	$2,421	$2,655	$2,396
$340,000	$2,689	$2,869	$3,056	$3,249	$3,449	$3,654	$340,000	$1,825	$2,038	$2,262	$2,495	$2,736	$2,984
$350,000	$2,768	$2,953	$3,146	$3,345	$3,550	$3,761	$350,000	$1,879	$2,098	$2,329	$2,568	$2,816	$3,072
$360,000	$2,847	$3,038	$3,236	$3,440	$3,651	$3,869	$360,000	$1,933	$2,158	$2,395	$2,642	$2,897	$3,159
$370,000	$2,926	$3,122	$3,326	$3,536	$3,753	$3,976	$370,000	$1,986	$2,218	$2,462	$2,715	$2,977	$3,247
$380,000	$3,005	$3,207	$3,416	$3,631	$3,854	$4,083	$380,000	$2,040	$2,278	$2,528	$2,788	$3,058	$3,335
$390,000	$3,084	$3,291	$3,505	$3,727	$3,956	$4,191	$390,000	$2,094	$2,338	$2,595	$2,862	$3,138	$3,423
$400,000	$3,163	$3,375	$3,595	$3,823	$4,057	$4,298	$400,000	$2,147	$2,398	$2,661	$2,935	$3,218	$3,510

Figure A2.1   Monthly payment table.

A LENDER'S WHOLESALE RATE SHEET
FIXED-RATE LOANS

15-Year Fixed Conforming (up to $227,150)					15-Year Fixed Jumbo (up to $650,000)				
Rate	15-day*	30-day	45-day	60-day	Rate	15-day*	30-day	45-day	60-day
6.125%	2.000	2.125	2.250	2.375	6.250%	2.750	2.875	3.000	3.125
6.250%	1.500	1.625	1.750	1.875	6.375%	2.250	2.375	2.500	2.625
6.375%	1.000	1.125	1.250	1.375	6.500%	1.750	1.875	2.000	2.125
6.500%	0.625	0.750	0.875	1.000	6.625%	1.375	1.500	1.625	1.750
6.625%	0.250	0.375	0.500	0.625	6.750%	1.000	1.125	1.250	1.375
6.750%	−0.125	0.000	0.125	0.250	6.875%	0.625	0.750	0.875	1.000
6.875%	−0.500	−0.375	−0.250	−0.125	7.000%	0.250	0.875	0.500	0.625
7.000%	−0.875	−0.750	−0.625	−0.500	7.125%	−0.125	0.000	0.125	0.250
7.125%	−1.250	−1.125	−1.000	−0.875	7.250%	−0.500	−0.375	−0.250	−0.125
7.250%	−1.500	−1.375	−1.250	−1.125	7.375%	−0.875	−0.750	−0.625	−0.500
7.375%	−1.750	−1.625	−1.500	−1.375	7.500%	−1.125	−1.000	−0.875	−0.750
7.500%	−2.000	−1.875	−1.750	−1.625	7.625%	−1.375	−1.250	−1.125	−1.000
7.625%	−2.250	−2.125	−2.000	−1.875	7.750%	−1.625	−1.500	−1.375	−1.250
7.750%	−2.500	−2.375	−2.250	−2.125	7.875%	−1.875	−1.750	−1.625	−1.500

30-Year Fixed Conforming (up to $227,150)					30-Year Fixed Jumbo (up to $650,000)				
Rate	15-day*	30-day	45-day	60-day	Rate	15-day*	30-day	45-day	60-day
6.125%	4.000	4.125	4.250	4.375	6.500%	4.000	4.125	4.250	4.375
6.250%	3.375	3.500	3.625	3.750	6.625%	3.375	3.500	3.625	3.750
6.375%	2.750	2.875	3.000	3.125	6.750%	2.750	2.875	3.000	3.125
6.500%	2.125	2.250	2.375	2.500	6.875%	2.125	2.250	2.375	2.500
6.625%	1.500	1.625	1.750	1.875	7.000%	1.500	1.625	1.750	1.875
6.750%	0.875	1.000	1.125	1.250	7.125%	1.000	1.125	1.250	1.375
6.875%	0.375	0.500	0.625	0.750	7.250%	0.500	0.625	0.750	0.875
7.000%	−0.125	0.000	0.125	0.250	7.375%	0.000	0.125	0.250	0.375
7.125%	−0.625	−0.500	−0.375	−0.250	7.500%	−0.375	−0.250	−0.125	0.000
7.250%	−1.125	−1.000	−0.875	−0.750	7.625%	−0.750	−0.625	−0.500	−0.375
7.375%	−1.625	−1.500	−1.375	−1.250	7.750%	−1.125	−1.000	−0.875	−0.750
7.500%	−2.000	−1.875	−1.750	−1.625	7.875%	−1.500	−1.375	−1.250	−1.125
7.625%	−2.375	−2.250	−2.125	−2.000	8.000%	−1.750	−1.625	−1.500	−1.375
7.750%	−2.750	−2.625	−2.500	−2.375	8.125%	−2.000	−1.875	−1.750	−1.625

Premiums

Fixed jumbo $650,000—$1 million maximum: +0.250% to rate.

Assumable (exclude CA, CT, FL, ID, MA, MT, ND, NH, NJ, NY, RI):
• 15-yr fixed only +0.500% to rate.

Second home conforming fixed note rate add-ons:
• Purchase 80.01–90% LTV +0.125%.
• Rate/term refinance 75.01–80% LTV +0.125%.
• Cash out refinance up to 65% LTV +0.125%.
Investor (fixed only): +0.500% rate, +0.500% fees.
Convertibility: +0.500% fees, +0.125% margin.

• High-rise condos (nonconforming fixed): +0.500% to fees.
• High-rise condos (all ARM products): +0.125% to rate.

* 15-day lock option not available until further notice.

Long-Term Locks—Add to 60-Day Price

	Fees due at lock
90-day purchase	+0.500 pts
120-day new construction only	+1.000
180-day new construction only (fixed)	+0.750, +0.250 to rate
180-day new construction only (ARM)	+1.500

Figure A2.2   Lenders' wholesale rate sheets.

INDEX